THE BLOODAXE BOOK OF
MODERN WELSH POETRY

Menna Elfyn is Wales's best-known Welsh-language poet. According to Tony Conran, she is 'the first Welsh poet in fifteen hundred years to make a serious attempt to have her work known outside Wales'. She travels the world giving readings, and her poems have been translated into many languages. Her books of poetry include three bilingual volumes: *Eucalyptus: Detholiad o Gerddi / Selected Poems 1978-1994* from Gomer, and two later collections from Bloodaxe, *Cell Angel* (1996) and *Cusan Dyn Dall / Blind Man's Kiss* (2001). She has also written plays, libretti and a children's novel set in Mexico, and lives in Llandysul.

John Rowlands is a widely-published novelist and literary critic who graduated from Bangor and received his doctorate at Oxford for a thesis on medieval literature. He is Professor of Welsh at the University of Wales, Aberystwyth, and is an Honorary Fellow at Trinity College, Carmarthen. A previous editor of *Llais Llyfrau* and *Taliesin*, he is now general editor of the series *Y Meddwl a'r Dychymyg Cymreig* for the University of Wales Press. He has won Arts Council of Wales awards, and is a frequent adjudicator of major competitions at the National Eisteddfod.

i

Tony Conran a Joseph Clancy
a wêl ei hurddas trwy niwl ei hadfyd

THE Bloodaxe Book OF
MODERN WELSH POETRY

20th-century Welsh-language poetry in translation

edited by MENNA ELFYN & JOHN ROWLANDS

BLOODAXE BOOKS

ISBN: 1 85224 549 2

First published 2003 by
Bloodaxe Books Ltd,
Highgreen,
Tarset,
Northumberland NE48 1RP.

www.bloodaxebooks.com
For further information about Bloodaxe titles
please visit our website or write to
the above address for a catalogue.

The publication of this book has been supported with
a translation grant from Cyngor Celfyddydau Cymru /
the Arts Council of Wales.
Bloodaxe Books Ltd acknowledges
the financial assistance of Arts Council England, North East.

Cover printing by J. Thomson Colour Printers Ltd, Glasgow.

Printed in Great Britain by
Bell & Bain Limited, Glasgow, Scotland.

Contents

Introduction

Why do I feel powerless as I stare at a blank screen fumbling for words to introduce this anthology? When I discuss Welsh-language poetry in Welsh, I feel no such lack of energy, and that is because I can engage with my subject without any need to be an apologist. To the outsider, being a literary practitioner in Welsh seems idiosyncratic, but within one's own language, one is whole and complete, and it feels as if the whole world is breathing in Welsh. Yet when I embark on the task of explaining Welsh literature in this global language, I suddenly find myself on the defensive. But why should I be? After all, my audience is not necessarily an English one, but an English-reading one, and I feel some relief in the fact that this book may be read by someone in Catalunya, or the Czech Republic, or by a French-speaking Québecois. Does size matter? And does a language's size depend on the size of its lexicon? Thinking these thoughts, I regain my confidence, and console myself with the eccentric-sounding idea that there are probably more minorities in the world than majorities.

Welsh is an old-new language. I will not attempt to trace it back to the mists of its Celtic past, but will say simply that the oldest surviving poetry composed in it dates from the 6th century AD, and therefore it predates all European literature apart from that of Greek and Latin. That poetry belongs to an area outside Wales, in what is today the south of Scotland and the north of England, which goes to show that Welsh was the 'old British tongue'. Welsh poetry was a highly oral art, aspiring 'to the condition of music' as Walter Pater would have put it. It was this orality which encouraged the development of *cynghanedd* (harmony), a highly complex system of alliteration and internal rhyme. As Simwnt Fychan said in the 16th century: 'A poem is only formed to provide sweetness for the ear, and from the ear to the heart.' It was as if poetry circumvented the cerebral and stirred the emotions with its music: *la poésie pure*, as Saunders Lewis once suggested.

Yet to counterbalance this romantic-sounding aspect, I hasten to add that the Welsh bards of medieval times were not the aesthetes which the above description might evoke, but highly practical people who were acutely aware of their social rôle. The backbone of the Welsh bardic tradition was praise, and that tradition persisted for over a thousand years from the 6th to the 16th century, and even after the bards lost their professional status, the praise tradition was revived time and time again, and is still alive today. However, it wasn't as monolithic as many commentators would have it, and the tendency today is to acknowledge the variety within the unity, and to listen to the undercurrent of humour and bawdiness counterpointing the high seriousness.

It was the Act of Union of Wales with England in 1536 which marked the beginning of the end of this thousand years of highly-polished virtuosic poetry, and yet at the beginning of the 21st century, many of us are kindled with the hope that the end is not nigh after all. Of course many things changed utterly from then on. The Welsh language and its literary practitioners became defensive, and yet it was at this point of crisis that the Bible was translated into Welsh (1588), and that our culture received a major boost as a result.

Free-metre poetry flourished, and we are talking here, not of blank verse nor of *vers libre* (those were later developments), but of rhymed metrical verse which gave such exuberant religious poets as Williams Pantycelyn and Ann Griffiths freedom from *cynghanedd* to express deeply spiritual experiences with passion. It was the Methodist Revival of the 18th century which transformed Welsh-speaking Wales and channelled its culture towards religion. By the 19th century, Welsh was the language of the ordinary people, *y werin*, a word whose literal translation as peasantry does scant justice to its rich overtones in Welsh. Welsh *diwylliant gwerin* or peasant culture was highly literate, fed as it was, not only by the Nonconformist chapels with their Sunday Schools, but also by the *eisteddfod*, a medieval institution which was revived as a much more popular festival during the 18th and 19th centuries. *Eisteddfod* (literally a sitting or session, deriving from *eistedd*, 'to sit'), became fused with Iolo Morganwg's *Gorsedd Beirdd Ynys Prydain* (the Gorsedd of Bards) early in the 19th century, whose pageantry was associated with the award of the two major poetry prizes, those of the Chair and Crown. In the biographies of the poets represented in this anthology reference is often made to these awards, and they are still the highest honours a Welsh-language poet can win, although not all poets cherish that ambition. The National Eisteddfod Chair is awarded for a long ode in strict metres, whilst the Crown is awarded for a long poem in non-*cynghanedd* metres, or a cycle of short poems.

The 20th century saw a revival in Welsh literature, or one might venture to say, a series of revivals, and the term *dadeni* (renaissance) has been used with increasing frequency to convey the *frissons* felt in our literature during the modern century. Despite the fact that the old Welsh language had been marginalised by 19th century pressures (its use was prohibited in schools during the era of the despicable 'Welsh Not'), and although English was quickly becoming the majority language of the people of Wales during the 20th century, Welsh-language culture was reinvigorated, especially in the literary sphere. And this was not a matter of clinging in desperation to past glories, but a true metamorphosis.

To call a nation schizophrenic may have no technical accuracy, but it does have metaphorical meaning. The Welsh were the original Britons, and yet their foothold had been seriously eroded by the English, and despite producing medieval classics such as the *Mabinogion* and Dafydd ap Gwilym, they lost their nerve as the British Empire gained its world hegemony during the 19th century. To be in the pocket of the Empire on which the sun would never set was not conducive to a high self-esteem, and so we nursed a huge inferiority complex. We sensed that we had something to be proud of in our native culture, but many felt like Matthew Arnold that it was something unpalpable and vaguely spiritual, with no relevance to the progressive and scientific modern age. It could be cherished in the heart, but might as well retreat from the practical sphere.

So in our scramble for progress, we established institutions of higher education far beyond our own needs, and what eventually became the federal University of Wales was in reality the University of England in Wales, a provincial university which could – and can – only survive through the influx of English students. The medium of instruction was English. Yet ironically this university provided the impetus for the revival of our literature, despite the fact that English was at first the medium of instruction even in the Welsh departments. Didn't I suggest we were schizophrenic? However, it was through an effort to cast out the demons of inferiority complex that Welsh poetry finally began to assert itself. This was not a simple matter of taking pride in the past and trying to resurrect it, but rather of being inspired by it and being spurred on to fashion things anew and to be almost militantly relevant.

It is true that the first Professor of Welsh at Bangor, John Morris-Jones (1864-1929) was something of 'a literary truncheon' as Bobi Jones has said. His pedagogic approach suited the mood of the times, and so 'he took the whole nation to school' according to Saunders Lewis. Coming to the Welsh language and its literature from his Oxford training in mathematics, he wrote his definitive studies of the Welsh language (1913) and Welsh prosody (1925) with the confidence of one who could set down the law on these matters. It is true that he was a talented poet and translator of poetry as well, although his 'machine-made poetry on hand-made paper', as one of his detractors put it, make it unsuitable for inclusion in this anthology.

The towering presence amongst the poets of the revival was T Gwynn Jones, a man of polymathic talents who achieved the distinction of being appointed Professor of Welsh at Aberystwyth despite the fact that he himself had received little formal education, and certainly no higher education. He was a self-taught scholar who steeped himself in medieval Welsh poetry, and wrote *cynghanedd* as if it was one of the many languages which he had mastered. His Chair poem of 1902, 'Ymadawiad Arthur' ('The Passing of Arthur') marks a new departure in Welsh poetry, and is the first of a number of long poems in the strict metres based on Welsh or Celtic myth and legend. He was long regarded as a romantic escapist, but a closer reading of his poems shows them to have a modern relevance, and he was in fact struggling between tradition and innovation. His 'Pro Patria', an excerpt of which is included in this anthology, is a less-known poem which gives us a glimpse of the realist streak in him. In his later poems, he ventured to fuse *cynghanedd* and *vers libre*, a seeming contradiction in terms, and devised stories with a modern provenance.

A similar creative tension between a nostalgic romanticism and a reluctant effort to face grim reality is also apparent in W J Gruffydd's work. But in the work of the two cousins, R Williams Parry and T H Parry-Williams, there is far more of a willingness to grapple with the angst of the modern sensibility. True, the youthful Williams Parry caught the imagination with his 1910 hedonistic poem 'Yr Haf' ('Summer') which is a self-indulgent expression of *art pour l'art*, but the tragic death of Hedd Wyn, the shepherd poet from Trawsfynydd who was killed in the Second World War, and who posthumously won the National Eisteddfod Chair, brought out a sombre streak in him. He is now regarded more as the Poet of Winter than the Poet of Summer. And this most noncommittal of poets was triggered by the burning of the Bombing School in 1936 (an act of sabotage by Saunders Lewis and two friends) to flirt with *engagement*, and to be the scourge of the Welsh philistines of the 30s. His cousin, T H Parry-Williams, was more of an introvert, who pondered philosophically the absurdity of existence, this being all the more poignant because of the ironic echoes of religious literature in his writing.

There was a definite shift away from pietism in the poetry of the first third of the 20th century, although it was more of an agnostic angst than a militant head-on atheism. But the remarkable thing about the work of the next generation is that it is imbued with a hard-won optimism, based on a stubborn resilience in the face of crumbling values. The key figure here is Saunders Lewis, the most controversial man of letters which Wales has ever produced. Born and bred in a bourgeois milieu in Lancashire, educated at a private school and at Liverpool University, where he gained a First in English, he seemed destined for an English academic and literary career, but underwent a "conversion" to the national cause during the First World War, and from then on dedicated himself to Wales and its language and literature. He looked askance at Wales from the outside and saw a once brilliant nation in a sorry state because of its lack of a sense of history and a lack of faith in itself. Saunders sought to inject it with self-esteem, to enable it to hold its head high amongst the mainstream nations of Europe. This entailed re-education, for it seemed as if the whole nation was suffering from amnesia, and hardly aware of its own independent past and high culture. Saunders Lewis's "vision" was problematic for many. He seemed to go against the grain of the kind of Welshness which had become the norm during the 19th century – Nonconformist in religion and Liberal in politics. Saunders himself wanted to push back the frontiers to a pre-Act of Union existence, where Welsh culture was led by a Welsh-speaking gentry, when Wales was more aware of the European dimension, and when the country was of course Catholic in religion. He himself was converted to the Catholic faith.

The ideology of Welsh Nationalism springs from his somewhat idiosyncratic view of Welsh history. He was one of the founders of the Welsh Nationalist Party (later Plaid Cymru) in 1925, a party which only had a small but dedicated following for about 40 years. By then socialism had become the dominant ideology in Wales, and the two ideologies seemed to be at loggerheads, although many early adherents of Plaid Cymru were staunchly socialist and working-class, and proud to call themselves *gwerin* – a term which Saunders Lewis himself abhorred.

Saunders was a brilliant artist, if a flawed politician, and his plays, poems, novels, essays, criticism and scholarship break over the banks of his own ideology. His example was an inspiration to many who didn't share all his prejudices, and there is no doubt that he injected Welsh poetry (and Welsh letters in general) with a robust sense of purpose. From the 30s onwards, poetry is much more committed than it had been during the first third of the century – the two main commitments being to religion and to Wales and its language.

I hasten to add that this was no throwback to the simplistic faith of the Victorians or to some sentimental patriotism. Gwenallt is the poet who best exemplifies the new spirit. His roots were in rural Carmarthenshire, but he was brought up in the industrial Swansea Valley, and was a committed socialist of the Marxist variety during his youth. He stood as a conscientious objector during the First World War, not as a pacifist *per se*, but to protest against British imperialism, and he was imprisoned in Wormwood Scrubs and Dartmoor. But his militant socialism became gradually translated into an ironic Christian Nationalism. His mature religious poems are sharp and acerbic, and he finds a place for the 'fist of Karl Marx' in the Christian church. As for his poems about Wales, they lash out with harsh vehemence, and have nothing of the idyllic idealisation which earlier lyricists were prone to.

Waldo Williams's name is often coupled with that of Gwenallt, although his mystical approach makes his religious poetry quite different in tone, and his leap-of-faith optimism about Wales and its language is persuasive and inspiring rather than denunciating. He is remarkable in the wide range of his palette, for he seemed to write instinctively and spontaneously as the mood took him – sometimes in a lyrical mode, then in a profound and complex mystical style; in *vers libre* and *cynghanedd*; alternately philosophical and humorous. In his best poems, Waldo is a different kind of modernist, challenging the reader to delve into the multi-layered meaning of his imagery.

The 50s saw the emergence of another two modernist poets, Euros Bowen and Bobi Jones, both of them extraordinarily prolific. Euros was an indefatigable experimenter, playing acrobatically with words, images and metres. Bobi Jones was a Welsh learner from Cardiff who seemed intoxicated with the adventure of being a Welsh-language Christian poet, and enjoying the rôle of *bête noire* on the respectable Welsh literary stage. His magisterial epic *Hunllef Arthur* ('Arthur's Nightmare') is the longest poem in the language.

This was the second wave of modernism, rejected by some as over-obscure and out-of-touch with the "ordinary" audience. The first wave, led by T H Parry-Williams, was never intellectually difficult, although it was emotionally complex, but despite the fact that the poetry of the second wave was generally positive and life-enhancing in its attitudes, it was often dubbed *barddoniaeth dywyll* (literally 'dark poetry') because of its mosaic-like juxtaposition of images. Of course this says a lot about the expectations of the Welsh poetry-reading public. The oral aspect presupposes that poetry is direct and easily-digested, and a retreat to the academic ivory tower is often frowned upon.

Paradoxically, it was a Welsh academic who managed to bridge the gap between the serious and popular. Gwyn Thomas came to the fore in the 60s, and writes almost entirely in a conversational *vers libre*. His *faux naiveté* sprang from his observation of his own children and his attempt to give voice to their inarticulateness. This, coupled with his basically deep humane sympathy, injected a welcome streak of humour into his poems, which have been popular as recitation set pieces at *eisteddfodau*. Gwyn Thomas also likes to introduce the *bric-à-brac* of contemporary life in the global village into his work, and he is passionately in favour of using modern media to introduce poetry to a wider audience. It was he who coined the word *llunyddiaeth* for television poetry. The word is a clever play on *llenyddiaeth* (literature), and roughly means 'pictorial literature'. Of course, the 60s are generally associated with the permissive society on the one hand, and disenchantment with traditional politics on the other. Wales had its own "60s experience", with writers going over the traces, and young people taking the law into their own hands in order to exert their belief in the future of Wales and its language. It was the period of the founding of the Welsh Language Society and the imprisonment of language activists. Paradoxically, Welsh poetry saw a revival in *cynghanedd* and strict-metre poetry. It is true that writing in such metres as the *englyn* or *cywydd* never ceased to be popular, especially amongst the so-called *beirdd gwlad* or folk poets. 'Bois y Cilie' (the Cilie Boys) were an almost legendary extended family of poets who had a vigorous social rôle in the rural community of Ceredigion. Bardic contests called *Ymryson y Beirdd* (Bards' Contention) pulled the crowds in the literary pavilion of the National Eisteddfod, and still do so, and they were also popular as a radio programme, now called *Talwrn y Beirdd* (Bards' Cockpit). Dic Jones belongs to this tradition, and is regarded as one of the most fluent practitioners of strict-metre poetry, although he also writes in the free metres, and is a polished prose stylist.

The revival of *cynghanedd* poetry in the 60s and 70s, however, was more politically motivated. In much of his poetry, Gerallt Lloyd Owen can invoke universal themes as well as any of the traditionalists, but the fire in his poetry was kindled by his loathing of the investiture of Charles as Prince of Wales by Queen Elizabeth II at Caernarfon Castle in 1969. The last Prince of Wales was of course Llywelyn, and Gerallt Lloyd Owen saw Charles as an impostor manipulated by political opportunists who wanted to smooth out the differences between Wales and England. His *Cerddi'r Cywilydd* ('Poems of the Shame') were scathing in their condemnation, but also a blatant battle-cry.

An almost anguished concern for the "fate of the language" is never far from the work of the exponents of the strict metres during the last decades of the 20th century. Alan Llwyd is not only the most prolific but also the most distinguished of these. He is not an explicit propagandist, but a sombre and bitter elegist of the old way of life with its humane Christian values and respect for art and culture. He can often seem like the prophet of doom, and he is certainly a clear example of a modern poet whose underlying theme is his rejection of modernity. His latest collection, *Ffarwelio â Chanrif* ('Farewell to a Century'), seems to say good riddance to the last century.

However, all is not gloom and doom. In fact, what characterises the poetry of the last 30 years is its exuberance. Iwan Llwyd, who doesn't shy away from the political here-and-now in Wales, has nevertheless a global perspective, and is very much influenced by American popular culture, including blues and jazz. His 1990 Crown poems, 'Gwreichion' ('Sparks'), were an oblique reaction to the referendum of 1979 when the Welsh people rejected their own elected Assembly. They are rich and allusive, and conjure up Aboriginal creation myth; it is as if Iwan Llwyd is trying to awaken Wales into a fresh existence with his 'songlines'.

The so-called second renaissance of *cynghanedd* poetry from the 80s onwards saw a new generation of young poets writing in the strict metres with a verve which is refreshingly ironic. The post-modern touches in the work of Twm Morys and Emyr Lewis shows their ability to pour new wine into old vessels with intoxicating effect.

These poets and their contemporaries are fiercely committed to their art. Outsiders might ask how authentic this fervour is, and how "real" the situation of a poet addressing a so-called minority of half a million can be. The reply would be a resoundingly affirmative one. Twm Morys, the son of Jan Morris, the celebrated travel writer who writes exclusively in English, would probably regard his potential audience of half a million as more "real" than Jan Morris's audience of many millions. Twm Morys refused permission for us to include translations of his poetry in this volume. He is content to address his Welsh-language audience, and adamantly regards translation as an aberration. Of course, a Welsh poet mingles with his audience. Poetry is heard at wedding parties, in pubs, on the radio, and there is a monthly poetry journal published by *Cymdeithas Cerdd Dafod* (literally 'The Society of Tongue Craft', meaning of course the Welsh oral poetic art), which has a membership of over one thousand. This gives the journal, called *Barddas* (another name for Welsh poetic art), a staggering circulation in comparative terms.

In introducing Welsh poetry to an English-reading audience there is always a tendency to over-emphasise the traditional and conservative elements, and of course any brief survey such as this one tends to be linear and two-dimensional, without taking account of the interweaving quality of any poetry, and of its multi-layered aspects. Although *Barddas* projects a rather middle-of-the-road image, the editorial policy is a surprisingly inclusive one, and a vehemently religiophobic gay writer such as Mihangel Morgan rubs shoulders with the evangelical nationalist Bobi Jones, and columnists include the rather conventional critic Donald Evans as well as the radical Iwan Llwyd.

Of course there are rebels galore as well, and one publishing house, *Y Lolfa*, has brought out a long series of poetry collections called *Cyfres y Beirdd Answyddogol* (The Unofficial Poets Series). Most of the authors would not be seen dead wearing an Eisteddfod Crown, and yet this is exactly what one or two of them have done. The borderline between various factions has been considerably blurred in recent years, and the gravitas traditionally associated with Welsh bards has all but vanished. The English media usually project a laughing-stock image of the mock-Druidical bardic ceremonies at the *Eisteddfod*, but most Welsh poets have long regarded them as charades anyway, but don't mind taking part almost in a Chaplinesque self-mocking spirit.

What we sometimes fail to emphasise is that poetry in Welsh is a fun thing. If anyone needs to be convinced of this, let him or her come to listen outside the literary pavilion at the National Eisteddfod and be bowled over by the raucous laughter. And a fairly recent trend has been the rise of performance poetry. Groups of itinerant poets (usually accompanied by musicians) have toured Wales and beyond to entertain an usually youngish audience in pubs or other popular venues. The most prominent of these troubadours is perhaps Twm Morys, who sings to his own harp accompaniment under the name of Bob Delyn (a pun on Bob Dylan, but of course *telyn* in Welsh means a harp). It is true that he and his group tour primarily as musicians, but the words are just as important as the music for him, and he has also travelled around with others to read his poetry. He and Iwan Llwyd have toured South America to write and perform for a Welsh television series. Iwan has also given readings in North America and elsewhere. This new wave of poets shows a renewed confidence in Welsh poetry and in Welsh as a language which can speak in tongues throughout the world. It involves no dilution of Welshness. The new Arts Council of Wales initiative *Llenyddiaeth Cymru Dramor*/Welsh Literature Abroad also helps to disseminate Welsh literature worldwide.

The most-travelled Welsh-language writer is undoubtedly my co-editor Menna Elfyn, who has given readings around Western and Eastern Europe, North and South America as well as the Middle and Far East, and she has also been involved in television projects and theatre productions and is also a librettist. She has published three bilingual volumes of poetry, two of them with Bloodaxe Books. Yet she is staunchly Welsh, and has been actively (and illegally!) involved in language campaigns. And I am suddenly struck by the fact that she is the first 20th-century woman poet I have mentioned in this introduction. Yes, Welsh poetry has traditionally been very much a male domain. The striking pre-20th-century exceptions which prove the rule are the erotic medieval poet Gwerful Mechain and the brilliant 19th-century hymn-writer Ann Griffiths. More women have invaded the pitch during the 20th century, two of them winning the National Eisteddfod Crown, but it was only as recently as 2001 that the first woman poet won the Chair. Women have been shy of using *cynghanedd* and the strict metres, and Mererid Hopwood's prize-winning poem is a refreshing example of *écriture feminine*. However, even the performance poetry referred to earlier, with its stand-up comic element, can sometimes reek of macho culture.

Yet Menna Elfyn has been very much involved with performance poetry, as have some younger female and feminist poets. It is true that her early poetry was informed by her fervour for changing things on various fronts, but to label her a feminist, a pacifist, or a political activist is to lose sight of the metaphysical scope of her later poetry, which easily crosses geographical boundaries. It was on my insistence (and our publisher's) that her poems were included in this anthology.

There may be observers from the outside who are still unconvinced that a lesser-used language with only half a million speakers can still produce a vibrant literary culture at the beginning of the 21st century. Are the enthusiastic young poets of today merely paying lip-service to the past, and artificially keeping Welsh poetry alive on a metaphorical life-support machine? Wouldn't any sensible person of talent practise his art in English? The implication is that only the untalented would cling to Welsh.

Gwyneth Lewis rebuts that suggestion triumphantly by writing alternately in Welsh and English. She is a truly bilingual poet who has no difficulty in gaining a wide audience with her poetry in English (she has won some major awards), and yet she divides her creative time between the two languages, not from a sense of duty, but because she seemingly follows her own instincts in this matter. Having now embarked on a three-year seafaring voyage around the world, it will be interesting to see whether her muse and *awen* will be balanced. Her artistic integrity will decide.

A few other poets vacillate between the dragon's two tongues, but the vast majority of Welsh-language poets stick to Welsh, because they feel that although they might be technically bilingual, they have no choice when it comes to writing poetry. Although a few of them occasionally translate their own poetry into English, most are happier to leave that to accomplished translators, a team of whom have been responsible for the dissemination of Welsh poetry to a wider audience through this anthology.

This is the first definitive anthology of 20th-century Welsh-language poetry in English translation. Menna Elfyn and I have attempted to present the broad sweep of poetry from T Gwynn Jones to Mererid Puw Davies. We did of course have to make difficult choices in the process, and many old favourites had to be left out. We have made an effort to choose the poems which translate best into English, and yet we haven't shied away from the task of making as representative a selection as possible. As many have remarked before us, poetry in *cynghanedd* is notoriously untranslatable, and the meaning divorced from its sound can seem as banal as a libretto without its music. Nevertheless we feel that our translators have made brave attempts, although they would be the first to admit that they had of necessity to reverse the Welsh dictum 'sound without meaning is preferable to meaning without sound'.

And finally, a brief word about the strict metres. This term means traditional metres where there is *cynghanedd* in every line. During medieval times twenty-four metres were codified, but although poets sometimes wrote a long *tour de force* to exemplify all of them in one long poem, only a few were used on a daily basis. The term *cynghanedd* has musical connotations, and means 'harmony'. A very complex system of *cynghanedd* reached its fruition in the 14th century, although it had developed over a number of centuries before that, with the free but extensive use of alliteration and internal rhyme. Now the rules were set down for posterity, although some modifications were introduced in later periods. The most comprehensive elucidation of them in modern times was John Morris-Jones's *Cerdd Dafod* (1925), which extends to almost four hundred pages. Obviously a brief note like this can only touch superficially on the nature of *cynghanedd*.

There are four main classes of *cynghanedd*, and these will be illustrated here with examples from Gerallt Lloyd Owen's 'Afon' ('River'). The simplest is *cynghanedd lusg*, where a word in the middle of the line rhymes with the penultimate accented syllable of the last word in the line, as in:

Pan feddwn dal**ent** / pl**ent**yn

In *cynghanedd groes* the line is divided into two, and the consonants in the first half are repeated in the same sequence in the second half:

Miwsi**g** **gwledd** / ym**ysg** **gl**oyw**dd**wr

A similar repetition of consonants occurs in *cynghanedd draws*, but this time there is a section in the middle of the line where no correspondence occurs, as in the following example:

Drwy'**r** **b**wlch / oedd ym mhen **dr**aw'**r** **b**yd

In *cynghanedd sain* the line divides into three sections, and there is an internal rhyme between the ending of the first two sections, and alliteration between the second and third sections, thus:

Maint fy m**yd** / oe**dd** h**yd** y **dd**ôl

Cynghanedd seems at home in Welsh, and although some poets have attempted to emulate it in English (and there are echoes of it in some of Gerard Manley Hopkins's poems), it does not exert the same power. One factor in its favour is the sharp articulation of consonants in Welsh, which is by its nature a musical language. This is obviously an aural device, and the visual representation of it above hardly does justice to it. Although this brief description might convey the impression of a fossilised ornamentation (as in Baroque music), this is totally misleading, and the best of young poets today display considerable versatility in their use of it, producing novel and striking effects.

The most popular strict metre is the *englyn*, a four-line monorhyme stanza of thirty syllables in all. It is often an epigrammatic verse, used on its own to convey some universal truth, or simply to describe an object concisely, or as an image to convey some underlying idea. It can be physical or metaphysical, satirical or humorous, and can also be used in a whole chain of *englynion*, each one linked to the next by a word or alliteration, and the ending similarly linked to the beginning.

Another widely-used strict metre is the *cywydd*, a series of accented/unaccented rhyming couplets. This was the most popular metre of the 14th to the 16th centuries, and its first distinguished practitioner was Dafydd ap Gwilym with his love and nature poems.

An *awdl* is a long poem in a combination of strict metres, which is a kind of symphonic poem in different movements, and it is such a poem for which the Eisteddfod Chair is awarded annually.

Despite this digression on strict-metre poetry, it must be emphasised that it co-exists today with poetry in the free metres (scanned rhymed metres, similar to the English "strict" metres), and also *vers libre*, or as we say in Welsh, *canu penrhydd* (literally 'unbridled singing'). To complicate matters further, a hybrid has developed, a combination of free verse with *cynghanedd*. Poets do not necessarily form opposing camps on the basis of their choice of metres, and a poet such as Alan Llwyd is equally proficient in all these types. In the last resort, the form is not an end in itself, and the total effect comes from a fusion of varying elements, not least amongst which is what might be vaguely called poetic vision. The varying rôles of poets as seers, craftsmen, political agitators, social commentators, satirists, comics and entertainers are represented somewhere or other in this anthology which attempts to reflect the variety of 20th-century poetry in the Welsh language.

JOHN ROWLANDS

NOTES ON TRANSLATORS

Joseph P Clancy (*b.* 1928) is a poet, critic and translator from New York City where he lived until his retirement in 1990, when he settled in Wales. He is Marymount Manhattan College's Emeritus Professor of English and Theatre Arts. He has translated extensively from medieval and modern literature and his anthology of 20th-century Welsh poetry appeared under the imprint of Gomer in 1982. He is also a distinguished and prolific poet. His most recent publications are *Other Words* (1999) and *Ordinary Time* (2000).

Gillian Clarke (*b.* 1937) is a poet, playwright and teacher of creative writing. She has published seven volumes of poetry and has also written poetry commissioned for the medieval garden at Aberglasney and the Botanic Garden of Wales. She has translated Kate Roberts's novel *Tegwch y Bore*, and her translations of Menna Elfyn appear in her three recent bilingual collections. She travels widely and has read her poetry throughout the world.

Tony Conran (*b.* 1931) is a poet, critic, translator and playwright. His translations became well-known when he edited *The Penguin Book of Welsh Verse* in 1962 (a revised edition appeared from Seren in 1986). He is also a prolific poet in his own right and a leading critic of the two literatures of Wales. In 1995, writers and friends collaborated to celebrate his numerous achievements with a book called *Thirteen Ways of Looking at Tony Conran*. Since then he has published another three volumes of poetry and another book is awaiting publication.

Martin Davis (*b.* 1957) was born in Llanrwst, but his family roots on one side are in Ireland and on the other in Hampshire. He was brought up in Stratford-upon-Avon, and it was annual holidays in Morfa Bychan which gave him the incentive to learn Welsh. He graduated in Irish and Welsh History at Aberystwyth, and is now a full-time translator. He has published a collection of poetry, a number of volumes of short stories and one novel, and is at present working on a trilogy.

Jon Dressel (*b.* 1934) is an American poet whose forebears were immigrants from Llanelli. He is a former Professor of English at Webster College, St Louis, and from 1976 to 1995 he was Director of the Programme for American Studies at Trinity College, Carmarthen. It was there that he met T James Jones with whom he collaborated on *Cerddi Ianws/Janus Poems* (1979) and *Wyneb yn Wyneb/ Face to Face* (1997). Although designated James Jones' translator in this anthology, he played a much more positive rôle in the composition of the poems than that word suggests.

Peter Finch (*b.* 1947) is a poet, editor and Chief Executive of *Academi*, the Welsh literary agency. He has published more than 20 collections of poetry, a book of stories, a series of guide books for new writers, including the bestselling *How to Publish Your Poetry*. He is much respected as an entertaining performer of his own work.

Catherine Fisher (*b.* 1957) is a poet and children's novelist. A full-time writer, she has published over a dozen books and has won many literary awards, including the Welsh Arts Council Young Writer's Prize in 1989. She has also won the Cardiff International Poetry Competition (1989), the Tir Na N-og Prize (1995) and has been shortlisted for the Smarties Prize and the W H Smith Prize.

Mike Jenkins (*b.* 1953) is a poet, short story writer and teacher. Author of numerous collections of poetry, he has won the John Tripp Award for Spoken Poetry and in 1998 he won the Welsh Arts Council's Book of the Year Prize for *Wanting to Belong*, a collection of short stories for teenagers. He is former editor of *Poetry Wales*, and is co-editor of The Red Poets' Society.

Nigel Jenkins (*b.* 1949) is a freelance writer and poet. His book about Welsh missionaries in India, *Gwalia in Khasia* (1995) won the Arts Council of Wales Book of the Year Award in 1996. His latest book is *Footsore on the Frontier* (2001). He is currently co-editor of Academi's Encyclopaedia of Wales. With Menna Elfyn he co-directs a Creative Writing MA programme.

Dafydd Wyn Jones (*b.* 1940) is a retired teacher, poet and translator. He has won numerous prizes at the National Eisteddfod for his own poetry, and writes exclusively in the strict metres. A former teacher of English, he has translated the work of his son Ceri Wyn Jones, another wordsmith of the strict metres.

Sally Roberts Jones (*b.* 1935) is a poet, critic, editor and local historian. She has published four collections of poems as well as critical studies, short stories and folk tales for children. Through her publishing house, Alun Books, which has over a hundred titles to its name, she helped to foster new talents. She is a former Chair of Academi, the Welsh writers' agency, and has been an indomitable supporter of the culture of Wales.

D Myrddin Lloyd (1909-81) was a scholar, literary critic and editor. A librarian by profession, he spent some years as Keeper of Printed Books at the National Library of Scotland. His many contributions include *O Erddi Eraill* (1981), an anthology of verse translated from eighteen languages into Welsh. With Tomas O'Cleirigh he translated a volume of stories from the Irish by Padraic O'Conaire. Other works include *A Book of Wales* (1953) and *A Reader's Guide to Scotland* (1968).

Christopher Meredith (*b.* 1954) is a poet and novelist. He is senior lecturer in English at the University of Glamorgan. He has published two volumes of poetry and three novels. In 1985 he won the Welsh Arts Council's Young Writer's Prize and was winner of the Welsh Arts Council's Fiction Prize in 1989.

Robert Minhinnick (*b.* 1952) is a poet, editor and essay writer. He has published and edited over a dozen books of poetry and prose. In 1993, his *Watching the Fire Eater* was the Arts Council's Welsh Book of the Year. This is only one of a number of awards he has won. He has travelled the world to literary festivals and ventured into many lands in pursuit of environmental issues. He has been editor of *Poetry Wales* since 1997. His *Selected Poems* appeared from Carcanet in 1999. [ADD HIS WELSH ANTHOLOGY?]

Richard Poole (*b.* 1945) is a poet and critic. Until his retirement last year he was tutor of literature at Coleg Harlech. He has published four collections of poetry and his poems have appeared in many periodicals and anthologies in Wales, England and the USA. He has written extensively on the fiction of Richard Hughes and on the English language poetry of Wales. He was editor of *Poetry Wales* from 1992 to 1996.

Meic Stephens (*b.* 1938) is a translator, editor, anthologist and poet, and was appointed a Professor at the University of Glamorgan in 2001. Amongst his numerous contributions to Welsh culture is *The Oxford Companion to the Literature of Wales*, a new edition of which appeared from the University of Wales Press in 1998. He runs the literary agency Cambrogos and is the literary executor of distinguished writers such as Glyn Jones and Rhydwen Williams.

R S Thomas (1913-2000) was arguably Wales's best English-language poet during the 20th century. Author of over 30 volumes of poetry, and winner of many prizes, he was nominated for the Nobel Prize for Literature in 1996. He was a fervent Welshman who became a Welsh speaker in adulthood, although English remained the medium of his poetry to the end. He was a staunch pacifist as well as a passionate bird-watcher, but he had a distaste for the changing human landscape. His later poetry, post-Christian in nature, grapples with the notion of the *deus abscondicus*.

Gwyn Williams (1904-90) was a poet, translator, novelist and critic. From 1935 until his retirement in 1969 he taught at universities in Cairo, Alexandria, Libya and Istanbul, latterly as Professor of English Literature. His translations were groundbreaking in making Welsh-language poetry accessible to a wider world. Amongst his publications are *The Rent that's due to Love* (1950), *An Introduction to Welsh Poetry* (1953), *The Burning Tree* (1956, reprinted as *Welsh Poetry, Sixth century to 1600* in 1973), *Presenting Welsh Poetry* (1959) and *To Look for a Word* (1976).

Rowan Williams (*b.* 1950) was Bishop of Monmouth and Archbishop of Wales before being appointed Archbishop of Canterbury. From 1986 to 1992 he was Lady Margaret Professor of Divinity at Oxford. He is a Fellow of the British Academy and the author of several books on theology, including *The Wound of Knowledge*, and he has also published collections of poetry. As a translator he avoids a literal rendering and attempts 'to recreate the progressions of imagery with something of the energy they have in the original'.

The following translators' work is included in this anthology, and their biographical notes appear above their poems: **Elin ap Hywel, Grahame Davies, Siôn Eirian, Emyr Humphreys, R Gerallt Jones, Emyr Lewis** and **Geraint Løvgreen.**

KEY TO TRANSLATORS:

Translators are credited after each poem with their initials:

EaH	Elin ap Hywel
JPC	Joseph P Clancy
GC	Gillian Clarke
TC	Tony Conran
GD	Grahame Davies
MD	Martin Davis
JD	Jon Dressel
SE	Siôn Eirian
PF	Peter Finch
CF	Catherine Fisher
EH	Emyr Humphreys
MJ	Mike Jenkins
NJ	Nigel Jenkins
RGJ	R Gerallt Jones
DWJ	Dafydd Wyn Jones
SRJ	Sally Roberts Jones
EL	Emyr Lewis
DML	D Myrddin Lloyd
GL	Geraint Løvgreen
CM	Christopher Meredith
RM	Robert Minhinnick
RP	Richard Poole
MS	Meic Stephens
RST	R S Thomas
GW	Gwyn Williams
RW	Rowan Williams

T Gwynn Jones

Thomas Gwynn Jones (1871-1949) had no University education himself, and yet became Professor of Welsh Literature at Aberystwyth at the age of 48. Both polymathic and prolific, he was a journalist, scholar, translator from many languages, novelist, dramatist, and scholar – but a poet first and foremost, and was in the vanguard of the literary renaissance at the beginning of the 20th century. He was contradictory in that he appeared a diehard romantic, but was in reality wrestling with modernism.

Argoed

1

Argoed, Argoed of the secret places…
Your hills, your sunken glades, where were they,
Your winding glooms and quiet towns?

Ah, quiet then, till doom was dealt you,
But after it, nothing save a black desert
Of ashes was seen of wide-wooded Argoed.

Argoed, wide-wooded…Though you have vanished,
Yet from the unremembering depths, for a moment,
Is it there, your whispering ghost, when we listen –

Listen in silence to the wordless speech
Where the wave of yearning clings to your name,
Argoed, Argoed of the secret places?

2

Away in Gaul, 'mid its splendour and famed
Riches, were the secret solitudes of Argoed;
There, there was inspiration and adventure,
And words, for truth's sake, chosen by the wise;
The heart of her people kept faith; richness
Of her history never lapsed to oblivion,
And sweet there and pure the old tongue continued
And custom as old as her earliest dawn.

Mystery, in that place, kept its repose
Under sleep lingering in her dark shades;
Her oaks and maples, the silent might of ages,

Sunlight, and warmth, and the crystal rain,
World-wonder, the wheel, the miracle of seasons,
Labouring green through innumerable veins;
Old history feeling its way out of them
(As it were) in perfumes and great mounds of colour
And many a murmur, till, being fused,
They became soul and quick of every inspiration,
A force, momentum of dreams half-remembered,
That to the thought of a poet gives form
When tumultuous senses have for long lodged it.

When Winter had fled the country of Gaul
And it was Spring there, come once more,
In the quiet, mysterious forests of Argoed
The old, irresistible miracle quickened;
Under the beating of its wing, slowly,
The countryside over, opened the eyes
Of buds innumerable: life broke forth
In a flood of colour, diversity of kinds,
Till the vigour of it raced in the blood of the beasts
And it rolled like fire through the hearts of men;
Which new vigour and virtue of Nature,
Despite bias of lethargy, grew in strength,
Withering, growing old, and yet renewing –
That inextinguishable flame that was given
To conquer anguish and the power of death.

Yet lovely also was Argoed when, over the trees,
Spread all the magic of autumnal pomp,
Colours innumerable, and sleepy hours,
Hours rounded in unruffled plenty,
Hours untroubled, as if the berries were ripe
On Time's branches, and the splendours of it,
Its sleep, its peace, had all been pressed into them
As the Summer gives to the juicy fruit of the vine
Its virtue and sparkle, and reckless power.

There, in the midst of her knotted oaks
And privet, was a stretch of open ground,
And webs of bright gossamer with dew upon it
Whether in Summer or Springtime, or Winter,
And under the dawn the uncountable dew
Was as if each drop were an opening eye

That glinted an instant, presently closing
As the yellow-gold sunlight rose before it
Like seaspray that dies even as it splashes,
Or sparks of a smithy, fading as they fly;
And on that open ground, a town at the wood's end,
Time out of mind the Children of Arofan
Had sustained their state purely, and never forsaken
The life of blessedness their fathers had known –
Hunting or herding, as there was need of it,
Living and suffering, as life required them,
Fearing no weakness, craving no luxuries,
Nor sought to oppress, nor feared the oppressor;
In such tranquillity, generation to generation,
They raised strong sons and lovely daughters;
Recited their tales of courage of old times,
Attentive to hear, to know the true sentence
Of words of wisdom of men that were good men
And all the mysteries hidden in musecraft;
They listened to the secret learning of Druids,
Men with the gods themselves acquainted,
Who kept in the mind, generation to generation,
A wisdom of wonder-lore, not proper to be graved
On stone or wood, or preserved in writing.

Oh then, how joyous were the days
In the quiet, mysterious forests of Argoed!
But she, in her ancient piety, knew not
Gaul was pulled down, under heel of her enemies,
And already the fame of her cities had dwindled
With coming of trickery, foreigner's ways,
To tame her energy, waste an old language
And custom as old as her earliest dawn.

Argoed, Argoed of the secret places...
Oh then, was not a poet born in that land,
One inspired to sing her old glory,
Turning the tales of courage of old times,
Words of wisdom of men that were good men,
And all the custom hidden in musecraft,
To fit a new song, whence glory grew
Of his country and its past, and praise of its language?

And Argoed was proud that her poet was gone
To the courts of Gaul and seats of her splendour,
Reciting there of the might and valour
And manners of men, heroes of old times,
Glory and legendary past of his nation
And the gods themselves walking the world.

Argoed, Argoed, of the secret places,
How great would be the day of his homecoming
Back to them, bearing his fill
Of the gifts and honour that rightly rewarded
The new song he had fashioned his nation
in the quiet, mysterious forests of Argoed,
Argoed, Argoed of the secret places!

3

One night, from a court of Alesia city –
A citadel that, in the day of her might,
Had held back the pomp of Roman soldiers
Nor stooped to cherish the yoke of her enemies –
One night, from this court of Alesia city,
From the good cheer of the feasting within,
From the unthinking crowd's dull tumult,
Women half-naked and daintified boys
Of that famed city, that danced therein,
Their flesh and their smiles passionate with wine,
From that tight throng and its wantoning friendship
And many an eye wandering ardent in lust,
Into the air of the night, cold and dark,
A man stepped forth; he was nearing the wall,
His features weary, as if with the knowledge
He was disgraced there, instead of honoured.

In grievous pain he stood for a moment
With a weariness on him like despair,
For in his heart that night he knew
His nation's valour and ancient glory
Was lost for ever, gone from the world –
He, that had sung the chief of that glory,
Turning the tales of courage of old times,
Words of wisdom of men that were good men,
And all the custom hidden in musecraft,
To fit a new song, whence glory grew

Of his country and its past, and praise of its language –
And now, at last, vain was the labour,
For Gaul was pulled down under heel of her enemies
With coming of trickery, foreigner's ways,
To tame her vigour, waste an old language
And custom as old as her earliest dawn;
Now they could grasp neither metre nor meaning,
Nor would his singing earn him ought better
Than the sneer of a slave, awkwardly mocking him
In a patois malformed from wretched Latin –
Ah now, at last, how vain was his labour!
Slaves must be slaves, then? Ay, he that sells
Of his birthright, his be the shame of it...
And yet, despite that, in Argoed also
Would there be heard this broken-down Latin
On the lips of slaves, defiled and unworthy?
A generation come there not comprehending
The words of wisdom of men that were good men?
An end in that place of talent and nobleness
And all clean living, oppressed by her enemies?
This jabbering to oust a dignified language,
And vile dishonour, where men had been brave?

Then did the bright fire light in his eyes,
The blood in him boiled as that servile laughter
Again burst from within. He listened, head bent,
For a moment stayed hesitant. Then,
Like a man that can finally see before him
The day of his hopes ended for ever,
With a kind of sob, a catch in his breath,
Did he laugh also, striding on his journey,
His path soon hidden in the cold, wet gloom.

4

And tribute from Argoed was decreed, three times,
And then, three times, Argoed refused it,
For never had Argoed at all given honour
To a foreign might or brutal oppression;
The heart of her people kept faith; richness
Of her history had not lapsed to oblivion;
And none but the vilest among them would suffer
An enemy's yoke without wincing in shame,
Or bear, without blushing, its naked disgrace.

'We'll not give tribute, let forests be fired first,
Let the last of the Children of Arofan die,
Nor mock our past, nor forswear an old language,
Nor custom as old as our earliest dawn!'

To the bounds of Argoed quickly the word went,
Each of her citizens was constant and sure;
The doom was pronounced, without one to cross it,
The course was ventured, no man flinched from it;
For all his trickery, no foreigner had tribute,
Chattel nor booty, nor man to be beaten;
Norhing was found there, or only a wasteland,
Desolation of ashes, where once were wide woods.

5

Argoed, Argoed of the secret places,
Your hills, your sunken glades, where were they,
Your winding glooms and quiet towns?

Ah, quiet then, till doom was dealt you,
But after it, nothing save a black desert
Of ashes was seen of wide-wooded Argoed.

Argoed, wide-wooded...Though you have vanished,
Yet from the unremembering depths, for a moment,
Are you there, unconquerable soul, when we listen –

Listen in silence to the wordless speech
Where the wave of yearning clings to your name,
Argoed, Argoed of the secret places?

[TC]

Pro Patria
(extracts)

'Thirty soldiers, exhausted and grim-faced
Cursing the heat to a man,
Our guns and our feet were like iron
And our throats were Sahara-like sand;
Over yonder we saw trees like beeches

With smoke drifting over their tops;
Our only desire was water
And that was the start of the rot!
Our bruised, battered feet sped on swifter
The guns on our backs felt light;
What matter the enemy, lurking,
Soon he'd be dead to the fight!
Water – some liquid to moisten
The fire in each parched, red-hot throat,
And if the guns started spitting
Then dammit, we'd push out the boat!

*

'When I woke, the sun in the sky said
I'd been sleeping an hour or two,
By now, the place was so quiet
As it had been before the to-do.
Two men were asleep beside me
Each quiet and still as a mouse,
Around twenty were laughing and swearing
Nearer to the house.

' "Hurry up! You're dam' slow at it laggards!"
Said one of the twenty, quite hoarse;
From the house came Jobkins and Jaggards
With their faces all red and coarse;
Juggins and Muggins and Snoddy,
Damning "these bloody Boers";
"Taffy!" called one, as I got up,
"Buck up! There's some fun indoors!"

'The five went towards them, laughing,
Two under the trees slept on;
To a rabble so lewd and lascivious
I doubt whether I'd ever belonged.
In sleep I had drifted from trouble
Back to my boyhood in Wales,
But when I looked up at their grinning mugs
I forgot all the fairy tales.
The seven and twenty were leaving
While the other two slumbered there
And I had every muscle tensed

For the danger I knew was near;
What pigs the two men sleeping
How ugly the whole blasted team;
And me in their midst, a man whose world
Had once been an innocent dream;
I raised my gun to my shoulder
Meaning to wake the two men,
If I really had stooped as low as that,
I should have been blamed for it then!
But I remembered Snoddy's cackle
And his cocky leer, the louse,
And I walked, with rising hackles,
To see what was in the house.

'God forgive us poor mortals
If any deserved that name,
Not naked, grinning devils
And me, maybe, part of their shame.
I remembered the sound of the piano –
Smashed now to smithereens –
And the floor – I'll never forget it –
Only God could have made it clean;
When I saw the sight before me
I nearly lost all control,
Then I heard something trying to rise up
And there, lying on the floor,
Was a girl with the clothes torn from her
And scattered around the room –
God! I memembered Shani
And her low, dejected moans!

'Twenty-seven of those devils had been there –
And she, who till then had been pure –
Damn it all! My soul was on fire
Though not much better myself, to be sure,
The sound of their lecherous sniggering
As the other two walked through the door
And the lust and the greed on their faces –
I don't recall any more.

'"Stand back!" I remember I said that,
"Or I'll brain you, by God, that I'll do!"
As I raised the butt of my gun up

I remember the oath I swore;
I don't know where I aimed each bullet
In that frenzied quarter-hour
But the noise grew quiet. I looked down
And saw two wads of brain on the floor!

'For a second, I stood and wondered
To see those two buggers' legs
Like the legs of a chicken, quivering
After you've wrung its neck –
But I felt my head a-swimming
And I rushed like a fool for the door
And after that, I remember
The darkness, and nothing more –
But Nurse, when I heard you singing
A snatch from that tune "Break of Day"
My head felt as if it were splitting
And my tongue coming clean away!
And that's the whole truth of the matter –
The tale of a Welshman who erred,
Who did wrong by his sweetheart – Oh Shani! –
Who broke his own mother's heart!
Who killed two bloody bastards –
I don't regret that, Lord above,
The pain that will stay with me always
Is the thought of those women's love.
So yes, I've told you my story
And no, I don't feel any worse –
But I trod the path of my choosing
And now I will pay for it, Nurse.'

[EaH]

The Meal

On a dish on the table, nothing but your head
in the midst of green lettuce –
all the rest gone into other folk's mouths.
Your eye dead, under its pale window
like a stagnant pond under ice,

39

and your mouth wide open
stayed
in a posture of weird laughter.
It's as if your destiny amused you,
having in your turn escaped
thousands of sea mouths,
to be caught by a vermin of the land,
and violated, stitched with leaves,
crafted by a fine cook
to pleasure the mouth and false teeth
and eyes too, under their fashioned glasses,
craving for every delicacy from sea and land
before I'm a titbit myself for littler vermin.
Isn't that funny?
Oh, indeed. He's laughing.

[TC]

Humanity
(extracts)

It was night in one of the old cities,
heiress of every daredevil deed of the long centuries,
she who had gilded herself
with the loot of the lands she despoiled
in the days of her power,
she who knew then she was no longer
the greatest city in the world...
it was night in the old city.

Fog enveloped her,
her streets lay empty,
dark and silent,
not a crack of light,
not a peep of pomp or poverty,
the network of sewers where ran
the pity and filth of life's twists and turns
from the veins of her wealth and its glance of glory,
day and night, no whit of fear
smoked still from the seethe and the swagger.

Tonight there was a strange difference,
an overwhelming darkness from outside,
a stillness no will could dismiss,
a gravity that dared but whisper
for fear of some fate not yet born
that lurked in the void above.

It was hushed, even in the hotels...
dinner a shade more spare,
no customary cheer and bustle.
Whoever spoke, spoke low.
The clink of crockery was quiet,
the knives and forks had lost
their tinkle on the plates.
Sobriety tempered the glasses
where wine's wild laughter had been.

Nothing came in from out there,
no sound, no familiar hum,
for a moment; suddenly
a sundering like thunder
shuddered the house and at once
all leapt in a frenzy,
huddled and pale
flocking like sheep when the sky cracks,
thunderstruck, shattering heaven.

And again, from out there, the first crack fading in the air,
came the burst of another bomb
further off, and a roar of walls falling
down into rubble
with a terrible growl...

Down to the cellars,
herded, terrified people
herding like animals to their lairs
safe in the bowels of the mother of us all,
the dark earth...

The ablest of their day,
with the last secret of their cleverness,
struck a deal between evil and need,
and their right to a place in the sun,
raining their vengeance from a blue black sky.

41

And there in the terror and tumult,
face to face with death, inflamed
as one thrill in the heart,
the desire of miserable flesh for flesh,
the lust to unite before death,
the quickening instinct to survive,
a moment of mutual revenge,
in an act of rampant rage,
a malign coupling...

II

Came the day,
day of human desire for a tryst with evil,
lust for a war of body and soul.
And she in her turn was born
to a world that matured her,
that armed her naked rage,
in her frailty, her fracturing,
in her muddle and madness,
at the door of despair.

Came her day,
her day among all the nations,
not one, or two, but all,
the judgment day for blind impulse,
lacked all instinct of the human race,
and from the enemy's venom in the blood,
the plague of a people's dispersal.

III

And Europe lying in her blood,
her cities already ablaze,
her people cap in hand
in penury and pain, and the poisonous gas
trapping and choking millions...
their dumb instinct turned
in the very depth of their being,
which knows itself,
that it's a human need to give and take,
this instinct turned itself
until flesh and sinew
were steely with rage...

*

One night in the old city
from a house near the promenade
Saint Peter went walking late
out of the old city, in flight,
and he saw that it was his lord there
in the darkness taken prisoner
and the suffering and the death
in the old city could have been his story.
The disciple had turned his back on him, –
broke down weeping and turned again
in humility
to face his destiny.

In that house was a hermit,
a solitary scholar reading the words
of that peerless story,
amid the clamour of the city
and the ceaseless sorrow.

And a man came to him in his cell,
in flight from many dangers,
his face pale and bloody.

And meek and merciful was the monk,
a man like his Lord before him;
and his heart filled with pity at the stranger's
story of suffering,
and nothing and nowhere remained
free from the tyrant now.

And the hermit took him into hiding,
and there he sat reading, studious
in the doorway by the light of the distant fires
burning the mother of all cities,
her treasure, her history,
turned to gray ashes.

Night fell…
        No one came
hunting the fugitive…
and there was nothing
nothing in the clamour of the storm.

The monk went inside,
called out to the man he had hidden...

One word from the place where he rested,
he did not come. He will not come again.

[GC]

Dyfnallt

J Dyfnallt Owen (1873-1956) was a Nonconformist minister who edited the
denominational paper, *Y Tyst* ('The Witness'). His innate lyricism as a poet was
tempered by his experience of active service in the First World War.

Hour of Fear

1

No going back:
I say no going back.
What could be crueller than the commandant's cursing scorn,
Or tomorrow morning, bullets fired at dawn;
I'm neither coward nor a reckless fool.

I was at Aisne:
Yes, the terrible onslaught at Aisne,
And on the Marne in the battle's dreadful fray:
Not the dark night of Hell nor Judgment Day
Like horrors such as these.

Gassed:
Oh, God, gassed.
A quick glimpse of a brother's blue-black face,
His fallen flesh flushed by his blood's red race:
I will never cross the ditch into that place
Again.

Flows the Nedd.
(Oh, to see the Nedd!)
Back from the country to its eye under the hill
At the foot of the Foel, before folding the call-up
Paper ordering me back to the stinking hole –
Better the grave.

2

And his voice hoarse:
And his gaze harsh,
He heard the woe of fire-balls in the heavens
His soul in the grasp of grim destiny
And he faced fate and power without bounds.

And his voice a wound,
His voice and heart a wound,
'Pray,' said a friend, 'before the Cross:
Only one knows pain's mystery,
The mad moment – only God.'

And in that place,
Unflinching in that place:
His hands folded together before the altar,
A picture of the Cross before him in blue-flame
He prayed, then brave-hearted he stood up.

And the night fled:
Yes, the frown of night fled
From its brow, and he stood tall,
Yes, stood like a king of the world;
He saluted, smiled, and turned his face to the trench.

[GC]

T E Nicholas

T E Nicholas (1879-1971) was known as 'Niclas y Glais' because he was a
minister in the village of Glais in the Swansea Valley for about ten years. He
was an unlikely combination of Christian and Marxist. In middle age he left
the ministry, and practised as a dentist. He was one of the founders of the
Communist Party of Great Britain, and was an unrelenting apologist for the
socialist cause – in newspaper articles, lectures as well as in his poetry, which
is unashamedly polemical. During the Second World War he was imprisoned
on false charges, and produced a volume of poems written originally on prison
toilet paper, *Canu'r Carchar* ('Prison Poetry', 1942).

To a Sparrow
(Swansea Prison, 1940)

Look, here's another bread-crumb for your piping,
And a piece of apple as a sweetener.
It gladdens me to hear your steady pecking;
It's good to see your cloak of grey once more.
You've travelled here, perhaps, from Pembroke's reaches,
From the gorse and heather on Y Frenni's height,
And maybe on grey wing you've trilled your measures
Above fair Ceredigion at dawn's first light.
Accept the bread: had I a drop of wine
Pressed from a distant country's sweet grape-cluster,
We two could take, amid war's turbulence,
Communion, though the cell lacks cross and altar.
The bread's as holy as it needs to be,
Offering of a heart not under lock and key.

[JPC]

Caernarfon Circus, 1969

For how long have you wanted a magician
    To conjure this kid from under his coat?
He's big for his age, a little Englishman
    Ready to stand on your shoulders and rule the roost.
As usual you've slaved under a spell,
    The rumour-mill your only philosophy;

46

But gossip has grown into a gospel
  And this is a nation in negative, living its lie.
Yet if the rich have no more guts than grass
  And the poor scratch a beggar's inheritance
Who is left to strike the dazzling stanzas?
  Without memory there is only madness.
They're stoics in their sties, yet this people calls
For made-up magic under castle walls.

[RM]

I D Hooson

Isaac Daniel Hooson (1880-1948) was a solicitor by profession, and a popular author of ballads and lyrics about animals and flowers, which were the staple diet of recitation competitors at *eisteddfodau* for many years.

The Flame

A red caravan, a greyhound bitch,
A lame mare sheltering under a hedge,
A girl dancing to a tune debonair,
As her sweetheart's fiddle glints to the fire.

Up and up the white flames float
Like an arm about a black cauldron's throat;
A tall gipsy seals a lover's oath,
On honey lips pledges troth.

And the moon climbs above the hill –
Like her, the fire's now dead and chill;
Flame's every gust and passion's fire,
In their turn, to ash expire.

[TC]

The Red Poppy

The morning dew was on your lip
In drops of silver, scarlet flower,
All afternoon June's sunlit hours
Poured gold into your brimming cup.

You and your dancing sisters seen
Cavorting on a coverlet of green,
Native ground to your pure ilk
Dressed in your flames of fiery silk.

But someone's careless hand has torn
You from the earth where you were born
To alien earth, and where you stood
By dawn is stained red with your blood.

[GC]

Dewi Emrys

David Emrys James (Dewi Emrys) (1881-1952) was an unconventional Non-
conformist minister who left the ministry to become a journalist. For some years
he lived a bohemian existence in London, but retired to Talgarreg in Ceredigion,
although he remained a colourful character to the end of his days.

Pwllderi
(extracts)

Up on the mountains where I live
With the little streams and the air above,
I can ape the moorbirds' forlorn cries –
The nightjar, corncrake, lark and snipe –
But I couldn't puff out a panegyric
Or weave a college-standard lyric;
And I'm not beset by gorgeous babes
Turning me hot and cold in waves;
And it's things like these make me quite sure

The muse never darkened my study door;
'Cause the schoolmaster's always giving out
They're what being a poet's all about.

Yesterday, sitting above Pwllderi,
Where eagles lived once, and bears, and bogeys,
I thought, those streetwise people down by there
Have no idea it's so wild up here.
The shop-counter poof with his tweeds so fancy
Couldn't keep his footing above Pwlldeͬri:
You stand up high above this dungeon
Looking down on a bottomless cauldron
Boiling between the greyish crags
Like churnsful of milk or foaming suds.
Just thinking of it this very minute
Makes a ghost walk on my heart.

This time of year it's dressed up nice,
The gorse all yellow and the thorns all white,
And the bluebells growing in sky-blue drifts
On the greeny slopes leading to the cliffs
Where the heather lies on the rock in sheaves
You'd swear that someone had fired the hills.
Like a cheeky angel, the summer's been by
With a cruckful of ribbons and frippery,
He's the only one would be fool enough
To waste his wealth on this patch of rough,
Chuckling to send the gorse on the ledge
To spendthrift its gold right over the edge;
A miser would sicken, might fall and drown
To see its sovereigns raining down.

*

And lord above, what a commotion!
Like howling dogs or hell in motion
Crying and whistling, a thousand ravings
Reverberating through all those caverns;
I'll never forget that night of dread –
The sailor on the rock, half-dead
Calling, calling: not a soul nearby
And only seagulls to hear his cry,
While those hawks, like devils in disguise,

Waited for light to leave his eyes.
It's things like these that come to mind
Above Pwllderi, in summertime.

There's only one house around these parts
An old barn of a place, but what a heart!
Tucked into Garn Fowr, Dolgar by name,
A fine spot for a welcome and a cup well-famed,
Or a bowlful of *cawl*, you can't beat that,
Full of leeks and potatoes and starred with fat,
The pot on its tripod boiling full force,
Fuelled by faggots of blazing gorse,
A ladle brim-full, and twice, and thrice,
Finer by far than any lobscouse,
And a wooden spoon to scrape your bowl
And a hunk of cheese from a huge great wheel.

You can park yourself on an oaken settle
And listen to the shepherd's tale,
He won't talk much of the knock he got
Rescuing a lamb from a perilous spot;
Far less admit it took rope and chain
To pull him safe to the top again;
But with a catch in his voice, he might touch on
What sent him down through rocks and thorns:
Not the animal's price in market sum
But its cry as it bleated for someone to come;
And he'll talk a while of another Man
Who gave his life to save his lambs:
And those are the things that come to mind
Above Pwllderi in the summertime.

[EaH]

W J Gruffydd

William John Gruffydd (1881-1954) studied Classics and English Literature at Oxford, and became Professor of Welsh at Cardiff. He wielded a considerable influence on the Welsh world of letters through the quarterly journal, *Y Llenor* ('The Writer'), which he edited for almost 30 years from 1922. In 1943 he caused something of a scandal by standing as Liberal candidate for the University of Wales parliamentary seat against the Welsh Nationalist candidate, Saunders Lewis. Gruffydd won, and served as MP until 1950. He always courted controversy, and was a revered and feared figure in Welsh life during the first half of the century, as critic, scholar and poet as well as public figure.

This Poor Man

Because there was disquiet in the wind
    And sound of old griefs in the beating rain,
Sad echo of erstwhile afflicted rhymes
    Turning their tunes unceasing through his soul;
Because the far sea's roar on a quiet night
    Related virtue of the lost generations,
       And because trilling streams
    Awoke the entire anguish of their passion –
Like one mute he went to a phantom silence,
    And one by one all his companions fled,
Leaving him rapt in his mysterious secret,
    To the strange voices listening alone.

Where his companions had invoked God's anger
    On an unclean world, he saw its beauty,
Refused their path to heaven, took instead
    The insubstantial echo of magic pipes,
The murmuring bees of Arawn from the vineyards
    Heavy with honeydew from down the vale,
       The nectar of hidden dwellings,
    Caer Siddi's gold enclosure on the hill.
Before he died, banquets were his to sit at,
    He listened entranced to the unseen choir –
The birds of Rhiannon in the porches of pearl
    That open on the old forgetful sea.

[TC]

The Yew of Llanddeiniolen

On the horizon where the sun descends
    Above the rocky country's farthest peak
The church of Llanddeiniolen stands, the dense
    Shadow of its long low nave, its hue of black,
Covering day's last rites with languid sorrow;

Surrounding it there spreads a dark green host,
    Unbending sentries of the grave's grim region,
Holding their gnarled and knotted arms upthrust
    To screen the joyful visage of salvation,
The sun of the living, from the sad dead's borough.

And in the midst of these, Death's courtiers, rises
    The sovereign yew of every church in Wales,
Swollen in shape from its unstinted courses,
    Its store of mortal provender never fails,
Mayor of dead-men's town, the parish's proud squire.

Proud squire of the churchyard, living in luxury
    Upon its feeble subjects' flesh and blood,
Without a fear of its mute tenants' plea
    Or that they might abandon its estate, –
This is their homestead, their ancestral shire.

Within this yew's surroundings come at twilight
    All youthful parish pairs to speak in secret,
To learn here at the king of terror's court
    The first steps in the troublesome pursuit;
The yew waits patiently; their turn comes round.

Their turn will surely come, – and yet what matter?
    The sweet free laughter is not quieted,
And not a single youthful wing is fettered
    By recollection of the wretched dead,
Their hands crossed, in their beds beneath the ground.

[JPC]

1914-1918 The Young to the Old

Because your hearts are ice
But your hate a flame
You are rabid dogs
And your souls are lame.

Because in your sad life
Hope finds nothing left,
All your kindness gone
And your faith bereft,

Because you worshipped the gods
Of blood and revenge,
Because you wasted the land
And made it strange,

Because you did all this
Because we died for you
In uncomplaining herds
It's time we said what's true:

In their safe routines
It's the old we condemn,
And on the council bench
The nodding aldermen.

We were young, we were fools
But will never understand
Why we were sent forever
To no-man's-land.

You were never like us
In the lovers' lanes
With instinctive spring
Thrilling in our veins:

You were never like us
With an appetite
That a breath or a flower
Or the dawn could ignite.

We made living itself
Our bravery's boast,
We were the chosen few
Of the Holy Ghost.

But there's none have survived
The bayonet charge
Or the howling trench
Or the mortar barrage.

No, we are not like you –
The motheaten men –
For whom love has whispered
Its ultimate amen.

But today there's a smile
Where a curse had stung;
We are not like you,
We are forever young.

[RM]

Gwladys Rhys

There was Chapel and Prayer Meeting and Dorcas and Children's
        Meeting,
And my father, night and day, nervous as the wind,
The wind that night and day writhed in the pines
Around the manse. Where it found my mother too,
Inscribing what she thought was the language of heaven,
And never a word from her mouth that wasn't a prayer.

But what could it find for me to do,
Me, Gwladys Rhys, eldest daughter of the house
Of the Reverend Rhys of Horeb on the Moor?
I waited my turn obediently,
My eyes eager on every corner of the fields
Until the day was a poor shadow of the night
And the night itself stretched out with no horizon.
But worse, the waning of winter afternoons
When I would close the curtains at four o'clock

On the wind's white migraine in the pines
To hear instead my parents' mutterment.

But one day, a Someone came to our house.
I felt a thrilling Something in my heart.
It was not the wind convalescent in the pines
And no longer did I need to sit watchful
Of every corner of the fields. A breeze
From beyond the frontier had traced my skin.

Ignoring my father's usual frown
And my mother's saga of the Temperance Society
I tore the curtains from across the glass.
Without a word to either I went out into the snow
And heard the wind's liturgy through the pines
On a night such as when our prayers are harvested.

And so, passer-by, you will find me now
In the shadow of Horeb on the Moor,
Me, Gwladys Rhys, thirty years of age, watching
Her father and her mother hurrying past
To all those ceaseless services
And to the committees of the Temperance Society,
While I must lie in an unremembered grave,
That breath I heard beyond the boundary
Only the sigh of the wind still lost among the pines.

[RM]

Isfoel

Dafydd Jones (Isfoel) (1881-1968) was one of 'Bois y Cilie' (the Cilie Boys), a
family of poets named after the farm near Llangrannog in Ceredigion where
they were brought up. Three generations of poets made the name of the farm a
byword for *beirdd gwlad* or country poets, an unique breed of bards for whom
cynghanedd was a kind of language within a language. They were particularly
fond of strict metres such as *englyn* and *cywydd*, which they used dexterously to
perform a variety of social functions, such as congratulating, praising, elegising,
satirising and leg-pulling.

The Tractor

What kind of constant racket
Breeds fear in the countryside!
An uproar through the furrows,
Outlandish croon on earth's skin,
Commotion's come, upheaval,
Clear its clang across the land:
No more will horse in harness
Plod the field with flowing mane,
Nor a lad behind the yoke
Sing bawdy on the meadow,
A bold steel keel, a smokestack
Does the work and cleaving now.
A smooth seat for the farmer,
A pillowy pedestal,
That's him, with his back upright
And his cigarette, four-square!

Lay the steed beneath the turf
Of the field, old and feeble,
Old hero, ploughshare soldier,
Gone back to the wilderness,
A brave lad crossed the border
To his heaven, and his home,
From pain and heavy labour
To old fields, blessed is he!

Mule equal to forty steeds,
This device is undaunted,
Machine of immense power,
Handy tool, dale's elephant
With plough piercing the topsoil
It sails on the bed of grain.

Old moorlands always idle
Bear the same shade as the dale,
To the hare's and alder's heath
It climbs with plough and harrow,
And from the scar of wasteland
Oats stand where a ploughshare plunged.

[JPC]

56

Wil Ifan

Wil Ifan (William Evans) (1882-1968) was a minister with the English Con-
gregationalists who wrote poetry in both Welsh and English, won the National
Eisteddfod Crown three times, and was Archdruid of the Gorsedd of Bards
from 1947 until 1950. His poems are popular and lyrical, but tend towards the
sentimental. His prize-winning poem, 'Bro fy Mebyd' ('My Native District',
1925) was the first poem in *vers libre* to win the Crown.

In Porthcawl

All day the doctrine of the dove
Is crooned from a cage behind the house.
What can it mean, such bittersweet
Language, that there is joyfulness in gaol,
Or that every generation grieves
No matter how distant the defeat?

When darkness comes, the roost's at rest,
All laughing thoroughfares are still;
But through the marram sways a psalm –
The dove is welcoming the dawn,
As captive in the hand of God
It dies for us beyond the dune.

[RM]

The Vale of My Youth
(extract)

Long days together I'd lie there on my back,
Cap over eyes, to shield me from the sun,
Listening to water:
Unravelling its separate strands of sound.
A cold, hard tinkle: that was spoon on cup
Now and again, a ringing sound as clear
As the bell on the Brewery shire horses' bridles;
Then drink poured out of flagons, great carousing;
A sound like a small child crying out in sleep,
And then the tenderest sound you ever heard,
The Sh! Sh! of his mother, comforting.

The river was my brother, love, companion.
I knew that there were bigger, deeper waters,
Had heard tell of the river at Llandeilo;
Had learnt, of course, the names of Thames and Jordan.
But as I first heard of Jordan in the loft at Sunday School,
I thought it was a river up in heaven:
It didn't count!
The sea, according to the Tre-cyrn farmhand,
Was a hundred times as big as the big mill pond
(Though he was always a devil for exaggerating).
Although there were greater waters,
The river was my kin.
I knew nothing of its story
Before it reached the Dan-dre garden,
Nothing of the country where it sprang;
To me, a secret world
Lay beyond the thorn bushes;
There was something about the grey mystery
I might have called holiness
If I had known the word.

And if you, my reader, are wise,
You will say nothing of a river's source
Nor seek its secret,
Nor enquire why it touches the strings of your soul,
For you will search in vain.
Yes, you may find the spring among the reeds,
Trace drop by drop from shining path to the raincloud
In the heights of heaven,
But your quest will be in vain.
For surely every river rises
From the throne of God and the Lamb:
A bright streaming from the laughter of His heart.

And if the hedge, and something higher than hedges,
Kept me from the secret of its journey's start,
There was nothing to stop me from following it on its way:
It flowed, openly, across the river meadow.

How often, in the golden, mellowing autumn
I floated half a nutshell under the bridge,
Then followed the smooth stones to the meadow's end,

The farthest end of Tre-cyrn meadow.
The boat by now
Bottom up, its sailors in a watery grave.

[EaH]

R Williams Parry

Robert Williams Parry (1884-1956) became known as *Bardd yr Haf* (Poet of Summer) after winning the National Eisteddfod Chair for his celebrated 'Awdl yr Haf' ('Ode to Summer', 1910) – an exhilarating long poem full of hedonistic *joie de vivre*, and a self-justifying aestheticism. But he gradually experienced a sea-change which turned him into a tortured Poet of Winter. His mature poetry is full of angst at the inevitable mortality of every living creature. Although a lecturer in Welsh at Bangor – partly intra-mural, partly extra-mural – he was disillusioned by the academic establishment, and wrote scathingly about the treatment of Saunders Lewis by the University of Wales after the 'fire in Llŷn' in 1936.

Spring
(The Butcher's Song)

After the bitter weather,
   The damp and drifted snow,
After the bull's hectic roping
   And the tempests of the cow,
Spring came with its light labour
   And weather soft and benign,
And then there's sweeter knife-work –
   The lambs do not complain.

When I see beneath my fingers
   The curling fleece in mud,
Why should I feel mournful
   More than there's any need?
After living like beggars
   To the end of a lean week,
Christians on a Sunday
   Will find my dinners sweet.

[JPC]

Hedd Wyn

I

Grave the bard underground overseas, hands
    That will never unclasp;
   Keen eyes beneath a close lid,
   Eyes unable to open.

Now it has been lived, your lifetime; your course,
    Now it too has been run.
   The time come to go gravewards,
   Come to an end, earth's journey.

Tender is the moon tonight, as it climbs
    Above Trawsfynydd's marsh;
   And you, sad beneath your soil,
   By the black trench are at rest.

Trawsfynydd! Once you toiled over its rocks
    On Eryri's bare slopes;
   Once you trampled its bracken,
   Far away from it you slept.

II

Brothers! Under many a moon's delight
    Do not forget the lad;
   Sadder than sadness it was
   To lay the frail bard in dust.

Bitter, to drive one so mild from his home
    And his haven of books;
   Bitter, his earth laid in earth,
   Most bitter, his distant death.

Leaving work and woods, leaving sheep-walk,
    Leaving the mountain stream;
   Leaving dale, leaving daylight,
   And leaving the green-leaved boughs.

Chair waiting in solitude there! Its arms,
    As in solemn listening,
    Reach silently out in peace
    For one who will never come.

[JPC]

The Geese

December through the high
Trees made a wretched cry
    Like waves breaking.

Below in a bit of field,
Heedless their fate was sealed,
    Geese were grazing.

Leaves were a feather-stack,
Blood-colour, pied and black
    On the green ground.

I explained to the daft geese
This moral of the trees –
    Death's sight and sound.

'Therefore, do not stay!
Fly on wide wings away
    Before, hark it,

The Goodwife takes her cheese,
Her butter and her geese
    To the Great Market!'

But fie on such falsehood!
Geese waddle under the wood
    In scornful order,

Unanimous in each
Frivolous and jeering screech
    Over and over.

[TC]

A E Housman

The wise man does not fear the world
    That waits beyond death's portal.
His dread is that he is alive,
    For to exist is lethal.

Not feigning that he grasps – how glib! –
    The madness of creation,
He broods upon his mortal state,
    His birth that was betrayal.

The wise man in his might bows low
    Before creation's wonder,
But in his weakness lifts a voice
    Against extinction's power.

His way through woods day never lights
    Will be enclosed by branches;
He will not give the sky his trust,
    Will not walk with the masses.

No blessing for him in the church,
    And in the cup no rapture;
No seat beside the orthodox
    Or foolish unbeliever.

He does not plough, none plough for him,
    But on the short-lived faring,
He makes his meditation food,
    Creates bread from his dreaming.

This man who did not choose the world
    Will turn away reluctant;
Because before decay and death
    He sought, and found, a comrade.

The insubstantial wind it is
    That shapes verse round his passage;
And the illusion that it weaves
    Will never fade or perish.

[JPC]

Pagan

May every reference cease
To man's fickleness; in homage
World-wide he chooses gods
He creates in his own image,
In his own pathetic image.

Wood and stone are *passé*
And the metal gods of old:
Enter God, which meant an end
To idols made of gold,
To sovereigns made of gold.

But in this day and age
Only flesh and blood will do –
The faithful need to touch and see;
Intangible gods are quite taboo,
Unseen gods are quite taboo.

Man is everlasting,
Steadfast in his design;
Gods are for past and present,
But it's man who will remain,
The one who shall remain.

[MD]

J S L

A bright bird lighted in the sheltered yard
Out of another sky and all his colours dazzled
Our native poultry. Above his head
There was consternation in the dovecote, the kind of fuss
You find among the well-fed and the tame.
The bright bird was unwise. He sang his own song
Unaccompanied, on a new scale
Without sympathy or support. Not so much wrong
As solitary. He was bound to fail.
That's you, my rejected friend. You were a fool.

As for us, sound men of learning, we serve tea
While you serve time. The afternoon is on our side
Nothing disturbs our classic calm, no parish pump
Concerns. No echoing sighs. No prison cells.
We munch with precision our trimmed and buttered toast
You sew your mail-bags for the General Post.

[EH]

Wales 1937

Arise, take up your bed and walk, O Wind,
Or else fly through the heavens wailing and empty-handed;
Create fretfulness throughout the world on your way –
No monarch's troops or governor's guard will restrain you.
Humanise once more the flesh that has been turned to steel,
Baptise the griefless with your tears, and rechristen the wise;
Give the lukewarm behind his wall an hour of madness,
Make the earth beneath Philistia's strong concrete quake:
Or with the strains of your disturbing violin
Teach the blameless repentance, and teach him hope;
Touch the self-sufficient through his couch's cushion,
And give the tough materialist a shudder of despair:
From Llanfair ar y Bryn or Llanfair Mathafarn
Blow him to the synagogue or blow him to the tavern.

[JPC]

The Strangeness of Dawn

Strange to reach Paradise without crossing Jordan,
     In a moment, all unwarned, to step into lovely day –
Hear the cuckoo's mountain voice in the trees of the garden,
     See the pigeon to the ash grove slip on her way;
Strange to meet a hedgehog across the peacock's lawn,
     And find rabbits nibbling the breadth of a field from their tunnels,
The carefree young hare in mid-meadow, without shelter or form,
     The incredible heron stark in the estuary channels.

Yet stranger still, O sun on the otherside slope,
    Did you stay where you were, and man in his houses impound,
And lest timely smoke rise again from his chimneys, stop
    Till the crowbars of grass topple them to ground –
Man rid of his woe, and earth of his aspect and savour,
Ere steeds be in harness again, and skies travelled over.

[TC]

The Propaganda of the Poet

To green Nature, not the world, the poet belongs;
    He has no truck with it: to make his mark
Does not climb pulpits singing fashionable songs
    Nor stands his box in the grass of Hothead Park.
Wasn't he born of a hag inhuman and unreclaimed
    Whose show of stars and sunset pomps amaze
Till the sick heart melts, till the healthy are tamed,
    Though she's not herself concerned in our shrunk days –

Save when her thunder's loose, and the word's there
    That frights from our fatal weaving the matter-of-fact,
Brings ghost to feast and phantom to the fair,
    And shows the worm in the wood, and the creation cracked:
Thunder that drives brave men to mosque and mascot,
Cloudbursts extinguishing sun on the roads to Ascot.

[TC]

Mortality

> *'Whatever the year brings, he brings nothing new.'*
> ROSE MACAULAY

Young rhymester, don't try to gag the old muse
From expressing his terminal heartache;
Stifling graveside elegies with odes to the
Glories of steel and infamous hardship.
Will divine airs blow to power the mills
Of our time or propel ocean liners?
Or scatter the people's woes which gather
Like last year's leaves in the dismal gutters?

Good God! The poet's now a pamphleteer.
And Branwen – did she die? or didn't she?
And will the barren fig tree flower again
When the west wind summons Arianwen?
Thus now, as it was in the beginning,
Death has no demise. This is the real woe.

[MD]

The Old Boatman

There were assembled, so the papers say,
    Seven and four score motorcars in conclave
To the solemn task, the day before yesterday,
    Of running someone dead towards his grave.
Though flashy's the paint on each fat, pampered cur,
    Yet at the funerals hereabouts, their guise
And conduct are as prim as if they were
    In God's Eisteddfod trying for a prize.

And when the body tires of the ferry road
    And the spirit its appointed end must meet,
Can we not quicker lay our brother's load
    In these luxurious vans than on two feet?
But on the flood that's shrouded from our dust,
Though boat be old and slow, Charon's not fussed.

[TC]

Hedd Wyn

Ellis Humphrey Evans (Hedd Wyn) (1887-1917) was a shepherd from Traws-fynydd in Meirionnydd (Merioneth) who had little education, but who became a poet under the influence of friends and the strong eisteddfodic ethos of his time. In 1917 he joined the Welsh Fusiliers, but was tragically killed in the trenches on the last day of July of that year. It was his long poem in strict metres, 'Yr Arwr' ('The Hero') which was awarded the Chair at the National Eisteddfod held in Birkenhead on the following September, and the empty chair was draped with a black shroud in his memory. A successful film (screenplay by Alan Llwyd and directed by Paul Turner) based on his life was nominated for an Oscar in 1994.

War

Bitter my life in times like these,
While God declines beyond the seas;
Instead, Man, king or peasantry,
Raises his gross authority.

When he thinks God has gone away
Man takes up his sword to slay
His brother; we can hear death's roar.
It shadows the hovels of the poor.

Like the old songs they left behind,
We have hanged our harps on the trees again.
The blood of boys is on the wind,
Their blood is mingled with the rain.

[GC]

The Black Blot

We can lay no claim to the stars,
Nor a yearning taste of the moon,
Nor the cloud with its gold border
In monotonous blue.

We can lay claim to nothing
But the tired earth's story;
And the turning of all to disorder
Amongst God's glory.

[GC]

T H Parry-Williams

T H Parry-Williams (1887-1975) was the son of the schoolmaster of Rhyd-ddu in Snowdonia. He had a distinguished academic career (Aberystwyth, Oxford, Freiburg and the Sorbonne in Paris) and eventually became Professor of Welsh at Aberystwyth. He won the Crown and Chair at the National Eisteddfod in the same year on two separate occasions (1912 and 1915). As a creative writer he excelled as both essayist and poet, and is often described as the first Welsh-language modernist, not on account of his technique, but because of his sense of dichotomy and the absurd.

Barrenness

There was only a wild world bare of trees
Up there in Snowdonia around my birth,
Just as if the giants had never ceased
Smoothing each slanting surface of earth;
And from infancy, through the amazing
Years of my boyhood in our upland home,
The mountains' primitive forms pressed in
Till their barrenness penetrated my bone.
And if something of me survives my end
Without vanishing away utterly,
And is found by a like-minded friend
At dusk near Snowdon accidentally,
No image will be seen in it, no design,
Nothing but barrenness's bleak outline.

[RP]

Tŷ'r Ysgol

The chimneys smoke despite each adverse breeze,
And now and then somebody sweeps the floor
And opens all the windows, though there has
Been no one, since the great dispersal, living there;
Save for a month's vacation, more or less,
In August, to leave town life for a space
And turn about a bit, till some express
Surprise to see us move around the place;
And everybody asks what makes us bother

To keep the old place up, a world away,
We, who have long since lost mother and father, –
But that is how it is, I don't know why,
Unless for fear the buried couple should
Sense somehow that the door was locked for good.

[JPC]

Llyn y Gadair

The jaunty traveller that comes to peer
Across its shallows to the scene beyond
Would almost not see it. Mountains here
Have far more beauty than this bit of pond
With one man fishing in a lonely boat
Whipping the water, rowing now and then
Like a poor errant wretch, condemned to float

The floods of nightmare never reaching land.
But there's some sorcerer's bedevilling art
That makes me see a heaven in its face,
Though glory in that aspect has no part
Nor on its shore is any excelling grace –
Nothing but peat bog, dead stumps brittle and brown,
Two crags, and a pair of quarries, both closed down.

[TC]

This One

Care about Wales? Well, I do and I don't.
The committed spring their own trap. I certainly won't.

One just happens to live here. It's a nice enough place
Not a boil on the back of beyond. As for the race,

If one dare make use of such an imprecise word,
Self-absorbed no doubt and hypocritical too. But in this world

Who isn't? Admittedly one can have too much melodious moaning:
It's important to distinguish between whingeing, wailing and groaning,

And maybe the constant twitter of nervously nationalist noises
Distracts our subsidised bards from promoting worthier causes –

But at least the sounds are local. Not media manufactured.
The smaller facts of life are less easily fractured.

So I'll make for the hills! Avoid all sententious chatter,
Get back to where I was born. The mountain and things that matter.

Here I stand. Not exactly Luther but relieved to get away.
Not a flag in sight. Or a hoarding. Just the light of common day.

There's the first peak I clambered: all the rugged truth of the land;
There's the lake, and the stream, and the crag: and right at hand

My father's house. Where else between heaven and earth
Can I recapture the sound of the folk who gave me birth?

Why am I shaking? Where's that scientific resolve
That keeps sentiment at bay? Homeland. Heimat. Bro.

These are claws of Cymreictod clutching at my breast,
Harsh signals to respond. Can I avoid the Test?

[EH]

Conviction

I stood, like a god, on the corner where
The old Red Trail to great Snowdon's summit
Turns left, level and stony, and there,
Like one who can boldly make fate submit,
I rolled a rock down the rough cliff-face
And watched as it galloped, lickety-split,
With a rabble of pebbles that joined the race
As it knocked them down along with it.
I knew very well that no one but I –
The god, though the fact's unworthy of mention –
Determined the shape of its destiny
When I set the simple stone in motion:
But I realised after it was gone
That I wasn't a god – I was the stone.

[RP]

Two Poems

(Which touch on something that came
Into my mind once, then went away.
I don't know what it was. – And what does it matter?)

I

I am deceiving you: deceivers are what we are –
  All, without exception. I confess this
Before God today. You will laugh, I know.
  My truth is nothing but a lie, my life a living death.

But you will not learn fear: not one of you
  Has yet learnt fear. That's how it's always been.
Come and listen, the raindrops tire of waiting
  For the sounds of a disturbance in the wood.

Two – there are only two colours, the white and the black –
  You and I. But for them the world is empty
As it spins in empty space; and they are merely
  A double nothingness – nothing spinning in nothing always.

The talent that was given you to fill the emptiness
  With your own self is your curse.
You taught me how to fill and colour the world,
  Void and two-coloured, with many shades and shapes.

But I am convinced. Truth is nothing
  But a lie, and my life a living death.
Listen to the raindrops' discontent. –
  We too are passing forms, and we wait as they wait.

Yet September was truly September.
  Arfon was mountains beneath our feet.
The mist was mist, and one and one made two,
  An hour and an hour made hours, and you were flesh and blood.

But I am convinced. September is only a month,
  And it ends without ever existing;
In Arfon today for me – for I am far away –
  Mist and mountain are nothing but forms that keep appointments.

And two colours – black and white. Black is not white,
    As the void knows well enough, and no wizard
Will ever unite them. Between black and white
    Lie distance, depth, vacancy, and immeasurable abyss.

I am deceiving you. My truth must to you
    Have been a lie, and my life a living death.
Between us, about us, enveloping us,
    The nothingness that's real to me is not so to you.

I am deceiving you. White and black will never become
    A single colour, any more than two are one.
Still, true or not, I know you will continue
    Forever to fill the emptiness with yourself.

II

I was deceiving you when I said
    I am a deceiver. Yes, oh yes – the wizard
Who works miracles exists, and will materialise
    From vacancies as if they were not there.

The voice I heard was not illusory,
    Nor were you yourself an apparition.
The flesh of your hands was substantial, and the breath
    Of the wind off the mountain scattered mist across our way.

Our laughter still remains on the road,
    Our unhappiness clings still to the hill,
And our silence, tidied away and locked
    In the coffers of Arfon's rocks, is absolute.

And there you are yourself – and so am I,
    Forever laughing, falling silent, grieving,
And there the precipices are, the mist is mist,
    September is always September, and one and one make two.

[RP]

From a Travel Diary

1 *On Deck*

A nun went past, and her girdle swung,
And I saw on the cross her Christ was hung –

A metal Christ on her rosary,
In anguish hanging on Calvary;

And like us all, the sea's Creator swayed
To an ocean swell Himself had made.

The Atlantic, Sunday, July 1925

2 *Death in the Channel*

Tonight an old man, around seven o'clock,
Found journey's end before reaching dock.

A service, a prayer, a splash as he sank,
And where he had lain, an empty plank.

The Ushant lighthouse flashed on the right
And the Evening Star to west of the night,

And between them the old man went to his Lord,
Wrapped in sackcloth, overboard.

The Channel, September 1925

[TC]

The Girl on the Quay at Rio

The tugs were pulling the ship out to sea
   And every last flag was whirling:
Of the hundreds there, I had eyes for none
   But the girl on the quay at Rio.

She bade farewell to all – but knew not one –
    In a hubbub of laughter and crying:
She sat – she stood: she twisted and turned.
    The girl on the quay at Rio.

She fondled the fur of a snow-white rat
    On her shoulder, and he too cast a glance
On everyone once, like the restless eyes
    Of the girl on the quay at Rio.

Perhaps some time or another she'd been
    To someone a Lili or Llio:
Now there was no one – none but the crowd
    For the girl on the quay at Rio.

Though she stood in a cluster of uncouth folk
    I never saw one abuse her,
Nor jeer at the emptiness of her farewells –
    The girl on the quay at Rio.

Who'll tell of her crazily waved goodbyes
    Or the timorousness that came on me
As I pitied the simple girl with the rat –
    The girl on the quay at Rio?

Rio de Janeiro, August 1925

[RP]

Life

O the blessedness of life! It's lucky, no doubt,
Man gets a taste for living by the time he burns out

And rides right into the Valley of Death in Sunday black
As the lights of heaven wink on his coffin plaque.

The world and life are both worthwhile things, and
Keeping life in one's bones is a duty that can stand

Comparison with any job when reckoned pound for pound,
Although a man must in the end go under the ground.

Infancy's days are unadulterated fun,
And everyone feels blessed as he dandles the blessed one.

Youth's a time for rollicking; next is middle-age,
A period of sobriety and ease; with old age

Consolation comes – the icing on the cake.
Who was Job to say that man was born for heartache?

But hold on a minute. What kind of rigmarole is this?
Black and White demand a better-balanced antithesis.

I've heard children scream and young people complain,
Glimpsed middle-aged faces white with visions of gain.

I've seen the old shrivelling, with cracks in their skin.
Yes, yes, I've seen more than enough sickness and suffering.

Man was born to affliction. Can that truth be gainsaid?
Job hit both rock bottom and the nail on the head.

[RP]

A Christmas Carol

It is close to a quarter of a century since then,
The Christmas morning my father crossed the glen.

A hell of a thing for Death on that holiday
To come by, like Father Christmas on his way,

And take him from us, and with a single stroke
Turn the Feast of Birth to a Feast of Death, as a joke.

We knew Death was about; but there was no need
For the sneak to show off his power, and suddenly

Leap sidelong from his carriage, like a monkey-on-a-stick,
Or a circus conjurer showing off a trick,

And this after we had learned all of our lives
My Lord Death was the well-bred model of how one behaves.

But possibly, nevertheless, in this matter I
Am taking him the wrong way. Who can say why

It came into the skull of the Lord of Terror himself to play
A trick on us on the Son of Man's Birthday?

Maybe His Grace, after all, intended no mockery,
But was investing his visit with public dignity.

I beg his pardon for doubting his meaning this way:
I saw him come from the glen with his summons a later day,

On a Sunday morning, to gather my mother to his breast, –
I was letting myself go; I take back what I said.

[JPC]

Return

Never can worldly tumults violate
Heaven's silence; earth's cries will not distress
The power of the peace that roofs the great
Expanses of unbroken emptiness;
And all of man's and world's disturbances
Cannot erase that quiet, cannot harm
The course and motion of those distances
Whose rapid whirlabouts produce such calm.
And since to travel from our wail at birth
Until our final whine is nothing but
A transient ripple, shadow of a scar
On that smooth stillness, mild and mute,
We merely, fleeing for good our frantic folly,
Slip back into that vast tranquillity.

[JPC]

Saunders Lewis

Saunders Lewis (1893-1985) is widely regarded as the major Welsh-language writer of the 20th century, and he was a controversial figure, revered and reviled in turn. He was brought up outside Wales, and educated at an English public school and then the University of Liverpool where he gained a First in English. It was during active service in the First World War that he became "converted" to Welshness, and from then on he dedicated himself to Wales and the Welsh language, as a dramatist, poet, novelist, critic, academic and politician. He was one of the small band who established Plaid Genedlaethol Cymru (the Welsh Nationalist Party) in 1925, and he was its main apologist during the next ten years. He converted to Catholicism in 1932, and the inspiration for his political and social ideals sprang from his idealised view of medieval, aristocratic, Catholic, European Wales. As a modernist, he was anti-modern, and the industrial revolution was anathema to him, as was romanticism in the arts. Yet he was a much more complex and profound thinker than any summary of his views might suggest. In 1936, he was one of the three who set fire to an RAF bombing school in the Llŷn Peninsula, for which he was imprisoned, and was sacked from his lectureship at Swansea. It was his 1962 radio lecture which was the inspiration for the Welsh Language Society. He dreamt up a new Wales arising like a phoenix from the ashes, but admitted failure, yet his ideals, complex as they are, live on in his creative work.

A Vineyard Placed in My Care

(extract from the radio play Buchedd Garmon – *The Life of St Germanus)*

EMRYS: God's nobleman, hearken,
　　　A vineyard was set by a man on a sunlit hill,
　　　He hedged her, and planted within her the noblest vines,
　　　He enclosed her strongly, and built a tower in her midst,
　　　And to his son he gave her, a goodly heritage,
　　　That his name might be known among men from age to age.
　　　But a herd of swine have broken into the vineyard,
　　　Have trampled the fence, and root and devour the vines;
　　　Is it not well for the son to stand in the breach
　　　And to call his friends to his aid,
　　　That the breach may be closed and the heritage made secure?
　　　Garmon, Garmon,
　　　A vineyard placed in my care is Wales, my country,
　　　To deliver unto my children
　　　And my children's children
　　　Intact, an eternal heritage:
　　　And behold, the swine rush on her to rend her.
　　　Now will I call on my friends,
　　　Scholars and simple folk,

'Take your place by my side in the breach
That the age-old splendour be kept for ages to come.'
And this, my lord, is the vineyard of your Beloved too;
From Llan Fair to Llan Fair, a land where the Faith is established.
Wilt thou not come to lead my host to Powys?

[DML]

Scene in a Café

From the flurry of the uniformed garrison
And their turmoil in Great Darkgate Street,
Amid the throng that was spilled from the market and the college
And the chapel vestries and the pubs,
Amid the motley horde,
The sad horde that has lost the goodness of intellect,
The living dead,
Amid the cheerless cackle and red claws of females,
Their brute lips like a wanton nightmare rending
The sleep of their gorilla faces,
Amid the horde in flight,
In flight from the death of the sky and the life of the bomb,
Amid the chatting skeletons, the strolling ashes,
We squeezed through the café doors
Concealing our vacant skulls behind our fig-leaves,
And snatched a table-corner from Babel's band,
And shouted above the bones and the tea things
To a girl near by.

How swift was the girl's service, –
She brought us oysters and Kosher vinegar and the burial rite on toast.
The rain fell like a parachute on the street,
But the civil guard of ash-bins
Stood like policemen in a file near their houses.
And an old hag went, a rope round her neck,
From bin to bin in the rain, and raised each lid,
And found them, every coffin, empty.
And at the bottom of the road,
In the presence of the ravenous ashes there in the café,
The ashes that had escaped from the bins,
Whitechapel's lard-bellied women, Golder's Green Ethiopians,
On a handy lamp-post, the hag hanged herself, with her rope.

We saw her shanks turning in the rain,
And we knew by her white gloves with their smell of camphor
That she'd come from the old land.
She was buried non-denominationally by the BBC
On the imperial wave-length.

[JPC]

The Deluge, 1939

1

From Merthyr to Dowlais the tramway climbs,
A slug's slime-trail over the slag heaps.
What's nowadays a desert of cinemas,
Rain over disused tips, this once was Wales.
Pawnshops have closed their doors. Clerks
Of the labour exchange are the chiefs of this prairie.
All flesh has tainted its way on the face of the earth.

The same taint's in me, as I second proposals
In committee after committee to bring the old land to life.
I'd maybe be better employed on a Tonypandy corner
And my eyes meditating up the valley and down
On the human wreckage adrift in the mire of despond,
One function common to man and the standing slag.

Eyes have been changed to dust, we know not our death,
Were buried by our mothers, had Lethe milk to drink.
We cannot bleed, no, not as former men bled,
Our hands would resemble a hand, if they'd thumbs to go on them,
If a fall shatters our feet, all we do is grovel to a clinic,
Touch our caps to a wooden leg, Mond pension and insurance:
Knowing neither language nor dialect, feeling no insult,
We gave our masterpiece to history in our country's MPs.

2

From empty docks the scourings rose
Over dry ropes and the rusted cranes.
Greasily civilised was the flood
Of the proletariat creeping to chipshops.
It crept like blood round policemen's feet.

79

The spittle of its silicosis spread like a lake
Through faceless valleys of the industry of the dole.

The rain poured down its diligent needles
On the soft palms of old colliery hands.
Hailstones spurted onto the leathern breasts
Of dry mothers and their wrinkled babies.
Even where girls' legs twisted with rickets,
They turned cow's milk into sticks of umbrellas.
They gave an old man's pension to the lads of the dole.

And still the moon was keeping her orbit;
Apollo still washed his hair in the dew
As he did when the wise counted their seasons
Centuries back, in the Sabine hills.
But Saturn and Jove, and the golden age of the Babe,
In their turn, are ended. Sorry destruction,
Ash in the chimneys and the pointless birth
Drown out the stars under the slime of the dole.

3

In the beginning, we did not see it like this:
We thought it was only the redeeming ebb and flow, the thrifty
        unsettling
That our masters blessed as part of the economic law,
The new scientific order, that threw over natural law
As Jove supplanted Saturn, in the undulating progress of being.

And we believed in our masters: we put on them priestly vestments,
Had them preach in plus-fours and tortoise-shell spectacles,
Preach the sanctity of the surplus of unemployed and the flexible
        providence of prices;
And one day in seven, not to break with a courteous custom,
We'd offer an hour to the pretty witchcraft of antiquity
And sing a psalm in the old Pantheons of our fathers.

Then, on Olympus, in Wall Street, Nineteen Hundred and Twenty-
        nine,
At their infinitely scientific task of steering the profits of fortune,
The gods decided, with their feet in the Aubusson carpet
And their Hebrew nostrils in the quarterly statistics,
That the day had come to restrict credit over the cosmos of gold.

They did not know, these latter-day gods of earth,
That the world's last floodgates they'd thrown open;
They did not visualise the marching of men,
The fists closed, and the raised blustering arms,
Through the agonies of Vienna rank on rank,
Or the deaf fury raving in Munich,
Nor the dragging steps of the unemployed,
Those tortured somnambulists, twittering in processions.

But it came about, though, the mothers wailing,
The noise of men like a whimpering of dogs,
A myriad myriad, without hope, self-thrown
To the starless ditch, the anonymous quiet.
Here failed the wisdom of the governors of nations,
Dragon's teeth sown over Europe's acres;
And Bruening went out, from their seething rages,
From Basle's derision, foul with usurers,
Husks and dead shells of the hosts at Geneva,
Went to his long mute fast and his exile.
And the fragile mob, the halfpenny populace,
Children of the dogs and the football pool,
Surfeited their bellies with lascivious pictures,
Chaff and dust of radio and press.

But the sky grew black over the districts of Ebro,
Blood became wine in the hunger of our passions,
And paralysis froze the defective will
Of the impotent rascals of Basle and Geneva.
We saw we were cheated. The fiendish disillusion
Festering our end, was the work of our gods:
Thrown down and raped was our peerless idol,
Reason's masterpiece, a man without fetters;
The planet-masters' magnificent creed,
Man's faith in man – that was extinguished:
We, poker-faced giants, measurers
    Of suns and of stars –
    Vain was that journey,
    Empty all laughter –
The deluge of hopelessness is our black haven.

And over the waves comes the sound of tanks gathering.

[TC]

Ascension Thursday

What's going on this May morning on the hillsides?
Look at them, at the gold of the broom and laburnum,
The bright white garment on the thorn tree's shoulders,
The attentive emerald grass, the still calves.

See, the candlestick of the chestnut tree alight,
The kneeling hedges, the silent birch a nun,
The cuckoo's two notes over the bright shushing brook,
The phantom of mist inclining with the meadow's censer.

Come out, people, out of your council houses
Before the rabbits scatter, come with the weasel to see
The raising from earth of the spotless wafer of grace
And the Father kissing the Son in the white dew.

[GW]

Mary Magdalen

'Do not touch me'

No one can know about women. There are those,
Like her, for whom their pain is a locked grave;
Their pain is buried within them, there is no fleeing
From it, or being delivered. There is no ebb
Or flow to their pain, a dead sea with no
Movement upon its deep. Who – is there anyone –
Will sometime roll the stone from the grave?

See the dust trailing limply along the path:
No, let her be, Mary is going to her peace,
Deep calling unto deep, grave to grave,
Corpse drawn to corpse in the cheerless dawn:
Three days she has been in a grave, in a world ended
In the afternoon outcry, the word Finished,
The cry that bled her heart like the point of a sword.

Finished, Finished. Mary fell from the hill
To the void of the final Pasch, to the pit of a world

That was merely a grave, its breath in a silent grave,
Mary fell to the stunned death of perdition,
A world without a living Christ, creation's dread Sabbath,
The pit of the hundred thousand centuries and their obliteration,
Mary lay in quivering creation's grave,

In the trough of the night of the senses, in the smoke's cauldron;
The rich hair that had dried his feet turned white,
All memory's flowers faded save the shower of blood;
Cloud upon cloud enveloped her, their stench
A burning coal in her gullet, and ravaged her sight
Till God was snuffed out by their piercing terror,
In the dying together, the burial together, disgraced.

See her, Christ's Niobe, dragging to the hillside
The rock of her pain behind her from the leaden Pasch
Through the dark dawn, the cold dew, the heavy dust,
To the place with a stone heavier than her broken heart;
Clumsily the stumbling feet make their way across thorns,
Troublesome tears doubling the mist before her,
Her hands stretching toward him in naked yearning.

One luxury is left to her under the heavens,
One farewell caress, memorial tenderness, one
Final carnality, sad and consoling, sweet,
The chance to weep once more, clasping his legs,
To anoint the feet and wash the savage wounds,
To kiss the ankles and dry them once more with her hair,
The chance to touch You, Rabboni, Oh Son of Man.

We have pity for her. He had no pity.
Surpassing pity is the pure, blazing love
That tempers the saints' iron by blow after blow,
That scourges the flesh to its fort in the soul, and its home
In the heavenly spirit, and its burrow in the most holy,
That burns and slashes and tears till the final skirmish,
Till it strips and embraces its prey with its claw of steel.

She little knew, six days before the Pasch,
Pouring the moist precious nard upon him, all of it,
That truly 'she kept this for my burial';
She did not imagine, so precious his praise for her task,
That she would never, never more touch his feet or his hands;

Thomas could place his hand in his side; but she, despite her weeping,
Only in the pitiful form of Bread would the broken flesh now come
      to her.

There she is in the garden at the crack of dawn;
She presses her eyes toward the cave; she runs,
Runs to her remnant of paradise. Ah, does she believe,
Does she believe her eyes? The stone on the ground,
And the grave empty, the grave silent and bare;
The first lark rising above the bare hill,
And the nest of her heart empty and bereft.

As monotoned as a dove, her lament,
Like Orpheus mourning for Eurydice
She stands among the roses crying insatiably
'They have taken my Lord, have taken him,'
To disciple and to angel the same outcry
'And I do not know where they have laid him,'
And to the gardener the same raving.

She was stunned. She was shattered. She sank herself in her grief.
The mind reels and reason goes astray, unless
One comes who will snatch her out of the flesh to crown her –
Sudden as an eagle from the Alps stooping to its prey –
With the love that moves the stars, the strength that is a Word
To raise and give life: 'and He said to her, Mary,
And she turned and said to Him, Rabboni.'

[JPC]

Et Homo Factus Est. Crucifixus...
(Christmas 1971)

And was made man. He was crucified,
What other course, what other fate
Could there be for heaven's son?
To kill is the primal instinct of mankind,
It's the amoeba's itch;
The most impassioned songs of the myriads of prey
Have been carols of pain and cantos of peril
Since the hewing of stone axes
In the doors of the caves,

The millions of generations of grief
Of an insignificant planet
Lost in the limitless void of being.

And here in the pit of darkness
In the winter of the earth,
Our shattered race's history's utmost hell,
We light a candle because a son is born to us
And we lift him from his cradle –
The frail baby is heavy,
He bears the weight of all the aeons of sin –
But we lift him up and we kill him,
I, Caiaphas,
You, Tiresias,
And set him aloft,
An altar hewn
From the world's anguish
To one who is, without him, an unknown God.

[JPC]

Chance Child

Chance befuddles prophets
And Marx's golden age, and Teilhard de Chardin's, demands a
        diceless evolution.
One can't get things set for a revolution
Or catch the future in a computer's
Net. Life doesn't climb
Step by step,
But gives a leap from the fishes' maw and has wings
Or gets up on two feet and has a hand.

The scientists today assert
There's a host of earths in the planets of the universe,
Their climates like that which nourished man.
They want to greet them, and fortify them.
But if man is an accident, a matter of luck, good or bad,
Perhaps there is only this
One in all the star-clusters,
Here a few hours,

85

The chance child in the eternal silence:
Is there no one, is there just one, will reach him a hand?

[JPC]

Prayer at the End

It's an experience everyone has that nobody else will know.
Each on his own in his own way
Owns his own dying
Through the millions of years of the human race.
You can look at it, you can sometimes recognise the moment;
You cannot empathise with anyone at that moment
When the breathing and the person stop together.
And then? Nothing reaches out to the then but a prayer groping.
Such a sorry creature is man, such a baby his imagination:
'In my Father's house there are many mansions',
As poor as our own, just as much earth-bound,
His intuition too in the days when he emptied himself.
And only this way can we ourselves picture hope:
'He is seated on the right hand of God the Father almighty' –
A general hailed with jubilation through the city of Rome
After the hazardous enterprise in a Persia of creation
And crowned as Augustus, Co-Augustus with his Father –
How laughable, the supreme assertions of our faith.
And around us remain silence and the pit of annihilation
Into which our universe will soundlessly fall some night.
Our words cannot trace the borders of silence
Or say God with meaning.
One prayer remains for all, to go silently to the silent.

[JPC]

Cynan

Cynan (Albert Evans-Jones) (1895-1970) was a graduate of Bangor, and he
served in the front line during the First World War, especially in Macedonia,
and was also a chaplain. He won the National Eisteddfod Crown three times,
and the Chair once, and later cut a dashing figure as Archdruid of the Gorsedd
of Bards. His romantic, lyrical poetry had a wide appeal, but he struck a more
realistic note with his depiction of war. This is particularly true of his 'Mab y

Bwthyn' ('Son of the Cottage', 1921) of which an excerpt is included in this anthology, under the title 'The Prodigal Son'. This is a long narrative poem about the traumatic effect of army life on an innocent young man from rural Wales. Yet the effect is somewhat dulled by the tear-jerking episodes about the innocence of rural life.

Monastir

In yesterday's Monthly Meeting, with its dry, financial theme,
I saw a shining river, and many a spire gleam,
Trembling, on mirrored waters above temples glinting white;
And the thin, clear air above them, like blue silk in the light,
Save where one cloud hovered, no more than the palm of a hand,
Mark of a hostile aircraft, openly scouting the land.
A rainstorm darkened the chapel and rattled on the slates,
Music for our accountant and his dull, long-winded rates.
  But in my heart desire is near
  For Monastir, for Monastir.

I march again, a soldier, with the column as before,
An echo of steady tramping wakes the dark valley floor.
I hear the same old singing and the same old salty wit,
Men hailing the Great Adventure, set free from duty's net.
The voice of the statistician cries like a long-lost wind:
'This year the fund collected amounts to eighty pounds.'
Better, my soul, to go freely, passing out of the world
In the midst of that Grand Venture, before my faith had cooled,
  Like the souls of many I held dear,
  Flown home to God from Monastir.

The chairman rose gravely: 'We have pleasure in asking now
For the deaconesses to join us, here, and take their bow.'
O, so sedate their garments, so neatly bound their hair,
So reverend their walking. But I saw a hillside where
Was Chloe with her yeanlings. Her hair was flowing free
From a band of silky yellow, the sun's light on her cheek.
She ran barefoot towards me, on her lips a ready kiss;
Only the sheep-bells ventured to trouble our secret tryst.

  Do you sometimes ask, bells so clear,
  For the story of two in Monastir?

[SRJ]

The Prodigal Son

(extracts)

It was all go with the jazz-band and all go with the dance,
And all go with the tables where they played games of chance;
It was all go with the whiskey, and all go with the wine
And all go with the tango, dancing knee to knee,
It was all go with the laughter and all go with the songs
And noise like fire crackling under thorns.

There were men there who despised the open air,
And women who were deaf to singing birds;
Men who chose on thistle stew to dine,
And women on the husks they feed to swine,
Men who were deaf to the tune of a stream,
And women for whom a child's kiss was a dream.

Paupers we were, without seeing we were poor,
Souls that having died dwelt still in carnal form,
Girls in the inferno dancing through the night,
For all the rose and lily that made their hair so bright;
And men whose raucous mirth escaped that pit of hell,
And down there in Gehenna was I as well.

In the room the curtains were all of them drawn;
There are men in London afraid of the dawn.
In the frail light of man his sin can survive,
But where in God's light can you see it still live?

At the edge of the curtain a faint light showed;
I looked up from Hell to see where it glowed,
And drew back that curtain to welcome the dawn.
And almost, it seemed, I could draw breath again.

There was thirst on me now, a thirst not for wine
But a fretful harsh thirst, the weary soul's sign.
As I gazed at the River under blue sky
I cursed the dry song of the jazz-band's shrill cry.

As I saw under paint the face of sin there,
And those dancing to jazz for just what they were;
Man and demon together, meshed into one
And the Fiend in the middle, driving them on.

I opened the window to let in the day;
On my feverish cheek felt the free currents play.
I looked out to the street and there, gazing down,
I saw how the dawn-light awakened the town.

Then a cart swayed by from a far-away place
On course to Covent Garden, to the market space;
And a heap of heather blossoms filled the cart.
O God! The pain that it brought to my heart.

I rushed out then, with that full, burning heart
To bathe my soul in the clean dawn light.
A heather sprig lay in the trough by the door.
I gave thanks to God for the beautiful flower.
And as I walked townwards, the sprig in my coat,
The old days came flocking again to my sight.

Slopes of heather! Slopes of heather!
Where there is life, not hollow matter.
Men in that place are clean and strong,
Their days as sweet as notes of song.
Women there are pure and serene,
Their children free from lust and pain.
No worldly poison ventures there
To corrupt that healthy mountain air;
No devil's sulphury lightning flash
To consume the homely cottage thatch.

O! Honest that life I call to mind,
A carefree lad on paths of the wind!
I could not have God's blessing now
As did the boy who sped the plough!

That was the time when my young heart
With all its songs held a merry note;
And all my life was pure and clean,
My happy soul devoid of pain.
The only dream of a country lad
Was to live by his sweat as had his dad.

Today behold me here in town,
A wealthy man, 'See, here I am;
Was nothing before I settled here,
Look how wealthy I am this year.'

For my fortune they envy me.
Yet now I'm deep in poverty.
Whoever is counted poor today
In London, I'm poorer. Gleaning, I stray
Hunting crumbs from the feast of the world,
While God in the country offers me gold
That my happy soul might rejoice!
A servant in my Father's house…
A land of famine that distant place
To one who knows the treasure of grace.

On the gorse is a store of wealth
That far surpasses bankers' pelf.
I treasured it in many a sack
Where neither moth nor rust attack.
But God knows where my key is now
To that treasure house of long ago.

And poverty comes not alone:
Sick of heart, my wounds bemoan
The thirst that's daily on my lips
Forced by the pain that haunts my steps.

Nothing will heal my weary soul
Till Felin Bach wellspring makes me whole.
How often in that slender rill
Have I Nain's pitcher held to fill?
As it filled with a myriad drops
I lay there on the soft green moss.
There I dreamed through the afternoon
While the pitcher filled to the brim,
Water lapping across its rim
Brought salvation's healing there
To cure each sickness and despair.

*

O Eden lost! O Eden lost!
Was all a dream that I loved most?
Why did I turn away, despise
Country and cottage, fail to prize
My father's prayers for me? And why
Disdain my mother's tearful cry?
I could not have God's blessing now
As did the lad who drove the plough!

[SRJ]

Alun Cilie

Alun Cilie (Alun Jeremiah Jones) (1897-1975) was another member of the
Cilie family in south Ceredigion. He spent his life on the Cilie farm, and his
delight in poetry was something he "caught" as if it was in the air. He wrote
fluently in both strict and free metres, producing *englynion*, *cywyddau* and
lyrics, often in response to local needs – whether to celebrate a birthday or a
wedding, to pull someone's leg, or to mark the passing away of a well-loved
person in the locality.

The Old Chapel

Old desolate place tonight,
A blemish on the landscape;
An empty, lightless building,
An old Meeting House long shut.
Insignificant, grey-faced,
Nobody comes to it now;
The dwelling of saints, speechless,
And the Bethel of their hopes.
Its door under twining thorns,
Briars in its fair courtyard;
The weeds a mesh around it;
In the yew, the roaring wind.
Under weather's whip the roof
Is flung apart, in fragments.

Gwerin, on a narrow lane,
Once raised it to their Saviour,
Lovely house to meet their Lord
And affirm the true Godhead;
Their hands' noble miracle,
Shapely, on strong rock sited;
And its majesty gave voice
To ancient honour's splendour.
On its face is their lasting
Trace of scrupulous patience,
Chisels' trace on the gables
And on its strong arches' frame.

When Sabbath's at its threshold
No longer a sound of praise.

Where are the old grave giants?
Not one of them left who once
Came to acknowledge the Lord,
A slow throng, on His morning,
From hill brows and valley floor
And cwm for the communion.
The uncolleged, modest flock
Of cottage and small homestead;
Faith's punctual, faithful men,
Men who were once its fortress.
Where are the gusts? the descant
And fervour of conversing?
The calling with eloquence
In times past for forgiveness?
The tuneful silver voices
Of the men doubling the song?
In a green glade was their fold,
Their candle in rough weather;
Their fellowship's Avalon,
The Lord's warm healthful island;
Great was the talk of grace there,
And of God's Word and his love.

Below, the crooked pathways
To the cwm's houses are closed.
And empty all the workshops
In the havoc of the thorns;
The humble whitewashed houses,
The snug houses, green their cloak;
The houses of saints honest
In zeal for their lofty Cause,
Houses of the ancient band
With faith in the Creator.

Gone the flame, gone the traffic;
And the pulpit now is mute,
Where once a sweeping outcry
Of Heaven's evangelists.
A distant place it is now,
In clay the small assembly,
Down in the depth of its earth,
In peace they all are resting,
In its soil's quiet acre,
The spot of their dear desire;

And cold and damp the chapel's
Stillness keeps watch on the dust.
And past the spot, unheeding,
The flighty crowd flashes by.

[JPC]

Gwenallt

Gwenallt (David James Jones) (1899-1968) was brought up in the industrial
Swansea Valley, and reacted strongly against his Nonconformist background,
and for a time embraced an atheistic Marxism. A conscientious objector during
the First World War, he was imprisoned in Wormwood Scrubs and Dartmoor,
and his experiences during that time formed the basis of his novel, *Plasau'r
Brenin* ('The King's Mansions', 1924). He graduated in Welsh and English at
Aberystwyth, where he later became a lecturer in Welsh. Gradually he relin-
quished Marxism and became a Christian nationalist. However, his poetic voice
is sharp and acerbic, and he has no truck with pietism.

Dartmoor

Bars burn again across your eyes. Doors
Clang upon your ears
Lags, lunatics, sow and reap their sighs
Break acres of remorse on those cold moors.

August you saw spread heavy sunsets
Like slaughter, blood into pools and ditches.
November came distributing mists
Imprisoning the prison. The nights belonged to witches.

You heard them. The congregation of the damned
Assembled and in session with their dogs
Their screech owls and their endless cries
Of pain and guilt. Shapes writhing in the fog:

But in your cell you gripped your necklace of goodness, your lucky
        charm,
The blue river Tywi winding between farm and farm.

[EH]

Adrift

Woe to us who know the words without knowing the Word that is there,
And sell our souls for the toffee and confetti of a fair,
Follow after every drum and dance after every flute
And drown the Intercession's hymn with the gabble of the Absolute.

Men in the South of Wales without food or drink or a fag,
The glory of their countryside under scrapheaps, cinders, slag,
The canal in villages dawdling, no ford, no movement, no sound,
And the big-bellied rats devouring the corpses of cat and hound.

In our lands fortune and fate and chance are now the gods on top,
And we ourselves are like moles that have been caught in their trap;
Beneath the paper floors of our world is neither hell nor devil,
Heaven's candles have been put out, and strangled is every angel.

Ashes are in this generation's mouth, and in its spit is pus,
A wolf-bitch in a wasteland howling for the moon's witless whorishness:
The barbarians' halls are full to the brim, and church and altar
        abandoned,
Our vessel is drifting in the fog, and drunk are the crew and the captain.

In the heart of heaven's darkness, O Mary, set Your Star,
And help us find the course back to His will by showing us Your chart,
And descend among the tangled ropes, and put Your hand to the tiller,
And pilot our rebellious craft into a heavenly harbour.

[JPC]

Wales

Why have you given us this misery,
The pain like leaden weights on flesh and blood?
Your language on our shoulders like a sack,
And your traditions shackles round our feet?
The cancer desiccates your face and form,
Your soul reduced to abscesses and scabs,
You are merely a nightmare in your own land,
And your survival but a witch's dream.

But still, we cannot leave you in the filth,
This generation's butt and laughing-stock,
Your former freedom is a sword in hand,
Your dignity a buckler on our breast,
And we will grip our spears and spur our steeds
Lest we should shame our fathers in their graves.

[JPC]

Sin

When we pull off ourselves each kind of clothing,
The cloak of respectability and sageness,
The linen of culture and the silks of learning;
How bare the soul, the naked filthiness:
In our poor stuff is the primeval mud,
The wild beast's slime is in our blood and marrow,
And the barbaric dance is in our tread,
Between our thumb and finger is the arrow.
Roaming the forest, free and primitive,
We sight between the twigs a bit of Heaven,
Where the saints sing anthems of grace and faith,
A full *Magnificat* of His salvation;
Like wolves we lift our nostrils, ravenous,
Howling for the Blood that ransomed us.

[JPC]

Rhydcymerau

Near Rhydcymerau,
On the land of Esgeir-ceir and the fields of Tir-bach,
They have planted the saplings
   to be trees of the third war.

I call to mind my grandmother at Esgeir-ceir
As she sat, pleating her apron, by the fireside,
The skin yellow and dry on her face
   like a manuscript of Peniarth,
And the Welsh on her old lips the Welsh of Pantycelyn.

A bit of Puritan Wales she was of last century.
Although I never saw him, my grandfather
Was a "character" – a brisk and twinkling little creature,
Fond of his pint;
He'd just strayed in from the eighteenth century.
They reared nine children,
Poets, deacons, and Sunday School teachers,
And each, locally, a man of authority.

My Uncle Dafydd used to farm Tir-bach,
And was, besides, a poet, the countryside's rhymester;
His song to the little cockerel was famous in those parts:
  *'The little cock goes scratching
    In the garden here and there.'*
It was to him I went for the summer holidays
To watch the sheep and fashion lines of *cynghanedd*,
Englynion, and eight-line stanzas
    of eight-seven measure.
He brought up eight children,
The eldest son a minister with the Calvinistic Methodists,
And he too wrote verses.
In our family we'd a real nestful of poets.

And by this time there's nothing there but trees.
Impertinent roots suck dry the old soil:
Trees where neighbourhood was,
And a forest that once was farmland.
Where was verse-writing and scripture
    is the South's bastardised English.
The fox barks where once cried lambs and children,
And there, in the dark midst,
Is the den of the English minotaur;
And on the trees, as if on crosses,
The bones of poets, deacons, ministers, and teachers of Sunday School
Bleach in the sun,
And the rain washes them, and the winds lick them dry.

[TC]

The Hedgehog

I saw him the other day as I went to Nanteos
    When he'd rolled himself up in his spiny skin,
The sun's cheerfulness was too much for him to bear
    And the chatter of the birds overhead a pain.

He had buried his head inside the roundedness
    And hung his feet on the inside of the prickles,
No need to move to gather bugs and toads
    Because there was a pantry of fleas on his quills.

Within the rounded dark the toads are hopping
    And frogs and bugs are chiming like a bell,
And the ancient instincts flow like waters,
    Divine, crimson, homosexual.

Within him are the primitive cults of the Congo
    The ready demons of tan wildernesses,
The music of idols in Malaya and Tahiti,
    Japan's cylindrical gods and goddesses.

He is the prophet of the ruins of Europe,
    Archetype of its fine arts and its lore;
He fills the void where once there was the Trinity,
    O! immortal ball. O! deity of thorns.

[JPC]

The Depression

Above our cupped world no tall stack opens
    Its smoky umbrella handled with flame;
    Neither crane's running din nor screech of the hooters
    Comes between us and the slow heights about us;
    The stars have all been scrubbed of stain.

No fog sinks down on the gardens near-by;
    On man's new Egypt, where locusts have been,
    Ventures the green grass, the weed grows thick,
    And the gipsy sheep more rarely come down to lick
    Buckets of tins of salmon and sardine.

Once more foam whitens on river and brook,
    And clears the scum from the speckled stone;
  Easier to find are trout, in the oily waters shaping,
  And eels to the edge of the stream are escaping
    The vitriol stink to tuck themselves home.

It is not heard, the morning alarum of feet,
    And, of an afternoon, round eyes laugh no more;
  A stranger now, the little something in the pantry;
  In each home the fare on the board's but scanty,
    The paint's grown shabby on windows and door.

Idleness a sour dog on every street corner,
    Workers tramp shadowless from place to place;
  There has come to the town's Eldorado this finish:
  Neighbourhood scuttled, and break-up of village,
    Roots of the South, a culture, a civilised grace.

[TC]

The Dead

With his fiftieth birthday behind him, a man sees with fair clarity
    The people and surroundings that made him what he is,
And the steel ropes that tether me strongest to these things
    In a village of the South, are the graves in two cemeteries.

I'd ride a bike pilfered from scrap, or with a pig's bladder
    Play rugby for Wales; and all that while,
Little thought I'd hear how two of my contemporaries
    Would spew into a bucket their lungs red and vile.

Our neighbours they were, a family from Merthyr Tydfil,
    The 'martyrs' we called them, by way of a pun,
And five of them by turns had a cough that crossed the fences
    To break up our chatter and darken all our fun.

We crept in the Bibled parlours, and peeped with awe
    At cinders of flesh in the coffin, and ashes of song,
And there we learnt, over lids screwed down before their time,
    Collects of red revolt and litanies of wrong.

Not the death that goes his natural rounds, like a gaol warder,
    Giving notice in the clink of his damp keys,
But the leopard of industry leaping sudden and sly
    That strikes from fire and water men to their knees.

The hootering death: the dusty, smokeful, drunken death,
    Death whose dreadful grey destiny was ours;
Explosion and flood changed us often into savages
    Fighting catastrophic and devilish powers.

Mute and brave women with a fistful of bloodmoney,
    With a bucketful of death, forever the rankling of loss,
Carrying coal, chopping wood for a fire, or setting the garden,
    And more and more reading the Passion of the Cross.

This Sunday of Flowers, as we place on their graves a bunch
    Of silicotic roses and lilies pale as gas,
Between the premature stones and the curb yet unripened,
    We gather the old blasphemings, curses of funerals past.

Our Utopia vanished from the top of Gellionnen,
    Our abstract humanity's classless, defrontiered reign,
And today nothing is left at the deep root of the mind
    Save family and neighbourhood, man's sacrifice and pain.

[TC]

Prosser Rhys

Edward Prosser Rhys (1901-45) left school at an early age becasue of ill-health and then worked as a journalist, mainly in Aberystwyth. He edited *Baner ac Amserau Cymru* for 18 years, and also established a publishing house, Gwasg Aberystwyth. In collaboration with John Eilian, he published a volume of youthful lyrics, *Gwaed Ifanc* ('Young Blood', 1923), and in 1924 he won the National Eisteddfod Crown for his long poem 'Atgof' ('Memory'), a poem which had a tempestuous reception because of its portrayal of the sexual awakening of a sensuous youth, and its allusions to the then taboo subject of gay sex.

Memory

(extract)

Our tight knot! Gentle boy with golden hair,
You know all that transpired between us there.
All the honourable trust and crazy
Purist plans which we dreamed up on that shore.
We deemed this earth as rotten to the core;
And demanded root and branch reform
For a world in which there would be no more
Talk of the twofold scourge of greed and glut.
We pledged to shun our base, innate desires.
The Body, Temple to a fertile Mind
Despite young cravings to make ardent love
We did not submit to such carnal joys,
For did we not hear the call from far away
That we strive to attain a Better Way?

A Better Way!…I recall one calm night
As together we walked the Bethel Road
No human sound to pound the silent air
The smell of hay pervading everywhere.
Our Mind needing no borrowed syllables
To complement our overflowing Thoughts,
When, from a nearby convent, an anthem
To the Virgin drifts serene to our ears.
We stood. Purging ourselves of the burden
Of our presumed disposition to sin.
The ancient beauty of that Latin chant
The age-old evensong of the chaste
To banish all thoughts of worldly delights
From the hidden recesses of their Minds.

Recesses of their Minds! We both believed,
You and I, that our Minds were squeaky clean
On that strange night when we slept together
The sacred song still ringing in our ears.
We slept…but one time, we were half aroused
And found ourselves wrapped in a tight embrace.
And then Sex had its wicked way with us
Its bliss receding swiftly as before.
Fully awake at last – what have we done?

My mind span like a tortuous whirlpool
Friendship once again trampled underfoot.
With the celebration of our passion!
I cried. Sex, get off my back and let me be.
I'm sick, I'm sick of wanting to Live.

To live…I so desire to taste sweet Life
But between me and life lies able Flesh
Pressing me to be his faithful servant,
And thwarting that which I desire. 'Poor Mind,
What are you, Flesh? You, who dissolves the heat,
Who thaws the chill, and blights the steel's resolve?
Who sleeps, who talks, who depends on money;
Who sees, who hears and who consists of pain.
What are you, Flesh? An accident of birth?
Had we not renounced libidinous Sex?
That Libido, which is a constant itch
In your veins, night and day! Just tell me, please!
And why place in such an ugly vessel
Substance which surpasses its container?

[MD]

Iorwerth Peate

Iorwerth Cyfeiliog Peate (1901-82) was a native of Montgomeryshire who studied at Aberystwyth, and became an expert on folk life. He was eventually appointed first curator of the Welsh Folk Museum at St Fagan's, Cardiff. His admiration for the Nonconformist and radical ideals of his background imbued his essays, and he expressed his independent opinions unflinchingly. Yet he was no modernist in his criticism or his creative work. His poems are in the lyrical mode, and show his fine craftsmanship and his love of rural life.

Nant yr Eira

There are owls tonight at Dôl-y-garreg-wen,
the grass covers the yard and the walls are grey with lichen,
and the cotton-grass spreads its sheet across the garden.

The plumes are a white shroud, over Cwmderwen's bare peat-marsh,
and the two ricks are like two eyes aglow no longer,
and the stars a host of candles there on the hill's altars.

Frail white-topped dwellers on the moors, what sorry enchantment
turned each memory to a skeleton, and the ancient moor to a shrine?
None, save Time's tyranny that withers all that is fine.

The old voices will not come back to Beulah through the sore
burden of six feet of earth; too much for them to bear.
Be tranquil, bruised heart, and expect them no more.

The old gentleness you loved, it fled on unreturning ways,
it vanished with the summers, the sweetness of former days.
Nothing remains but the trembling of cotton-grass in the breeze.

[JPC]

Roncesvalles

Do you remember, mountains of grey,
    the turmoil lost to long-gone times?
'Those deeds, to us, were but yesterday,
    one of the scented wind's pastimes.
From that voiceless age no soldier tall
will stride through the mist to Roncesvalles.'

Did you see the armies of Charlemagne,
    envoys of the utter nullity of man,
and the glory of France, the pride of Spain,
    Roland and his men, the grand Suleiman?
'They are nothing but mutes, their power spent,
In Roncesvalles what endures yet

is our mountain might, the grass and heather,
    the bells of herds distantly tinking,
and the humble men bending together
    as the knell sounds before sun's sinking.
The stars and the dawn, the mists and the night,
in Roncesvalles are the beacons of might.'

Across the valley the darkness spread
   (o! famous men, how brief is fame),
we hear the cattle breathing deep breaths
   (o! life, how small the realm you proclaim):
I wait until the shadow comes to call,
and the night that was, in Roncesvalles.

[NJ]

Museum Piece
(The old-time kitchen in the National Museum)

Slowly the clock is ticking the long hours,
silent is the wheel, its spinning done,
quiet the baby beneath its coverlet,
no one bends over the Great Bible now.
The gleaming dresser full of bright blue dishes,
and all the china in the little cupboard,
bowls on the board await the servants' company,
the kettle, nonetheless, completely mute.
Will you come again, old people, to your kitchen
from fold and cowshed, from tending to the crops?
(Hurry up, my girl, and fetch the bellows
to kindle flames within the glowing peat.)
   My only answer is the ticking of the clock,
   are they all away from home?... tick tock, tick tock.

[JPC]

Airstrip St Athan

God in his wondrous grace a garden did sow
between sea and mountain, whose paths would ease
the wearied people to meadows whence would flow
the waters of Bethesda, Eglwys Brywys's peace.
Many a cheerful village he sprinkled there –
Llan-faes, Aberddawen, Y Fflemin Melyn –
dazzle-white gems in the grasslands' care,
and hedge, lane and dune with tales beyond telling.

103

But now they're as dust, all passion broken on the wheel –
unhappy man whose wants he cannot quell
turning leisurely roads into highways of steel
that deliver nothing of Llan-dwf's peace or Llangrallo's spell.
    And the gracious Vale, from Barry to Porthcawl,
    is raw meat to greedy hell's mechanic sprawl.

[NJ]

J Kitchener Davies

James Kitchener Davies (1902-52) was a native of rural Ceredigion, but spent most of his adult life as a teacher in the Rhondda Valley. He was an indefatigable campaigner for Plaid Cymru and the Welsh language, and courted controversy with his play *Cwm Glo* ('Coal Valley', 1945) because of its allegedly lax morality. The long poem translated here was written in 1953 in response to a BBC commission, when the poet was dying of cancer.

The Sound of the Wind that is Blowing
(extracts)

Today,
there came a breeze thin as a needle of a syringe,
cold, like ether-meth on the skin,
to whistle round the other side of the hedge.
For a moment, I felt a numbness in my ego,
like the numbness of frost on the fingers of a child
climbing the stiles of Y Dildre and Y Derlwyn to school,
only for a moment, and then the blood flowed again,
causing a burning pain such as follows numbness on fingers,
or ether-meth on the skin after the first shiver.
    It did not come through the hedge
though I could recognise its sound blowing,
and feel on my face
the foul breath of graves.
But the hedge is thick-trunked, and high,
and its shelter firm so that nothing comes through it,
– nothing at all but the sound of the wind that is blowing.

*   *   *

Ha!
You are the one who always boasted
you had no fear of dying,
but were afraid of having to suffer pain.
You've never had a chance
to fear either dying or suffering pain
– never once, because of the hedge's shelter around you.

Yes, yes, like everyone in your time,
you've seen people in pain –
and seen people dying – other people –
without the wind that is blowing getting to you deeper than the skin,
with nothing at all occurring within what you are.

To you, something for them, the others,
is suffering and death,
every test of faith, indeed,
just like acting in a play.

*   *   *

But fair play now,
be fair to yourself, and confess
you did your best to set yourself
in the teeth of the wind, so it could lift you
and shake you free from the safety of your rut.
You climbed the stoutest beech to the topmost branch
in fair summer weather
to run a race with the squirrels in the green leafy twigs,
daring to leap behind them from bough to bough;
and you climbed, in winter, the stark bare trunk
to the spot where the eye was fearful to follow you
swaying on the slimness like a crow on the crest,
your knees and your arms riding the wood
and your eyes closed with the astounding surging
like a baby sleeping in its cradle's rocking.
Be honest, now;
not everyone dares to ride the wind,
the wind that is blowing where it will.

*   *   *

No!
there was no need for you
to dare the Empire and the Hippodrome packed on Sunday evening,
– you a dandy bantam on the dung-heap of the spurred cocks

of the Federation and the Exchange –
but you ventured,
and ventured in elections for the Town Council and the County
and Parliament presently
against Goliath in a day that knows no miracle, –
the giant with picks of posts as a sweetener on your bread,
while you reached out your slice and begged like a clever slave.
Well no, I am not ashamed to admit
that the garden near the house has been turned over through the years
and diligently weeded, till the back was near breaking;
but the soil is stronger than I, the convolvulus
like cancer twisting itself through the bowels
squeezing life to the ground, inch by relentless inch.
The deeper I dug, the swifter would wind
the snake-like convolvulus through the loose soil,
climbing each stake and bush beneath my hands
and strangling the roses and the beans in their flowering
and raising their pure white bells like banners,
or like girls with petal-like lips
baring their teeth to smile whitely
with no laughter reaching their eyes, nothing but rancour in those pools.
    I wanted to save Cwm Rhondda for the nation
and the nation itself as a garden that had fertility.
'How often I desired to gather your chicks but you did not desire it.'
But it was a boost to the heart to hear passers-by over the garden wall
begging me – 'Stop killing yourself, simpleton;
you're working too hard from morning to evening,
from spring to autumn, and your garden's soil will not pay you.'
Then as they turned to their strolling I heard:
'There he is, doubled over, so foolish, so foolish.'
And the furtive weeds stealing bed after bed
so that only a single bed was clear of their ravening,
my home, my wife, and three little lasses, –
Welsh-speaking Welsh and proud as princesses.
    Yes, I confess that I tried to hurl myself
into the whirlwind's teeth to be raised on its wings
and be blown by its thrust where it willed
as a hero to save my land.
Since it not only blows where it will, the tempest,
but blows what it will before it where it will;
'Who at its birth knows its growth,' I said.

*   *   *

O shut your mouth with your lying self-pity
and your false unctuous boasting.
You know it was a giddy game with squirrels
to slip from bough to bough;
and a more reckless game to hover in the wind
like a paper kite, a string tying you safe to the ground,
where the crowd gathered to marvel at your feats
on the pantomime trapeze and your clowning in the circus.
Not riding the whirlwind, but hanging to the mane
of a little roundabout horse, that was your valour,
a child's wooden-horse in a nursery,
and the sound of the wind no more to you than the crackle of
        recorded music from vanity fair's screeching machine.
You suffered not so much as a scratch on your skin
by following the squirrels – the soup-kitchen and the cobbling –
when your alms were pus in the septic wound,
inflamed sores, on the wretched souls of the Means Test.
The flag-waving marching, the eloquence and electioneering
were nothing but stunting your plane in wayward loops
instead of flying straight on your journey to your hangar,
like fliers of the authorised parties.
'If he,' they said, 'would fly straight for the mark, like us,
stopping his flourishes, he would go quite far, –
there would be offices and honour and a seat in Parliament
and a chance to work wisely for Wales
within the only Party that matters.'
'And as it is,' said others, 'they will shut his mouth with office soon,
and buy him off like the rest with ribbons.'
Of your own free will you provoked the whirlwinds
dangling humorously to amuse the open-mouthed rabble.
Your shovelling with a sand spade and a seaside bucket
in the garden, chopping the convolvulus
– the cancer of Englishness that is twining through Wales –
that was nothing at all but a chance to listen closely round the hedge
to the unconcerned passers-by so gentle in calling you simple;
but you never heard their words after they turned away, –
the Welsh are too courteous to speak the truth to your face, –
'the stupid fool, the half-wit, the idiot,' they said,
'it will be more than he can do to keep a single bed free
from the convolvulus, – his home will turn English in time
like all our homes when the children reach school age.'
And so it would, very likely,
had the Welsh School not come to sustain your home in your stead.

The tempest's roar in the distance is music
to your ears when its sound is blowing.
But who at its birth knows its growth, you said.
Well not you, despite your boast and your false and deceitful pitying...
but it is another thing to answer it.

*   *   *

Yes, perhaps,
but you with your sandpaper tongue,
the rasp of your criticising and the file of your distrust,
only scrape and scratch the brightness of the polish on the furniture
of truth.
'Tell me, what is truth?'
O wind of truth, come in your pomp and power
to blow with your spirit where you will,
is the answer for Pilate and for you.
    How like an appended story
of John the Evangelist concerning Peter
going to fish by night,
having tired of the promise of the Kingdom that did not come,
and the King cursed outside the city.
Every footstep beneath the window of the Upper Room
was the tramp of Roman soldiers, or the stealthy sound
of the High Priest's spies, to put them in prison.
Though so mystery-filled the three years in the marvellous company
till he longed to raise a tent at the shining Transfiguration,
yet how irresponsible in years of responsibility, and in maturity
to raise a house on the chimera of adolescence's sweet thrilling hour.
No, I am going fishing, said Peter,
back to the boats, and the nets, and the fickle contrary sea;
there is safety's assurance.
Like the glass-cupboard dishes, too expensive to be risked
on the kitchen table each day, is the adolescent excitement, so
        splendid, so splendid.
    And that night they did not catch a thing.
A miracle.
A trip on the sea, one dark night, in the boat without the Company
was enough to estrange them from knowing Him in the morning on
        shore,
since they were forced to turn home empty-handed, a failure.
If only the nets were full and the boat brimming with fish!
That night
– despite their skills with the gear of their craft, and the ways of the sea –

they did not catch a thing (O Miracle!),
lest Peter succeed in slipping slickly,
like one of his own fish, from the palm of the hand that held him,
and turn to boast at the crowing of the cock.

In feasting at the feast that was prepared
joining Society and the company together,
He
took bread and gave it to them
as a sacrament,
and the fish they caught the same way,
the fish of their experience becoming part of the sacrament
with the bread He gave.

Then the questioning.
Do you love me more than these,
more than your fish and your nets,
more than the changeable sun-and-shower of the April of adolescence?
Did you wish to turn your steadiness now to them, and in maturity, –
to the safety before the thrill and the excitement,
before the sound of the wind that is blowing strikes sharply upon
        your ears?
There is a choice for you, Peter, one final choice:
when you were young you girded yourself
and walked the way you chose,
but when you grow old, another will gird you
and lead you the way you would not choose.
'But where and when will I reach journey's end on Your shelterless
        back road?'
'It is not for you to know the seasons or the times,
but to follow me.'
And this he spoke, signifying
with what kind of death he would glorify God,
commanding the wind that is blowing
to blow him before it where it would.

You as well have been begging and praying
for an experience such as Peter's to lift you before the wind,
for it to blow you again to the font
so the baptismal water on your forehead would be wiped out
and the name of Man that was given you,
and there you would be plunged in the Spirit's baptism,
and a saint's name placed in your heart.

And it's worse for you to announce that in public!

*   *   *

May God who is slow to anger forgive my presumption,
pulpiteering, singing hymns and praying to Him
who wore about Him the breeze of the day,
to come to tickle my ribs to wake me from my dozing.
I asked for the wind that was probing the skeletons
to breathe into my dry bones the breath of life.
I pleaded with the tempest to winnow with the whirlwind
my desert's draff, and drench with its rains
my wasteland's parched ground till it bloomed as a garden.
I appealed with fervour without considering –
without considering (O terror) He could take me at my word,
He could take me at my word and answer my prayer.
And answer my prayer.
    Listener to prayers, be merciful,
and turn a deaf ear from hearing my false petition,
from having to create a saint from my fickle earth.
    Steadfast One, with never a shadow of change,
do not smother me with single-minded devotion,
but let me gather honey with dilettante piety,
from flower to flower in Your garden while the weather is fair.
    Supreme Doctor,
who carve with Your scalpel between the bone and the marrow,
hold Your hand from the treatment that would carve me
free from my fellows and my neighbourhood,
wholly apart from my household and family.
    Pilgrim of the wilderness,
do not set my steps on the martyrs' wandering path
and the loneliness of the soul's pilgrimage.
    O Father of Mercies, be merciful,
leave me my comrades' company, and my acquaintances' trust,
and the strength that is mine in my wife and children.
    Familiar of grief, do not grieve me
by baring the soft soul, leaving it skinned
of the protective shell that has been settling for half a century
as a layer of sloth over the spirit's daring,
so that not a grain of sand would disturb the core of my ego.
    I am too old and too weak and too happy in my world,
too comfortable, too self-satisfied,
to be shaken into the unknown in the teeth of Your whirlwind.
Let me lurk in the shelter of my hedges, and the nooks in my dyke.
    King of kings, legions of angels flying at Your summons,
volunteers glorying in Your livery – Your crown of thorns and Your
        five wounds –

stop pressing me and conscripting me to the hosts that are Yours
on the Sea of Glass and in the Far Country.
Atonement who purchased freedom,
leave me in the cocktail parlour to shake them and share them
with the trivial customs of my civility
and the manners in fashion among my people.
Do not tangle me in my prayers like Amlyn in his vow,
do not kill me at the altar by whose horns I have blasphemed, –
but let me, I pray, despite each wound, however hideous,
fail to be a saint.
'Quo vadis, quo vadis,' where are you going?
Stop pursuing me to Rome, to a cross, my head towards the ground.
O Saviour of the lost,
save me, save me, save me,
from Your baptism that washes the Old Man so clean:
keep me, keep me, keep me,
from the inevitable martyrdom of Your elect.
Save and keep me
from the wind that is blowing where it will.
So be it, Amen,
    and Amen.

[JPC]

R Bryn Williams

R Bryn Williams (1902-81) was a native of Blaenau Ffestiniog, but the family
emigrated to the Welsh colony in Patagonia where he was brought up. He came
to Wales for his university education, and became a Nonconformist minister,
before joining the staff of the National Library of Wales at Aberystwyth. Much
of his published work is about Patagonia, including children's novels, plays, an
important history, as well as his Chair-winning ode in the strict metres (1964),
an extract from which appears below.

Patagonia
(extract)

Fragile *Mimosa*, through the flood of months,
Fared at the mercy of the fickle winds
Her frail shell braving the seas' expanse,
And piloted by the dream of multitudes:

Sallying from the region of the loveless mists
And sailing for the land of tremendous riches.

And her wondrous band also ventured out of
The mud and filth of poverty of their lives,
From a powerful Lord, from dreadful oppression,
And the futile ploughing of a rocky soil,
Earth that gave not the diligent its wealth,
But gave indolent men its luxuries.

Somewhere beyond the horizons there
Were regions gold with reward for the bold:
From their mystery, hope would come to the heart,
For the strong of will an Avalon fortress;
Love would flood the far corners, from the fields
Would come joy and abundant harvests.

In their dream there was every kind of longing,
Without bloodshed or pain, their lives would prosper;
Ploughing a field with no lord to oppress them:
From sickly poverty, the nation would grow,
And Welsh be honoured, without contrary word,
No anguish would come in worshiping Jesus.

They come to the paradise of all their yearnings,
A solitary band, to the edge of the waves;
They land, their eyes on the wilderness ridges
In the desolate region, and the barren hills:
Through tears see it ugly, lacking in splendour,
Not the promised land of their fervent prayers.

An orphan crew on the beach, so persevering,
With the rain pouring on the frigid banks;
Cold their shelter in the new world's caves,
Yet with the loss of their cheerful spirit;
They'd give no refuge to the feeble doubts
That make hearts break in hidden battles.

Again, unchecked, they venture forth and step
Assured of soul across a desolate pampas,
Valley by valley with the fickle winds,
Freezing and flailing in the yielding gravel:
Since a miracle sustains them, they entered their journey
With fervent joy and kept a steady course.

112

In wide-acred Camwy they put up cabins,
Till its soil underneath the Southern Cross:
From reaping sufferings would come success,
Their seed and their memorial in sunlit summers.

[JPC]

J M Edwards

J M Edwards (1903-78) was a native of Ceredigion, followed a teacher training course at Trinity College, Carmarthen, and then spent the rest of his life as a teacher in Barry, Glamorgan. He was a prolific poet, and many of his poems are based on reminiscences of his early years in mid-Wales. They combine the native tradition of the "country poet" on the one hand, and the influences of such poets as Emile Verhaeren and Robert Frost on the other. He won the National Eisteddfod Crown three times.

The Few

These are the few who love her as she is
And are readying themselves for the last stand.
For everywhere the weather has grown strange;
All that's left untouched are the contours of the land.

These are the few who knew her as she was
Before the wind burned out the blossom of her skin;
The ones who have pledged their spirits to the cause
In this battle only words' weapons will win.

These are the few who have heard her make complaint
That the worst betrayal comes from those close by.
But all's not lost;
Because hope, eager as eyebright,
Will always be the last of her to die.

So before the head and the heart's jury
Give their final verdict,
And before her royal jewellery
Is indistinguishable from the dust,

Surely every one
Of these few's fortresses
Must be stormed and overrun.

[RM]

Christmas in Europe: 1945

It's darker tonight than when those shepherds watched,
And the wind is colder too.
But I'm sure, my friends, that this year, as ever,
You are on the way to Bethlehem
Though the path is perilous this time
And there's a wasteland now
Between yourselves and the stable
When Christmas itself is in exile
Its loss is as vast as a child's.

This music is quieter than the choirs
In starlight's steepling galleries.
Every belfry is dumb this year
And the mapmakers working in blood.
In France of the silent festivals
Only the graves are built to last.
So how might we reflame the fire
Of the peace that warmed our lives?

This road is harder than the road of kings.
Where we gather for a birth is a continent of graves.
But how the dead still dance in our minds
Though they lie tumbled by the wind's fusillade.
The lights we knew are in bloody eclipse
While to the east the great sadness starts.
There will be no gifts on our stable floor
If the kings cannot find their Christ.

This is hardly the country of goodwill.
Who leads us now is harsher than Herod;
That Lord of Lack
Will give us all short shrift.
Yet through Brittany and Greece, and over the banks of the Rhine,

In these unpropitious times,
Yes, my dear friends,
Is the journey to Jesus.

[RM]

T Rowland Hughes

T Rowland Hughes (1903-49) was born at Llanberis, Caernarfonshire, the son
of a quarryman, and is mainly known as the novelist of the slate-quarrying dis-
tricts of north Wales. His five novels were written during the last years of his life,
when he was suffering from multiple sclerosis. Although he won the National
Eisteddfod Chair twice, he was not a prolific poet, but some of his lyrics gained
popularity as recitation pieces at *eisteddfodau*, or when set to music.

Hymn

You, who gave colour to the dawn,
    Magic to the twilight hour,
You, through whom scent and sound were born
    That woods in spring might flower,
O guard us, lest we lose for good
This miracle that lights the world.

You, who gave music to the brook,
    Its lullaby to the grove,
You, who made sharp the wind's attack,
    Put the lark's notes high above,
O keep us from that fatal day
When our hearts' song is locked away.

You, who heard stumbling feet go past
    On the road to Calvary,
You, who saw how the blood fell fast
    As He walked, incredibly, by,
O keep us lest there come a loss
Of crown of thorns, of pain, of Cross.

[SRJ]

Crib Goch

Yell.
You won't scatter the scree's flock,
waterfall of stone sheep
panicking without fear or bleat,
their transfixed, headlong rush;
shepherded by glaciers,
fleeced by ice and frost and fog,
storm-sheared
in the world's burst of birth.
You won't scare these.
Scream. Fling your rope
(though the wind snaffles your spindly voice)
a thousand plummeting feet
round the peaks of the bull of dark whose
bulk butt out dawn.

Shout.
Words don't count here.
Weren't they born yesterday
babbled and gurgled in some cave
not so far off?

[CF]

Salem

Siân Owen Ty'n-y-Fawnog's the old wife
Who wears, with borrowed dignity, that shawl,
Old woman, plain and strong in all her life
As Cefncymerau's rock above their hall,
Those country worshippers beyond our sense –
Siân Owen, William Siôn and Owen Siôn,
And Robert Williams from Cae'r Meddyg once,
And Laura Ty'n-y-Buarth – sweet her tune.

I meet so many worldly, knowing men,
Important, busy, driving boldly out,
Horses in front, their harness bells a din

That's not one second hushed, a regal shout.
And afterwards, how fresh your silent tone,
Siân Owen, Ty'n-y-Fawnog, William Siôn!

[SRJ]

Gwilym R Jones

Gwilym R Jones (1903-93) came from the Nantlle Valley, and was a journalist by profession, working on various papers in north Wales, culminating in his editorship of the Welsh-language weekly, *Baner ac Amserau Cymru* from 1939 until 1977. He was a versatile and prolific poet and prose writer, and won the Crown, Chair and Prose Medal at the National Eisteddfod. Although a master of the strict metres, he preferred the freedom of *vers libre*.

The Quiet Valley
(from the radio poem 'The Atomic Factory')

Where are you going, son of refugees,
your saloon car humming on the hill,
exhaustion in your eyes?

I'm searching for the Valley
beyond all valleys,
for the Quiet Valley;
a small bowl of meadow
ringed by black pines,
where no voice speaks
but to console
and nothing is out of place.
There I'll talk with my soul,
re-order my goods for the dark journey,
finger the fine things
made with craftsmen's care
whose patina satisfies.
Quietness laps that lakeshore,
a hedge breaks the wind's blade;
there the finest of spun chains
will hold me tight to the doorposts.

117

I'll search there for laughter,
for once face my heart,
the mercies
of my father's house.

Men don't endure;
the leaves still dance
after our passing.
I've seen those whose light
faded from their eyes before night,
who knew too much about death.
Some like their fathers went to Flanders,
brought back only a mirage of poppies.
Others in Germany
had the skin peeled from their bones
by barbed wire;
dock leaves sprout now
through their donations of dust.

So we are the ones who fear death and life;
the schoolmaster's stick,
grin of the bogeyman,
fear the bailiff's knock:
authority's scowl.
In dread of the jackboot,
Munich and far Belsen,
for the hell of the gas chambers
their pits of heaped corpses;
and we see in nightmares
a shadow of the lamp made from skin,
soap squeezed from men's grease.

We've lost harmony;
no longer rhyme.
Worry, like a shadow from peak to bush
follows us close.

Unpreventable evil
glowers at us daily,
we're apprehensive of headlines,
whispers in soup kitchens,
screech of a sudden brawl,
the note in the paypacket one Friday afternoon.

We gossip and gossip
to cover terror.

And the Dark Dancer who drags his feet
is up to the heels of our happiness.
We're dead in the hell of our houses,
mummified
in shrouds of skin.

Life had more flavour;
the leaves were green twice over
in earth's infancy.

So before the short-lived struggle
that turns on its loop
like a child's train,
before arriving at death's dim lodging
I intend to live.

Which is why I see the Valley
beyond valleys.
The Quiet Valley.

[CF]

Caradog Prichard

Caradog Prichard (1904-80) is best-known for his novel *Un Nos Ola Leuad*
('One Moonlit Night', 1961), which has been widely translated, and is available
in English in the Penguin Modern Classics series. But he was also a prolific
poet, and most of his creative work is autobiographical in one way or another.
He began his career as a journalist on Welsh-language papers, but eventually
worked on London newspapers, including the *News Chronicle* and *Daily
Telegraph*. An unusually sensitive soul, he never knew his father (who was
killed in the quarry before he was born), and his life seemed to be ruled by the
obsession which he had towards his mother who ended her life in a mental
asylum. Prichard won the National Eisteddfod Crown three times in succes-
sion at a very young age (1927-29), and also won the Chair later in life. His
themes include madness and suicide.

Earthly Turmoil

(extract)

This is my testament, the voice of one
returning to his earthly, native soil,
stripping off his fairer dust to wear
once more the indifferent maggot's guise;
this is my body, harassed and abused
by the choleroid bile of its brief years,
costly, flimsy matter, which when fused and
desiccated to almost nothing, dies;
this is myself discarding the relics
collected, on the journey through the fair
begging for them frail lyrical refuge
in the twilight temple of yesteryear;
this is my blood and flesh – let them be sweet
grapes from the desert void, bread from the rock.

By what hard means shall I ascend the Quiet Tower
and by this venture secure its orphan-deity?
The Tower which transcends every joy on high and low,
the deity which triumphs over eye, ear and mind.
But do not the Just, in their infinite wisdom, deem
my chosen dwelling to be both vile and subversive?
Its top-dogs contemptible; its heaven a cellar,
the grave and its clutter a perpetual pleasure.
Let the Just speak out – I will not relinquish my word
until I have reached the heights of this inverted world,
for there, a cool humour will pervade my darkest hour
watching mortals in the anguish of their darkest hour,
and knowing my dust will be eternally secure
from the earthly bloodhounds which are following its trail.

Many a path has been taken, since the chase began
through the uncivilised forests of the world, by those
who would cheat the dogs and reach that high and secret place
far from all the unruly howling and hunting horns;
and though their journey often takes them over rocky voids
and sometimes through fertile lands of ruddy abundance
the intrepid trails they blaze remain as bloody webs
in the pattern of the clay crust which covers their day.
Thus yesterday, and each weary today which follows
it to the long labyrinth, will also fade and die;

the day after next pursuing tomorrow until
the two frayed ends of yarn conjoin at the journey's end,
at that time when hounds and rusty hunting horns are mute
as mute as in laughter from the man in the moon.

The long haul of the Hanging Road; a rope in the gap,
its oval noose weighed down by the stars in the heavens;
of the black-and-white night-shot, only the frame remains
when, without a cry, a human neck fills up the noose.
But the covert voice of incitement insists: 'Despite
your gradual death in my embrace it is guaranteed
that you'll never return to familiar ground, nor tread
again in torment the stones which pave the loathsome road.'
A sudden icy blast and I saw a companion
turning towards me and a new image now filled the frame.
Like a fleeing coward I turned and hurried away
from this sanctimonious creature with its false salaam
and repulsive grimaces in ridicule of its friends
beneath the languid orbs of its cold, unseeing gaze.

A rapid river which issues from the dark Essence,
each streamlet the powerhouse for the clockwork of some heart,
a sluggish flow, congealed in the indivisible
black stagnation when the persistent tick-ticking stops;
and in due course both the vine and hazel bear their fruit
and each heart beats swifter for the feast of nuts and wine,
until at last their allotted term also expires
and the floodgate opens wide quelling their merriment.
O! Life, this is not the way I will cross your threshold
to attain a lofty repose from the weary struggle;
fearful of the exposed vein under the knife's sharp blade,
is the miracle which turns blood to wine so futile,
when the self-same act is performed in the fields of France
with the constant terror of disgorging arteries?

The thunder and lightning of the years does not desist
with the grudging and generous forfeit of our age;
the flash and booming continues beyond the mountains
swelling the peaceful ranks of the unlucky fallen.
Before the storm clouds are finally torn asunder
with renewed fury over freshly blossomed land,
I'll demand a fairer, bolder term than casualty
and a surer road towards eternal peace and ease.

I'll demand it from the swift bullet – clean and classic
leaping abruptly into my new-found domicile,
to attain, not the poor warrior's oblivion,
but the land I have ordained, above the smoke of war,
if I but knew that I would nor forever regret
the ceaseless echo from a single deafening shot.

My cup is full, as it was full in Athens when the
father of the true quest placed its hemlock to his lips,
but in the space twixt the cup and me on the table,
lies the endless procession of angry centuries;
new altars have been raised for the burning incense of
the lethal gases of the conquistadors of science;
awesome, outlandish weaponry forged for purging
the lifeblood of every nation from this black earth.
Fill up the ancient Acropolis and market place
with a blast of poison from this mean civilisation, –
one last breath from the ends of some distant battleground
one pitiable cry a mote of dust weighed down –
and brave Socrates himself with worthy parables
would scorn the cheap chalice and smash it to smithereens.

I raise up mine eyes. Yonder is the promised haven
its red beacon ignites the horizon at nightfall,
an ancient dream city beyond all baleful slaughter
its gleaming windows shut fast against the wailing dead.
I row my boat towards its port, now deeply fearful
that the sea lane will not lead its pilgrim to the shore;
the city in decay, elegant columns quaking
waves lapping at the bedrock of my pallid mirage.
A voice, part bidding, part forbidding, calls from the deep
and doggedly trails my boat as it returns to land:
'We will give you sweet sad melodies to break your heart
and a fine elegy to lull you to a long sleep.'
Far off, like a vulture of battle, the poor seagull
wheels and gyrates mournfully above a sanguine sun.

There is but one white road which leads to my dwelling place
and to join it, I will make my way through the lowlands,
through limewashed villages and past deserted bothies, –
the days and years of carefree youth never to return;
until I reach, through the nuts and berries of bush and tree,
a forest clearing that is to my mind ever green

for small boys, who understood the riparian tongue
and knew well the tricks of the trout and all its dark ways.
And the place where I would hurl my young body and swim
in the sun and shade sheltered beneath the great Maen Mawr.
This day brings a gentle amnesia to soothe the brain
in the quiet firmament of a world turned upside down
where lightbeams and clouds joust towards the high mystery,
and the untouchable deity of the Quiet Tower.

The deep is now called height and the height is now called deep,
and dead – as in stone dead – bestowed on the half deceased;
a voice rises from the lake and in its smooth mirror
I perceive someone like me but more godlike in form.
The muted unfamiliar strain from afar offers me
the tranquillity of the land under the water,
ethereal words evoking unspoken pleasures
and peal upon peal of laughter as yet undefined,
where once the little merman would listen rapturously
floating on his back, gazing upwards with confidence,
he has now turned over and has prostrated himself
before the old wizard who has been counting his days,
counting his days, one and two and three and four,
his unrefined tongues sing a deep, unrelenting tune.

[MD]

The Bargain
(In Memory of Robert Williams Parry)

> *'The Minister of Works said they had under construction an ultrasonic
> vibrator to scare away the starlings roosting around Trafalgar Square.'*

Listen, you chattering society that roosts by night
    And begs by day in the precincts of Trafalgar Square,
A plot is afoot to turn you out of your opulent yard,
    And here is the secret, according to its vengeful deviser;
They will send through hidden wires beneath your roost
    A wavelength of sound transcending our human deafness;
It will turn your sleep into pain and your grey rest to a nightmare
    When it pierces your sharp ear. Too high-priced will be your
        charity.

123

If there is among you a starling who heard it mentioned
    By father or grandfather, that day when he drifted
From the summit of Nelson's column down to its base
    And found there a Welsh welcome he did not forget,
I will strike a bargain with that starling and give him
    A matchless chance to vilify the deviser,
And to be a scout for his comrades in search of a spot
    To evade the hell being readied with devilish sounds.

But for fear there is none, I will tell you how it was
    When a bard from Eryri came cautiously to your abode
And stood amazed to watch the wonder of feathers
    That flooded the Square one afternoon in June.
One starling drew near as if it had always known him
    And dallied, big-beaked, and ate its fill from his hands;
Never was a couple happier keeping a tryst
    Than the bard and the bird I saw caressing each other.

That is how it was. And since an astonished murmur came
    Of the bard's humiliation in the valley last night,
From my heart to the folds of my brain a cry has been sent
    Like the one being plotted by your destroyer;
Beyond sound's earthly limit and transcending hearing
    The keening swells, wave upon wave, to deafen me,
As though it wished to bridge the abyss between the living
    And the mute friend placed in a box to be laid in earth.

And this is the bargain. From your number elect the one
    Prepared for a journey, a starling whose wing is daring;
One who will not count the miles, will not reckon man's distances
    And will not fear the wild duck's solitudes' cry;
He will be my messenger to the door of one whose cell will not open,
    Whose breast is pale and dreamless in the soil of Eryri,
To listen with sharp attentive ear for the distant notes
    Of a shapeless earthly poem's low mournful joy.

Should he hear that, his journey will not be worthless,
    His ear a witness that the rainbow-bridge is in place,
And my ultrasonic lament has pierced the shallow grave
    And crossed the border between death and resurrection;
The brain's cry will fall silent and I can turn old leaves
    Of memory's Bible, dying and living the years again,
And the speechless and the speaking cross the bridge in turn
    To play hide-and-seek with death among the mountains.

Therefore, comrades under a cloud, your reward will be generous
   When your chosen one returns with joyful beak from his journey
To tell of a green place transcending your sorry roosting
   And to lead you back to the road of the muse's lodgings,
Where only the mad wind's wavelength in its elation
   Will shed its dance and song above your cosy eaves
And scatter the lavish crumbs of each memorial feast-day
   Kept with the gentlest of the band of shades.

[JPC]

Waldo Williams

Waldo Williams (1904-71) was born near Haverfordwest in Pembrokeshire, and spoke English as a child, but learnt Welsh after moving to north Pembrokeshire when he was seven. He studied English at Aberystwyth, and then became a teacher and extra-mural lecturer, mainly in his native county, but with one period in England, where he escaped to on the untimely death of his wife after only one year of marriage. He was a dedicated pacifist, and was harassed by the authorities and imprisoned for non-payment of tax during the Korean War in the 50s. His poetry is extraordinary in its range, encompassing humour and irony, melodious lyrics and sublime mystical meditation.

Preseli

Wall round my boyhood, Foel Drigarn, Carn Gyfrwy, Tal Mynydd,
At my back in all independence of mind.
My ground, from Witwg to Wern and down to Yr Efail the Smithy
Where the sparks flew that are older than iron.

And on farmyards, on hearths of my people –
Breed of wind, rain and mist, flag iris and heather,
With the earth and the sky they wrestled and carried,
Bent as they were, reached and gave children the sun.

Both memory and sign. Reapers on a neighbour's slope.
Four swathes of oats felled at each sweep
On the one swift way. Then, straightening their backs,
A giant's laugh to the clouds, one shout, four voices.

My Wales, brotherhood's country, my cry, my creed,
Only balm to the world, its mission, its challenge,
Pearl of the infinite hour that time gives as pledge,
Hope of the tedious race on the short winding way.

It was my window, the harvest and the shearing.
I glimpsed order in my palace there.
There's a roar, there's a ravening through the windowless forests.
Keep the wall from the brute, keep the spring clear of filth.

[TC]

A Summer Cloud

'Durham', 'Devonia', 'Allendale' – those are their houses
And every name is the same name,
Name of the old place and the slow source of time
In the cave that is brighter than air,
The house that is out in all weathers.

A fistful of larks thrown here and yonder
To summon the playmates of day
And among them a much-pedigreed notable –
Greet the great travelling stallion, his mane a sprung bow,
His action lovely, a strictness, a pride of lineage –
We thought he was showing off, too big for his boots!

And see, up from the river
A mildness, a milch dignity, like night
Bending the rushes with her udders
And on her horns carrying the sky.
And among us, lords of words, were those
Greater than history-kings and queens.
In every weather, security was the weather.
Love and kindness was the house.

A spectre of a huge giant came down once
Through the summer sun, in an hour you'd not think it –
Struck from their ropes of music the mob of climbers,
No play of mist, neither play of night,
A dank and grey stillness,
The one that is waiting for us –

No coming at all, look, it just came.
Mountains closed on each side of the gap,
And back, back
Like years, mountains moved further and further
In a world too silent for life.
The rushes grew into trees and ended
In a world too huge to exist.
There is no there. Only I is here,
I,
Without father or mother, without brother or sisters,
And the beginning and the end closing around me.

Who am I? Who am I?
My arms reached out and there, between their two stumps,
Terrified to think about myself
And asking the basis of all asking:
Who is this?
A noise of water. I waded into it for an answer.
Nothing, only the cold flow downward.

Home – if there is home – through the stream,
In my doubt touching the gate post, the mass of it,
And Oh, before I reached the back door,
Sound of new earth and new heaven being built
On the kitchen floor, were my Mam's clogs to me.

[TC]

Welsh and Wales

These mountains, only one language can lift them,
Give them their freedom, against a sky of song.
To the riches of their poverty only one pierced
Through a dream of ages, small moments of vision.
When, through thin air, sunlight etches the rocks
Strong over chasm, sure above playgrounds of chance –
How *do* they endure, unless the confines of time
Hold them in a turn, an eternity of dance? –
A home fit for her, their interpreter! No matter what,
We must claim this house, never asking the price.
And she is danger's daughter. Her path the wind whips,

Her feet where they tired, where they fell, those of the lower air.
Till now she has seen her way clearer than prophets.
She'll be as young as ever, as full of mischief.

[TC]

After the Mute Centuries
for the Catholic martyrs of Wales

The centuries of silence gone, now let me weave a celebration
Because the heart of faith is one, the moment glows in which
Souls recognise each other, one with the great tree's kernel at the
      root of things.

They are at one with the light, where peace masses and gathers
In the infinities above my head; and, where the sky moves into night,
Then each one is a spyhole for my darkened eyes, lifting the veil.

John Roberts, Trawsfynydd, a pauper's priest,
Breaking bread for the journey when the plague weighed on them,
Knowing the power of darkness on its way to break, crumble, his
      flesh.

John Owen, carpenter: so many hiding places
Made by his tireless hands for old communion's sake,
So that the joists are not undone, the beam pulled from the roof.

Richard Gwyn: smiling at what he saw in their faces, said,
'I've only sixpence for your fine' – pleading his Master's case,
His charges (for his life) were cheap as that.

Oh, they ran swift and light. How can we weigh them, measure them,
The muster of their troops, looking down into damnation?
Nothing, I know, can scatter those bound by the paying of one price.

The final, silent tariff. World given in exchange for world,
The far frontiers of agony to buy the Spirit's leadership,
The flower paid over for the root, the dying grain to be his cradle.

Their guts wrenched out after the trip to torment on the hurdle,
And before the last gasp when the ladder stood in front of them
For the soul to mount, up to the wide tomorrow of their dear
      Lord's Golgotha.

You'd have a tale to tell of them, a great, a memorable tale,
If only, Welshmen, you were, after all, a people.

[RW]

What Is a Man?

What is living? Finding a great hall
Inside a cell.
What is knowing? One root
To all the branches.

What is believing? Holding out
Until relief comes.
And forgiving? Crawling through thorns
To the side of an old foe.

What is singing? Winning back
The first breath of creation:
And work should be a song
Made of wheat or wood.

What is statecraft? Something
Still on all fours.
And defence of the realm?
A sword thrust in a baby's hand.

What is being a nation? A talent
Springing in the heart.
And love of country? Keeping house
Among a cloud of witness.

What is this world to the great powers?
A circle turning.
And to the lowly of the earth?
A cradle rocking.

[EH]

In Two Fields

Where did the sea of light roll from
Onto Flower Meadow Field and Flower Field?
After I'd searched for long in the dark land,
The one that was always, whence did he come?
Who, oh who was the marksman, the sudden enlightener?
The roller of the sea was the field's living hunter.
From above bright-billed whistlers, prudent scurry of lapwings,
The great quiet he brought me.

Excitement he gave me, where only
The sun's thought stirred to lyrics of warmth,
Crackle of gorse that was ripe on escarpments,
Hosting of rushes in their dream of blue sky.
When the imagination wakens, who calls
Rise up and walk, dance, look at the world?
Who is it hiding in the midst of the words
That were there on Flower Meadow Field and Flower Field?

And when the big clouds, the fugitive pilgrims,
Were red with the sunset of stormy November,
Down where the ashtrees and maples divided the fields,
The song of the wind was deep like deep silence.
Who, in the midst of the pomp, the super-abundance,
Stands there inviting, containing it all?
Each witness' witness, each memory's memory, life of each life,
Quiet calmer of the troubled self.

Till at last the whole world came into the stillness
And on the two fields his people walked,
And through, and between, and about them, goodwill widened
And rose out of hiding, to make us all one,
As when the few of us forayed with pitchforks
Or from heavy meadows lugged thatching of rush,
How close we came then, one to another –
The quiet hunter so cast his net round us.

Ages of blood on the grass and the light of grief,
Who whistled through them? Who heard but the heart?
The cheater of pride and every trail's tracker,
Escaper from the armies, hey, there's his whistling –

Knowledge of us, knowledge, till at last we do know him!
Great was the leaping of hearts, after their ice age.
The fountains burst up towards heaven, till
Falling back, their tears were like leaves of a tree.

Day broods on all this beneath sun and cloud,
And Night through the cells of her wide-branching brain –
How quiet they are, and she breathing freely
Over Flower Meadow Field and Flower Field –
Keeps a grip on their object, a field full of folk.
Surely these things must come. What hour will it be
That the outlaw comes, the hunter, the claimant to the breach,
That the Exiled King cometh, and the rushes part in his way?

[TC]

A Young Girl

The skeleton of stone was once a young girl.
Always she's done it, she holds me now –
I go back for every year of my age
A century, to the world she knew.

Hers were a people who lived in peace.
The bounty of earth was theirs to win,
Pondering secrets of birth, marriage and death,
Keeping the ties of the brotherhood of man.

Early, they pitted her down for ever.
Twelve times she welcomed in the May
And then the dark companion took her.
Her voice was in the mountain no more.

The wide expanse of the sky was deeper then,
Bluer the blue of it because of her.
Stronger the house invisible and timeless
For her sake, on the hilltops here.

[TC]

Three English Poets and England

I

Supreme love poet through the vale
That severs heart from heart's delight,
Whose sleeping God wakes not at all,
A God seeing neither black nor white.

Behind his house, June on the moor
And nothing stirs all the long noon.
What is the quiet waiting for –
Reedbed and birch, the rush, the broom?

One with the choir of Ages, can
The Mercies upon His ear break
And turn to joy? And what is man?
In the mind of God is he to wake?

II

Harvesting barley by Winchester town,
Evening whitens stubble and lea.
England, when your vaunt is gone,
This to your Maker is what you'll be.

Here, one harvest, your giant came,
Five foot tall, sure amid mockery,
And the great days were a springtime
Will last for ever as leaves of his tree.

How yearned the sun upon its way
As evening shed its rosy light.
A meadow of beauty was the day,
A vale of soul-making the night.

III

Asleep are the great meadows of hay
Where ancient Ouse drags through the mud,
And so they were upon the day
When like a stag, he fled the herd.

But from his refuge heard the cry
Of his brothers betrayed from far –
Black slaves under an alien sky,
White slaves in the squalor of war.

And in the silence, by his song,
By his weakness, alone he stood
And for man's brotherhood, challenged wrong
Through the mysterious ways of God.

IV

Not for your great ones, England, though,
I give you my thanks now – because
Of your exchange of pleasant speech
That with me in my great years was.

Your bird song and leaf of the wood
Sang round about my Linda blest,
Together sang of her with me
Who bore the privilege in my breast

As when the sun rises on a hill
And his gift of warmth reaches down
And sets his bright shaft through the vale
And clears the mist on shining ground.

[TC]

Die Bibelforscher
for the Protestant martyrs of the Third Reich

Earth is a hard text to read; but the king
has put his message in our hands, for us to carry
sweating, whether the trumpets of his court
sound near or far. So for these men:
they were the bearers of the royal writ,
clinging to it through spite and hurts and wounding.

The earth's round fullness is not like a parable, where meaning
breaks through, a flash of lightning, in the humid, heavy dusk;
imagination will not conjure into flesh the depths
of fire and crystal sealed under castle walls of wax, but still
they kept their witness pure in Buchenwald,
pure in the crucible of hate penning them in.

They closed their eyes to doors that might have opened
if they had put their names to words of cowardice;
they took their stand, backs to the blank wall, face to face with savagery,
and died there, with their filth and piss flowing together,
arriving at the gates of heaven,
their fists still clenched on what the king had written.

Earth is a hard text to read. But what we can be certain of
is that the screaming mob is insubstantial mist;
in the clear sky, the thundering assertions fade to nothing.
There the Lamb's song is sung, and what it celebrates
is the apocalypse of a glory
pain lays bare.

[RW]

Euros Bowen

Euros Bowen (1904-88) was a native of Treorchy in the Rhondda Valley who
received his higher education at Carmarthen, Aberystwyth, Swansea, Oxford
and Lampeter, and became a priest with the Church in Wales. Most of his adult
life was spent as rector of Llangywair and Llanuwchllyn in Merioneth. He won
the National Eisteddfod Crown twice, but failed to win the Chair with his long
poem in the strict metres, 'Genesis', because it was deemed too difficult by the
adjudicators. Bowen was unperturbed by such criticism, as he propounded an
aesthetic which went against the grain of crystal clarity. He was an experimenter
par excellence, enjoying verbal gymnastics, playing with metres, and often writ-
ing 'through a glass darkly', yet paradoxically he was also a staunch traditionalist.

The Nightingale

Was the nightingale killed in the groves?...
We heard the heart rise with her syllables
Up the stairs of quiet splendours, –
Passion voicing the flesh's scents
And enticing the ear to caress the poem:
The bird's vitality colouring night's bed
With roses, violets and the lily,
And the song in the warm, tight concealment of leaves
Makes the rod to blossom under the lips of stars.

We heard the uninhabited places in the sap of branches
Crushing the brain, drying up the breath,
And the trunk in the ground's stranglehold
Is rough with the thorns' bites,
So that fruit did not rain on the treetop
And so that taste did not fall on the bud,
Totally, expressively full,
Shining and consonantal from the round throat…
Is flesh hardening like an empty nut?
Is the wine in the glasses nothing but a stain?
Is the world from now on emptied of its intoxication?

[RGJ]

Nettles in May

Do nettles mutilate May
When bracken's crooks are swans' heads?
There is a breeze haunting between the grave walls
And limpness on the churchyard's late daffodils,
Like the scent of bluebells
Turning to follow the wind:
Long-necked is the briars' tenure
Floating
On rhododendron's rippling,
And the green of the whitethorn's blood
Is a sadness the hue of pain's lingering,
The long evening's sadness.
Does thunder destroy early summer
When it hauls its nurturing on a mountain
And the day lies heavy on the lake bed?
No, not so.
A flash breaks on the land's astonishment,
Like stinging a hand's tiredness,
The needle in the gatherings of cloud,
Injections in grass stems – pain's restoration.

[JPC]

The Power of Song

Today on the field and on the footpath
the sun shows its quiet and gentle mastery
over the dead leaves,
a brightening in time for spring,
like snow on the bare hill,
or – to one's surprise yesterday –
like the free running tide
all light over drab flats
turning the muddy beach into a sea of pearls,
or as last night one could ponder,
under troubled clouds,
the still motion of reconciled stars,
or tonight opportunely one may see
the presiding element above the earth,
slow and undisturbed,
a golden moon in pools of water,
in puddles on the road
and in the debris of ditches,
as also tomorrow, as ever before,
the power of song shall purify woe.

[AUTHOR]

The Youth of the Language

Open the windows,
that we may listen to the leaves whitening
and hear the thrush's sparkling.

Let us smell the youth of the language
ploughing the earth,
putting a new skin on school and camp
and washing the colleges' breath.

The glass is winter's haze,
the windows are the stain of old smoke,
and the panes everywhere turn grey.

The grass follows the blood,
the soil marries the pavings,
and the stars blossom on the crests of the halls.

The generation of water's rights is rising,
spring's colours on the apple tree,
its voice growing like hands,
its words electricity
between border and shore in the land.

Here is a fellowship of new music,
like old prayer,
as old as the Middle Ages,
as new as sending messages to space:

Open the windows,
for the healthy air to come in.

[JPC]

In Chartres

And here are the famous colours.

I listened to them striking up their chords on wall and pillar, in the bays and on the floor.

I saw the musical instruments in the windows, an intense violin blue, red impassioned trumpets, a yellow fluting alternating with harps in their setting bright and gay.

The panes sang heartily, pouring rubies of light, sapphire notes of sunshine, the beautiful sound of topaz, over the vision of the place between the confessional tones of the pillars and the quiet absolving roof.

Suddenly the great organ beamed forth, a blue penetration in all the aisles, its sound red in the bays, yellow in the chancel, white on the choir screen.

Presently the candles of the deep trembled.

The heights were an agitation of lightning.

And then thunder poured forth a darkness from the uttermost mystery on blinded eyes and unforgettably deafened ears.

[AUTHOR]

Aneirin Talfan Davies

Aneirin Talfan Davies (1909-80) embarked on a career as a pharmacist, but changed direction after his chemist shop in Swansea was bombed during the Second World War, and became a well-known broadcaster. By 1966 he was Head of Programmes for the BBC in Wales. He also joined the Church in Wales, and was an eminent writer on theological and literary subjects. His studies of such authors as Eliot and Joyce helped to widen the horizons of Welsh readers, and he also published literary studies in English. He was the editor of the literary magazine *Heddiw* ('Today'), and with his brother, Alun Talfan Davies, he established a publishing house called *Llyfrau'r Dryw* (Wren Books).

I Looked You in the Face Last Night

I looked you in the face last night,
Death,
and found only
my darling's face,
its tender contours
civilising the jeer
of your surly skull's
mocking grimace.

She would not want me to squander tears –
she who wanted no one to penetrate
to her hidden disease's ugliness,
but smiled and attended to everyone's needs,
everyone's death a greater matter
than her death.

I saw you as you were, my darling,
before Death clawed your flesh
from your frail bones,

I watched the struggle
in every line of your body
and your dear face,
unable to raise a hand
to strike a blow in the battle.

[JPC]

Books
(for ME)

'What more is there for me to do...'

Ranked solid on my shelves
the books
stand witness to a life of labour;
of gleaning
sparse pennies
through bleak adolescence,
going without this and that,
hungry sometimes,
till the careful coppers were counted over
and I took the tattered spines
into my palms, like sacraments, channels of grace.
No wonder they crowd my walls in their fingered finery
blue and scarlet, sepia, black and green,
closing me in like an orderly army,
shields
against the siege of despair,
or maybe, if I'm honest,
squadrons
of antiquated idols
I thought I couldn't live without.

Once though, when I found myself caressing their skin
I gave them straight to a friend to admire.
Heard my voice say
'Take them brother'; in the words heard a knife
slice flesh,
separate a sick limb.

O surgeon of grace,
how many more amputations
for your merciful blade?

[CF]

Pennar Davies

Pennar Davies (1911-96) was a coalminer's son from Mountain Ash in south
Wales, and English was his mother tongue, yet most of his literary output was
in Welsh. Widely regarded as a polymath, he had a brilliant academic career,
graduating in Latin and English at Cardiff, before going on to study at Oxford
and Yale. Then he became an Independent minister, a Professor at theological
colleges, and eventually became Principal of the Memorial College at Brecon
(later Swansea). He wrote innovative novels and short stories, and his poetry is
characterised by its wide-ranging allusiveness, its sensuousness and its mystical
overtones.

When I Was a Boy

When I was a boy there was a wondrous region
the other side of the mountain:
the sun livelier there, in its prime;
the moon gentler, its veil of enchantment
resting chastely on hill and dale;
the night like a sacrament,
the dawn like young love,
the afternoon like sliding on the Sea of Glass,
the evening like a respite after mowing;
the faces of ordinary folk like china dishes
and their voices like the soliloquy of countless waters
between the source and the sea,
and the people sons and daughters of old,
princes and countesses in the court;
and all the lines of nature, thought, society
and talent and will and sacrifice
and the saving and the wretchedness and the peace,
all the lines of venture, claim, compassion,
meeting at eye level there
in an unvanishing vanishing point

called Heaven:
and all on the other side of the mountain
in Merthyr, Troed-y-rhiw and Aber-fan
before I crossed the mountain
and I saw.

[JPC]

I Was with Ulysses

I was with Ulysses, Odysseus son of Laertes.
We besieged the ancient city of Troy,
valiant and adventurous men
and wiser than our comrades,
since we saw the end before the beginning,
all the emptiness of heroic boasting,
all the futility of consuming wrath.
We went to war at last to spare the son,
Telemachus, better wisdom's final battle.
Laughing mockingly, we gazed at the marvels,
the arms of Achilles, the arms of Hercules,
the hateful deceit of the Wooden Horse.
We applied ourselves to cutting to bits and to killing
without the comfort of a feeble conscience
or any of Big Ajax's childish purity.

I was with Ulysses on his journey home,
home through the perils of wind and wave,
home in spite of envy and revenge,
home in spite of barbarian atrocities.
The goal was home, the home that the lustful
plundered and polluted and ruined.
We headed homewards,
thankful for the cunning of Penelope
and the fervour of Telemachus,
for the devotion of Eumaeus and the old dog Argus,
vowing to establish in Ithaca
a purer heritage, a more mannerly tribe,
and a land that would be a joyful paradise.
We held there was nothing better
than fashioning from the chaos of the age
home patch and recognition and lineage and a stubborn nation.

I was with Ulysses, the man of many wiles,
who naked aroused the naked Nausicaa,
the privileged adventurer on sea and land
who defied all the sleights of the persistent ravager,
unsparing, unwearying, unyielding death.
I almost ate the lotus,
the Cyclops almost dined on me,
I nearly became a meal for the people of Lamus.
I remember feasting in the halls of Circe.
I ventured safely to Persephone's Grove.
I heard with longing the song of the Sirens.
I sailed astonished
between the gullet of Charybdis and the hideous heads of Scylla.
I know that Odysseus wasn't completely alone
when he landed after the storm on the isle of Ogygia
and when he lingered long in Calypso's luxurious cave.
Between glittering terror and fearful entertainment
and imagination and yearning
I wasted gifts and days.

I was with the Ulysses Dante knew.
I turned my back with him on wife and son
and the feeble old man, my father,
to cross the ocean and explore the nations' shores
and weigh the good and the evil in earthly cravings.
Outwards, questioning the distances, we sailed
to the west, past island and promontory,
across the cunning smiles of the bright waters,
through the Pillars of Hercules to the deep beyond,
with the words of the Prince always in our hearing
talking of the unpopulated regions beyond the sunset
and man's appetite, compared with the poor beasts,
for the splendour of knowledge and achievement.
As we rode the cruel seas
we saw the heavens alter their appearance
and marvelled until we saw in the furthest reaches of the south
the greatest mountain that we'd ever seen,
its summit beyond our eyes and our hope
with mist half-concealing the steep hillsides:
the Mount of Purgatory, probably,
with an invisible paradise above.

142

I was with many another Ulysses
down to our own time:
Tennyson's, the Ulysses who boasted
of his courage and his comrades
before venturing on the last mad quest;
Kazantzakis', the Odysseus
who saw the fall of other cities
and sought other worlds until he met
a little Negro fisherman
and recognised him as a mirror
of the Fighter who left his bloody footprints
on the long path of the ascent of human kind;
and the one Joyce hurtled through a day
in Dublin,
the unheroic hero, the many-sided Jew,
with the yearning in him for a son transfiguring
the ordinariness of Adam's race.

I wonder whether it's the disappointment and the comfort of every
          Odysseus
that it's in the son Telemachus, after all,
the final battle will be fought?

[JPC]

Ave Atque Vale

I love you
     though, possibly, we haven't met.
If you're reading this poem of your own free will
     you belong to the minority
     who presume a poem's worthwile.
It's a pretty good basis for the relationship
     between us.
I love you.
I greet you as a friend.

But because you have been born
     you've been condemned to die.
Every greeting's a goodbye.

Someone's probably told you sometime
   it's the body that dies
   and the soul "escapes"
   or "flies off" or "moves on".
Forget it.
   The body's not a prison;
   and the stuff of the body doesn't die.

By the grace of the worms – or even the fire –
   the elements of the flesh have a future
   after they've stopped being
   parts of you.
They're not your body.
   Your body is the image and the shape you have,
   and the passion and the pain and the trembling,
   the yearnings and the impulses, the life,
   your life.

You can't live without your body
   but
   if you're determined to live,
   to keep your body,
   you will.
I don't know what sort of stuff will be given you.
   There's no scarcity of stuff or kinds of stuff.

So in saying goodbye I greet you.
   Every goodbye's a greeting.

[JPC]

The Dung Beetle
Geotrupes stercorarius

Your life has a simple pattern,
dung-beetle.
You gather manure in spring and turn it to pellets
to store away tidily and enjoy as food;
and after summer's siesta at work once more,
you gather and bury manure again to nourish the grubs,
placing the tastiest morsels next to the weakest mite
of new-born life
to fatten it nicely.

I marvel at your tenderness and fidelity.
I marvel at your foresight and strict perfection.

Is it not the utmost goodness that defecation
rouses your humble devotion?
Is it not supreme wisdom that excretion
stirs your awareness?
And you are a shaper of buds as well, your filthy pellets
obedient to the primal laws of all art;
and though creation's shit is your medium
what end and purpose is there but the precious love
that gave the rose
its form and colour and fragrance?

Not insignificant, your family connection
with the ancient Egyptians' sacred scarab,
beautiful, powerful, shapely beetle,
revered one who consecrates our filth.

Noble relations are yours, and among them
the pegasus dung-beetle so exalted by Aristophanes
when he described the patriot peacemaker
in his ride to the heavens on the happy adventure
that freed the goddess of peace
to reign over the earth.

Welcome, dung-beetle, comrade of saints.
You have doted on what we despise.

[JPC]

J Gwyn Griffiths

J Gwyn Griffiths (*b.* 1911), a native of Porth in the Rhondda, has had a distin-
guished academic career, educated at the Universities of Wales, Liverpool and
Oxford, and is now Emeritus Professor of Classics and Egyptology at Swansea.
He married Kate Bosse-Griffiths who was also a scholar and a well-known
fiction writer in Welsh. He has written widely in his specialist field, and is also
a literary critic and a political thinker, as well as a prolific poet.

There Are Limits to Brotherly Love

There are limits to brotherly love, as I've observed more than once.
There was an earthquake in Eastern Turkey
with an entire village scattered into the desolate hill-country
and thousands buried under rocks and rubble
with no hope of escape.

Help came, to be fair, from all points of the compass
and planes flew in laden down
with food and clothing and medicines
to help the wretched survivors
and get the weak back on their feet.

Yet there, on the ground, there was a curious bottleneck
with the Turkish Government slow to act
where the world had been quick.
At last the reason emerged:
these victims weren't Turks
but Kurds
and Kurds to the Government
were Nationalists and Separatists,
Freedom fanatics,
accursed extremists.
Hellfire,
they didn't deserve to be helped!

Jesus, in your limitless and overflowing love,
take pity on mankind.
Make another earthquake happen
and raze to the ground
the mountain that spits flames of prejudice and oppression,
the Vesuvius in the heart of man.

[RP]

Rosa Mystica

(The first line is quoted by Annemarie Schimmel from the Koran in a book introducing two mystics from India)

Everything but His Face perishes.
In the midst of disintegration there is One

Who is unmoved. In storms he will cause us
To see Him flying beyond the clouds – the Moon itself.

Where beauty was, there's barren desolation;
Where flowers smiled, extinction's flames consume
The ages' dowry; yet, despite misfortune,
The Mystic Rose comes, smiling on each wound.

Everything but His Face perishes.
The creed attracts, but the sad fact remains
That but by faithful eyes the Divine Essence is
Unseen. He persists beyond hurricanes

And flowers, beyond the gaudy pageant strewn
With gentle faces, beyond skies that fix
Each miracle of night and mist and noon.
And yet His Face came to the Crucifix.

[RP]

Two Are Embracing
(in the Ashmolean Museum, Oxford)

Two are embracing, a strange act,
in a corner of the Museum
near the entrance to the Library
by a small new exhibition,
Neolithic Configurations in Southern Italy.

Is it appropriate, I wonder,
in such an ambience, where yesterday
is of greater importance than today,
where the matutinal arts of these predecessors
make the masterpieces of ages appear inferior,
and the sun of adventurous early centuries
fills the room?

Well, one must confess
that it's a quite shy embrace –
a tender kiss on moist lips
like lovers in a statue

such as Pyramus and Thisbe
or Psyche and Eros –
restrained, neither impetuous nor ardent.

And I remember myself in a Museum –
the same one in fact –
being infatuated once
and declaring I love you.
Ich liebe dich too,
speaking in a whisper
out of respect for the setting,
the tears almost springing to my eyes.
After that, kissing occurred
well away from the public domain.
By Eros, that kiss was
a hundred times wilder!

[RP]

Parasites

There are worms in the dark recesses of my gut.
    But, come to think of it,
I'm a worm myself, one among millions
in the bulging belly of the world.
So what?
The world's a worm too
in the gigantic gut of God.
The intricate geometry
of concentric bellies
makes each one of us a parasite
on God.
For it's in Him that we live,
move,
and have our being.

[RP]

Gwilym R Tilsley

Gwilym R Tilsley (1911-97) was a Wesleyan minister who won the National Eisteddfod Chair twice. Although not a prolific poet, his long poems became popular as recitation set pieces and also as words to be sung to harp accompaniment at *eisteddfodau*. He was a master of the strict *cynghanedd* metres, as seen in his ode in praise of the coalminer, an excerpt of which is anthologised below. In such poetry, the medium is the message, and the message all but evaporates in translation.

An Ode in Praise of the Coalminer
(extract)

The boy strides boldly from his June of youth,
Fine his desire, but feeble his grasp,
The harsh rock's his instead of college,
A shovel for his hands, a floor for his knees;
He comes, raw lad, to the coal-face, to live a slave,
Gentle and docile under supervision.

And hard will be his labour in the mine,
And he'll spend his life in the busy pit,
He'll learn its oppression and measureless spell,
About task and meals and idle months,
He'll know injury, how to hide pain, and at times
To spread his hands for a friend in pain.

He'll know how time's spent among the pillars
Imperilled by the presence of hanging rocks,
Know the worry of water collecting,
Or the risky fleeing and the rope breaking,
And he'll know the impassioned cry when the detonated
Seam has been shattered, with someone beneath it.

[JPC]

W R P George

W R P George (*b.* 1912), a solicitor, practising in Porthmadog; senior partner in the firm established by his uncle David Lloyd George. He has written two acclaimed studies of his uncle's background and early career – *The Making of Lloyd George* and *Lloyd George: Backbencher*. A Fellow and former Archdruid of the National Eisteddfod, he won the National Eisteddfod Crown in 1974, and has published a number of poetry collections in Welsh. In 2001 his autobiography *88 Not Out* was published.

Armstrong and Aldrin on the Moon

*(My reply to a question from my little daughter, Louise-Gwen,
as we watched a historic telecast – 'Are they spirits, Dad?')*

Spirits of man's escapism,
phantoms in the cauldron
of man's rebirth
on the lowest rung
of the ladder that climbs
to the restless settlements of the cosmos.

The first to imprint their footsteps, hesitant
on the milky way:

they must appear
blind drunk
to the eyes
of the defenders of Caer Arianrhod.

Twilit precursors
of exodus
into the wilderness of space,

when our world's
on the brink of plunging –
like an ember
that got too hot
for man to handle –

down a shaft
of the old lead mine
of Creation.

[RP]

Harri Gwynn

Harri Gwynn (1913-85) was born in London, brought up in Merionethshire, and spent years in the civil service in London before settling down as a semi-retired farmer in Eifionydd, whilst still dabbling at journalism and broadcasting. His experience of farming is chronicled in hilarious vein in *Y Fuwch a'i Chynffon* ('The Cow and its Tail'). He published two volumes of poetry.

The Creature
(extracts)

Welcome
Black beetle
In your sackcloth.

You whose greeting
Is really a goodbye
To the one who hears the movement
Of motionless feet,
The sound of a soundless voice that says
That the noose that swings
In death's outhouse
Needs a neck.
So still your delirium,
My black beetle.
It's only a day or two
Until a foot falls on you
In excommunication.

I've trodden on so many of your kind.
And the more pointless the death
The bigger the thrill:

The thrill that runs through my head like a neon filament
And spells out in death's alphabet:

'To be hanged by the neck until dead.'

I could get a taste for such words.

How simple it would be
To tread on you,
Black beetle.

A sharp little click
And you no more than a stain
Like the stains of all your black fathers.
As simple as that.

As simple as squeezing the white neck
Of my lover:
The slight, downy throat
Above her full breasts.

As simple as squeezing you between these fingers,
Between these thumbs
In a white knuckled grip.
And once again, that sick
Little click, and then, better,
Flesh's wild perfume from a wound
Like an open mouth.

My little beetle,
Has the hurricane roared through you
And swept away what was withering?
Naked no more, you're now
One of a band of burning brothers,
Every one of them pledged to passion.

So did you feel the whitehot surge –
Lovelust's momentous moment,
The torture that is rhapsody –
Driving before it through your veins
The hallucinating blood?

And did that pulse throb in you
So fiercely you had to dance to it,
And keep dancing, further, further,
Until you thought you'd lost your mind,
A crimson ululation
Between your ears?

Then you must have reached that place
Where killing and creating
Are the same thing?

I saw two wet lips
Deployed by desire.

Two lips that would drink from love itself
But were seeking instead
The suck of some
Other's mouth.
So don't do as I did, black beetle.
Through the redness of her lips
I tasted a false tongue.
And that's when I felt a funeral inside me.
I was the sovereign who married the sow.
She made a swine of my soul.
But once there was a prince enthroned in me –
Before any priest
Signalled sacrifice
And any cry was raised
Over ancient altars.
There's one who rests
In the seed's lodging
And the tree's root,

There's one who pulls the green flames
From spring trees, one who knows
There's a leopard's heart
In every woman's purring breast.
And there's one who unsheaths from a lion's fist
The equalising claw.

This is what I'm itching for,
My little beetle.
To press my tongue
Against that cherryskin mouth.

Ah, black beetle, when you rise from your bed
In the buried city, it is still dark.
So do you know how to reach me
In the kingdom of the night?

The night,
When guilty hands close the curtains
And light is a refugee
And there is whispering
Under the hedges
And dementia in the ditch
And hands that grasp
And fingers that grope.

Don't you know the night is lurking
Disguised as daylight
Under the stairs
And in the cellar
And beneath the bed
And in the church porch?
Don't you know it is biding its time?

And can't you calm
That crepitation in the mind's cave?
It's the night beetles
Scratching at the walls,
Burrowing under the floors,
Awaiting their time.

Child of the dark,
Didn't you promise my kind
How to understand this inheritance?

Then why so silent?
Why this dumb
Insolence?

Don't you recognise
There's a kind of creation
And an effigy of God?
So won't you honour him,
My darling black one?
But you're crushed
By the presence of your lord.
Crushed so low
It's impossible to change.

I'll show you how
To reveal your respect,
How to humble yourself
So you resemble a creature
Crept close to its lord.

Stand straight for once,
Little fleshling,
Next to his honour, our judge
In his goathair and gown,
And there

In the witness box
See the milling
Of the malign
As they all take the stand,
Feel the derision
As they urge each other on,
And hear their conspiracy like a breeze that steals
Through the eyeholes of the dead
In some nightmare.

Here are some of those faces
I recognise.

The corn-fed con-man,
Avoiding the cracks as he winces
His way over the pavements of his town,
Sated and soft
With a wad in his wallet,
And always a different doxy
Who's good for the holiday.

The face of the pinched prelate,
Pawing in his piety the maiden ladies in the porch.
He understands that the parable
Of Saturday night is not
The parable of Sunday morning
As he peddles the bargain
Of God's soft soap.

Then the owl-faced schoolmaster, behind his desk
In the classroom's sanctuary,
Offering us the secrets
Of blood and swords and our imperial fathers,
All that *dulce et decorum est*,
As if he had been part of it.

And there's the copper-cropped soldier
Who taught me how to drive the bayonet shaft
Through the map of the guts,
Ambassador of espionage
And devious death, an arm
And hand his only weapons.
Such a good teacher.
Such successful work.

While's here's that old woman for you,
So kind to her pets
But she bays like the bitchwolf
About how the rod and the rope
Should chastise the likes of me.
Then she dozes off into her royal dreams.

And now that butter-wouldn't-melt
Book-keeper, back after spending the Sunday
With the lodging-house daughter.
What a fine time they had of it,
Translating their paternosters
Into pillow talk.

Then look at the crowd
Snuffling the trail
Of tragedy in the Sunday morning scandal-sheets,
And later, dousing themselves
With the adulterous dark
Of the cinemas'
Second-hand sins.

*

So before you, black archbishop,
My philosophical friend,
I abase myself.
Here is my confession:

God never made a bigger mistake
Than when he breathed life into us.

Like the perfume from a bottle
It has leaked into the world.

So take it
As your lords would wish,
For your lineage in the labyrinths.

Because
It was he who threw whole worlds aside –

Cold corpses –
On to the dunghill of creation:
It was he who struck out the stars
Like the pinching of a cheap candle.
But shouldn't he keep his bile
At least in this world
For the beetle-lords and their scrabbling lives?
Shouldn't he put his foot on them
So they are no more
Than a vanishing stain,
And the holy flood
Can sweep their remains from the surface of his earth,
Washing that poxed army
Into the gutters,
While the hunchbacked ape proclaims
Amen
And the owls
Whistle the *Nunc Dimittis*?

Now cratering the silence
Comes the tramp of feet
And I wait
At the door of my cell.

The key screams in the lock.

Here comes a creature
To put a rope around a creature's neck.

And what arrives
Are the same hands and face
Seen at Golgotha
And in Buchenwald.

It was one like this,
My dear beetle,
That nailed our God to the cross
As a collector crucifies a moth.
And because of his loneliness,
God took a beast
And created a god-doll out of it,
To comfort himself.

But how quickly
Is the divine imagination
Bored. So God dangled his creature
From a beam between men like me.

Black beetle, it's not easy
To doublecross your own kind.
And it's no child's play
To give up your own soul.
Yet what's this life
But the bottle's beery whiff?
I swear that there must be
A sweeter scent than that.

And again, for a second,
I can feel the rope lie slack
About my throat.
Then earth's trapdoor opens.
The night slams down.
And in that moment I recognise
The faces of all the beasts I've seen,
Mingling together in their mockery,
Feel the shiver of their satisfaction
Before they go their separate ways,
Blessing their bellies
And scattering the seeds
Of their kind into eternity,
As if their God was applauding
Christ and the Christ-killers too.

So come, my dark evangelist,
And take the word to all your kind
About these lords of yours.
Have the beetles congregate
To your gospel.
Unless of course they've already found
Their place in paradise.

[RM]

Moses Glyn Jones

Moses Glyn Jones (1913-94) was a native of Mynytho in the Llŷn Peninsula, and he spent his career as a science teacher in Caernarfonshire. He won the National Eisteddfod Chair in 1974, and published a number of poetry collections, where the old is fused with the new, and where there is often a combination of *cynghanedd* and *vers libre*.

The Old Light

Two things remained constant:
the chamber of stars
and the tombstone's weight.

'Goleuni Parc y Blawd'
on the purple moors of Tynffynnon
where the stream speaks parables
between the flowers' bowing heads,
our muffled sight as fog descends,
though the moon buffed
green moss with the old light.

Yet also, those rays shone
on the lanes and rough tracks
of a struggling birth:
candlelight the midwife
in the glowering shadow
of the Schoolhouse, the foetus
revealing the navel's secret.

Stillness under the stars
and crop of stunted stones,
grief in the hillocks of heather,
knelling of each tiny bell.

Old is the light,
older than curlew's cry
and the oak's druid-cloak,
the flux of its brightness
filling every crack and crevice.

[MJ]

The Living Spring

Here, there were pilgrims
born of the waves
kneeling with sunset in their eyes.
Cian, Iestyn, Pedrog and Tudwal
laying down their knotted sticks of hands, they lapped
silence from cold waters.
From a land beyond their vision
where their prayers could reach,
came news which lifted them:
news of a living stream
which flowed without ebbing
and never lost its clarity
however much of washing and drinking.

Gorse-flowers have been extinguished
on the mountainside, Cian
and the stream of Tudwal
has become sluggish with silt,
the rill of Oerddwr
runs dry till moss is white;
orchid and mint are choked
and horsebane strangled by slime.

But listen, Iestyn and Pedrog,
if you eavesdrop you'll discover
that land and water are one.
Creatures of both, the toads,
leap on their web of stones
just as in your time.
Raiding storms from the sea
which besiege the clifflines
did not end with you.

[MJ]

The Candle's Fly

On the fifth of September
you journeyed
                    like a stray helicopter,

160

landing on our antique table
as a timely reminder.

You come here for the last days
at the close of our summer
and I don't regret your arrival
despite what you carry,
your invisible leather
will so soon disappear.

On our sumptuous feast you've fallen
a harvest gathered here.
Take your time, for it is almost over,
the candle's smiling clear.

[MJ]

Sand-time Measuring

Hours of my youth spent dallying,
clumsily needing
in the roll of things.
Long day and into the night
sand running through the slim waist
from top to bottom
filling full of todays and tomorrows.
The treacly texture of it,
stickiness on my hand –
clutch of cold glass.

The shorter falling
in the high chamber after
of virginal brides
led from the wedding feast,
flecks glimmering their locks,
on tinselled high heels –
glass blown, full-bodied.

But there were days
when the shiny sand
slipped through the wide waist,
days gone with grains

lost in a pit,
easy as water from fist's grip.

[MJ]

Alun Llywelyn-Williams

Alun Llywelyn-Williams (1913-88) was a doctor's son, brought up in Cardiff,
and graduated in Welsh and History at the university there. He worked variously
as a librarian, a radio producer with the BBC and Director of Extra-mural Studies
at the University of Wales Bangor, and was awarded a Personal Chair in 1975.
He served with the Royal Welsh Fusiliers during the Second World War, and
is one of the few Welsh-language poets who wrote about his war experiences.
During the 30s he established the literary journal *Tir Newydd* ('New Ground'),
and as a poet and critic he was sensitive to contemporary issues, whilst at the
same time emphasising the universality of human experience.

When I Was a Boy

All the day long and each day the sea would gleam, steeped in
         blueness;
the sun did not foretell tomorrow's storms, did not bewail yesterday's
         guilt;
I walked the quay in the white morning, examining the masts,
questioning and seeking beneath the rude seagulls' racket;
and there it was, my Gwennan Gorn, foam's foal, piercer of billows.

I would lie in the bow of the boat and drench my hands in the water;
the unbearable pureness of the island lighthouse came nearer
where the fish would quiver and dart beneath the soundless cliff;
how gladly the sail would leap to the azure heavens,
how prettily sink again in the pit of my adventurous sinews!

The blue land beyond would hang like a dream between my lashes,
the furrows of the sea did not clock my boyish course;
bitter, after the returning, to tread the motionless earth,
cross the heaviness of the clay
and hear, from its cell now, the mortal pulsations of the flesh.

It was an unreturning return; those suns wore down
to their late, long setting; but the light in the gloom across the bay,
that remains, like a miracle that snatched to the virgin spire

the eye that warms the world:
just as before time's watchmen besieged me, it shines
on a sea-voyage ever unended.

[JPC]

On a Visit

Peace has surely come by now to heal it completely,
and turn the stricken house to a home of joy once more;
if I could return some winter twilight
and walk again through the noiseless lane's silent snow
to where I once was, there would be a change in time and a new
order, and I would not know a world as strange as summer.

And perhaps it was a dream, when I knocked at a haughty
door long ago: the Baron himself came to open it
and courteously eyed my uniform:
'A, *mon capitaine*, *mille pardons*, come right in,
out of the blizzard: the days are dreadful, and till the calamity
passes, a man's most courteous welcome would be uncouth.'

He spoke the truth: I remember that the house leaned
above a steep and pine-dark secret valley, on a clear slope,
a mansion lacking antiquity's magic, of hewn grey
rocks, strong, like the forceful gesture of someone who
dreamed of stones, till he declared his dream a fortress
and a temple for his secret heart against the angry gods.

So I crossed the threshold of a reluctant host.
'I have heard,' he said, 'there was a great battle in the hills
in a snowstorm, for three days on end:
victors over weather and man desire rest, and lodging
for the weary: but, sir, we sorrow for the scar
we ourselves have had, and the aerial scourge of our faith.

War will not spare today poor defenceless people;
from the far sky devastation comes without warning, in bursts
of steel and fire more scathing than the whip
of a God of vengeance. Would you care to see fate's joke
on all cordiality?' He turned surlily towards the stairs
and bade me follow him up in the half-darkness.

The east wind was piercing the wide glassless windows
and spewing snowflakes on carpet and mirror and chest:
on the bed's costly coverlet was spread
the north's sullen white shroud and the freezing wind's paralysis.
How softly the man's groan came to my ears: *'C'est triste!'*
Sad! the grey blight was swirling from room to room.

But I said, 'Let us go to your living quarters.' In anguish
he looked at me, and turned without a word, and led me away
back to the naked stairs and the hall. My boots now
beat out grim heavy-heartedness on the wooden floor,
but lightly he stepped in companionless dignity,
alone, like a stubborn invalid determined to mortify the flesh.

When he opened the unnoticed door, the cheerful light leapt
to embrace us, and the warmth to caress us: from her cosy
seat by the generous fire, a woman rose
startled, and was shining anxious eyes upon us,
and 'Madam,' said my guide, 'be of good cheer;
here is a soldier, a stranger who asks, reluctantly,

shelter with us in his weariness.' She bowed her head,
but said nothing. I remember that an image of Christ
was hanging on the wall through the silence:
lit by the leaping flame, the wood was glowing, turning pale,
as though the blood spurted from the sorrowful, faltering heart.
And then I saw the handsome piano, and the books thickly

cluttered on top. Peevishly, I scrutinised their taste;
and smiled: 'I see now, Madam, you are a romantic;
Liszt – and Chopin: there's been many an alliance, I know,
between France and Poland: the rigid frontiers of our earth's
disillusion do not apply to music.' And I saw the great tears
gathering in her eyes, like a lake filling with stars.

Oh clumsy fool, not to have seen their secret! He
was the first to speak. 'My friend, forgive us
our discourteous manner; we are mourners
because the musician will never, never more come back home;
we did not wish to share our pain with anyone.' We three stood silent,
till the man turned to the piano as if challenging its strength.

For a moment, he sat there, in humble prayer
before attempting the music: then the gracious melodies
flowed from his hand, prelude and dance and song so bitterly sad,
so carelessly joyful, and gentle and full of compassion –
till the sound grew soft, a communion where angels walked,
honouring our wound and setting our captive hours free.

[JPC]

In Berlin – August 1945

I *Lehrter Bahnhof*

Heledd and Inge, when the torches are red –
Inge, or Heledd, which? the years play tricks with us –
see how we meet, at an interweaving of the swift threads,
the distant travellers, by chance beneath the clock.
By chance, I wonder? From the station, there is
neither start of a journey, nor its end, unless one has found
in its broken platforms the end of all further journeying.
Book your sorry ticket for wherever you wish;
long, long the waiting for this crowd,
long its patience and without a murmur,
because the blind bullet that flung my stupefied carcass
to its sulk on the rust of the rails
ricocheted too, shattered the convex glass, ripped the fingers away
that appointed the coming and going
of the harsh wheels' stately bustle.

The whirlwind went by –
and from the cleft in the wall, from the crack in the pavement,
the water pours without echoing the song of the brook.
The night drips around us.
You forgotten travellers, since you are so quiet,
I will gather together my terror, and lay it a while
here at the edge of life, lift it from the damp floor,
and share your waiting for the station master.
Let the quiet flow between us; let us watch again,
after the worthless centuries,
the lava trickling slowly along the road,
the spreading of sand across the tombs of kings,
and praise the hearth's purity beneath the grey lichen's blight.

(That was long ago, the memory isn't clear
whether each time our fate has been the same;
but before the bridges blew up, you too were in flight.)
Sharp is the breeze; Heledd, do not shiver, do not weep;
take courage: concealed on the handy bed of the rubble,
as a gift for savouring the cigarette, for sucking the chocolate,
you can extend your love to the lonely conqueror.
The night drips without mercy.
When will he come, when, when, the blue official,
with his spruce uniform, with his detached good taste,
to sound his horn and start the crowd once more?
This was always a gross, pompous city
and fit to be ruined;
have you heard, Heledd, – no, wounded Inge, –
the greedy eagle's fierce laughter,
have you seen, in his half-shut eyes,
the preordained image of all our fragile cities?

II *Zehlendorf*

Death had come to the public garden:
I saw the shallow grave, the tiny cross of wood
between the footpath and the lakeside
on the tiny headland where the tall pinetrees grew:
strange if it were done in Roath Park, in Kensington Gardens,
this useless and sorry gesture.

Kneel, Inge, and kiss the soil:
if you wish, spread the blossoms tenderly on the brave:
do not give him a name –
the children fled from that spot long ago, a broken toy,
a sorry boat with a mast, is what is left of their games.

Familiar, no doubt, when it comes, is the death
that mercifully climbs to our bed at the long day's end,
that awaits us on the farthest corners of our consciousness,
on Everest's highest peak, there to greet our strength:
that gave in the days of old
long sleep and everlasting song to the guardian of the ford,
the defender of the border.

Ah! the wretch did not say, here, at the anonymous cross,
if it was the fear struck him down in flight,

or the drunken despair of the lonely challenging,
or if the devouring flame of Belsen's fires consumed him.
The grave has been simply marked, and above it
the prophetic trees will not venture to promise
that the spring will come back in its turn.

III *Theater Des Westens*

It keeps on raining. Somewhere in the roof
    the hidden pool overflows at the tip of a crack,
and through the captive darkness, the steady unhappy
    drops trickle to soak the slack carpet.

So be it. Let us be content to watch Inge dancing,
    dancing where the harsh electric light is focussed;
stronger than the fear that lurks in the rain's pulsations
    is the music that fosters the assurance of her supple arms,

that governs the joy of each disciplined gesture.
    In the prints of her nimble steps, the clover grows –
for the burden at her breast, let the mother again be joyful,
    let the weary doctor be cheerful on leaving his friends!

Because the training has been long, and her instruction thorough
    in many an ancient city; and many an age
has fashioned her delicate art, the craft that incarnates
    the spinning of the notes, that purifies the primal wound.

Here, there is a garden to be tended, a disease to be isolated;
    after swearing the irrevocable oath to its high order,
how lightly we too tread the hard stage, and feel
    the force in the firmament, the strength in the green shoots.

[JPC]

Geraint Bowen

Geraint Bowen (*b.* 1915), brother of Euros Bowen, graduated at Cardiff, and
was then a teacher and later an Inspector of Schools. A sparse poet, he made
his name with the ode in praise of the farmer, which won for him the National
Eisteddfod Chair in 1946, and which achieved the same kind of popularity as
Gwilym R Tilsley's ode to the coalminer. Bowen has published only one vol-
ume of poetry, but is a prolific scholar and critic.

Ode in Praise of the Farmer
(extract)

The Poet's Prelude

The anyone of his birthplace – partner
    To the pasturage, he worked hard;
  The man who gardens the greensward,
  Who sows the field; pure his world.

Pure the world that he harvested – the grain
    Grown from his levelled furrows;
  The man who saw tomorrow
  In the turn of the harrow.

Row on row following the tether – turning
    The steaming horses, feather-
  Foot under the reins' leather,
  Daily, whatever the weather.

In all weather, hear the chains sing – the plough
    How late from the tilling;
  The sight of her line, her wing,
  Crows where horses were hauling.

The hills were green-breasted – to the skyline
    Secure and quiescent,
  On ploughland where seed was cast,
  Would come the time for harvest.

September, harvest the seed – turned to gold
    Gilding the spine of the slopes;
  Ocean-waves under the oaks,
  Like grains of the sea – corn seed.

Ceding his blade to the wave – in the lull
    A light-headed breeze hovering;
  His stoop like a stack stoved over
  At evening in some haven.

A haven where he'd come smoothing – came
    Then old ripeness for birthing
  And heavy pregnancy filled
  The breasts of the fields.

Kindly he keeps the fallow; – the hay felled
    In the field and the meadow;
  And creates, in joyful brio,
  Building the stacks in the sun's glow.

Day in, day out on the farmland, – brave
    Above the hoofed and the horned,
  When summer grew shadowed
  And winter in summer returned.

[GC]

Eluned Phillips

Eluned Phillips (*b.* 1915?) hails from Ceredigion, and her university studies in London were interrupted by the Second World War. She has written professionally for English periodicals, and did not make her name as a Welsh poet until she won the National Eisteddfod Crown in 1967, a feat she repeated in 1983. Her second Crown poem describes a poignant scene from the Falklands war.

Ties

1865

From the mist came sounds of moving in Pant Glas
and the wail of a woman weeping.
Then, silence of remembering –
the gate to the sheepfold closing.

No herdsman calling in the sty. In the barn,
the mice are merry.
An anchorless family cut free
as a helmless boat on the sea.

A ruthless squirearchy broke
a home without mercy.
Their orphaned furniture borne away
on a cart down a muddy track.

He was voted in, big bellied squire,
by forelock-tugging followers, and then
his treacherous cuckoo-servant sent
strutting in to steal the nest.

Man of God, the faithful hand, who honoured
his rented acreage of land,
for his children took his stand
`against tyranny and eviction.

The bailiffs meant business. Tools
and stock went under the hammer. All
day was like a day of funeral.
Work on stop, fun under a pall.

*   *   *

Not for them was chancing Liverpool,
but 'Llynlleifiad' *Y Faner*, a whirlpool
of emotions lashed them,
the nightmare of fear pierced them.
The ties bound them closer, the hearth
of Pant Glas round them like a cord of *hiraeth*.
Slow was the *Mimosa*'s way
to Patagonia's paradise.
A voyage of plague and sickness.

To turn away from the nation of their oppression
for a land of freedom from humiliation.
To awaken conscience, community,
to start again in a wide open country.

Long centuries of seafaring,
and the ache of *hiraeth* like a sting.
To sing in a choir in the English tongue
with those who couldn't know their longing.

On board the ship of adventure, children
free of pain and innocent,
wild in the restless tempest.

*   *   *

1982

The mansion claimed by clambering bramble,
rats took to the byre and stable.
A hippy commune, the cellar no longer
locked by the squire, is their lair.

Capitalism came to the fair land
to buy a fleet of homes for summer.
Every parish tie's unbound.
The carthouse is a boat's shelter.

Y Felin became a retreat,
retired couple, no children :
sold for 40,000.

No one lives in Betws now
but a mannered German *frau*
with a goat that dotes at the door.

Gravestones grown over with umbellifers
and the graveyard gate ajar
like a gaping jaw.

The weeping yew tree sighs
over the bones of old hands.
Indissoluble are the grave's ties.

                    *   *   *

Pant Glas's boy is on the Beacons now,
a soldier in his khaki suit.
He swallowed the lie – travel, go,
see the world, fill your wallet with loot.
He left the plough and harrow to the rust,
to learn to fire a gun, a bayonet's thrust.

                    *   *   *

The urgent order came from the War.
A green lad from the life-spring of his home.
Farewell to the sight of a ewe in labour
in a corner of Cae'r Eithin, birthing her lamb.

The *Sir Galahad* is like a monster,
mouth agape as the jaws of a whale.
The tanks into her bowels sinking,
sullen guns on her shoulder bristling.
Military pride in her kind on the ocean,
the tethering anchor alive to her searching.

The Pant Glas boy is a stranger here,
a number, a surname, mere
killing machine, one of the rank and file
on the voyage to hell.
A green boy with a gun at his side,
his intimate partner day and night.

*   *   *

When waves lose their temper he remembers
the tale of their journey, reaching Patagonia,
after months in the belly of the *Mimosa*.

He, sailing to the same destination
his ticket paid for by the nation.
In his heart the same old yearning
to reach land, but for a different reason,
to see the vast continuous ocean – the whale
like a beast from the Book of Revelation.

Cold comes like the cold of ice on the day of war
because of the old ties with Patagonia.
Each small country under another's rule,
and their anguish cruel.

There'll be no tears and no memorial stone
in No Man's Ocean over his bones.

*   *   *

The Welsh in coldness and in heat
on Buenos Aires streets.
A people descended from heroes
who emigrated from their woes.
Here they celebrate a holiday
on Eisteddfod Friday.

The Capital is alive with celebration
and they're dancing in the Casa Rosada.
After long war killed all such emotion,
back in their hands, the Malvinas.

Came the day of Armageddon
its darkness on the white wave.
Day of the black sun, day of the torn breast.

A mirage of gunfire, and death
is dropped from its claw
as it flies home over the rocks.

Sir Galahad in flames.
The rush into the waters of bedlam
from the mouth of the flames.

A bee-swarm of helicopters
suck the living into their mouths
as hope closes its eyes.

Cruel death to the frail ones
who scream in the fire. From
their Catraeth they will not come home.

*   *   *

On a day of madness to swallow the truth.
Abandoned, every deception's excuse.

Two countries reap the lightning of Cain,
Argentina and Britain.

To bury the dead who will not see summer,
in the June of their winter;
and bear them broken
to a shed where meat was frozen.
In haste to move them onward
to a makeshift hospital ward;
and boys who'd been enemies
suffered side by side.

From the mouth of a bottle, British
blood flows into Argentinian veins.

Today, blood of two patriots
merge and mingle in a soldier's flesh.

*   *   *

Who is this who sees only the darkness
of the shed in San Carlos?
A boy and his long night, for always.

He listens to sounds of activity
seeing no one, his gaze empty
in the horror of tragedy.

Sightlessly staring,
endlessly looking, looking
into the long night of sighing.

When morphine soothes the pain
he still walks the old lanes
from Pant Glas through Cae Meillion fields,
and a beautiful girl runs into his arms.

To see love carved in the bark of an oak,
to see blood-beads cluster on the mountain ash
to see Jesus of Bethel hanging on a tree
in the shadow of a yew to see death lurk.

To see a field dance with new lambs
to see the mother he'll never see again.

Who visits him
in his cold bed?
A lad from Buenos Aires.

A boy from the world of poverty
of those who fled adversity
in Cwm Hyfryd, one winter day.

Wonder on the tip of the tongue,
small words, their value holy among
the difficult sentences.

The one-armed one greets the blinded one,
harmony, despite the conflict
between two nations.

Celts of one blood-line.
Their birthright the mother tongue,
two of a kind.

Ties are stronger than wounds.
Will they weave a way across the void?

Fragmentary their talk
before they part.

Is the future forever dark?

*   *   *

Nothing's left but memories of pain,
a widow's mite to heroes of a poor nation.
Lean days to finger the remains
of memory carved in an oak tree bark.
Cae Meillion's door is locked. A girl
is an illusion, a passion that breaks the heart.

> The frail tie, the last tie,
> for the boy who would not see summer.

[GC]

Rhydwen Williams

Rhydwen Williams (1916-97) was the foremost chronicler in Welsh of the life of the Rhondda Valley in both novels and poetry. It was in the Rhondda that he grew up, and he returned there as a Batpist minister, but later in life he worked for television, and also made a name as an actor. He won the National Eisteddfod Crown twice, in 1946 and 1964, and was a prolific poet.

Dogs

The whole of doghood I've seen in my time
Dogs great, dogs small, dogs comic, dogs godly and good;
Dogs under-arm, dogs under-arse, dogs dull, dogs devoted to crime,
Dogs highbrow, dogs a-grovel, dogs dishevelled, dogs a plague in flood.
Yes, I've seen and heard the whole canine catalogue,
And I have still in my nostrils the smell of two generations of dog.

Well I remember yesteryear's dogs in the long ago Valley
Funny little old mongrel dogs; dogs of every size and format;
Dogs happy, dogs bereft, dogs that would dog you up any old alley,
Dogs fearless of both man and devil – except sometimes the devil
       of a cat!
Carrying messages and cocking legs, the little old dogs of our boyhood,
More alive to me now than ever – though gone, a long time since,
       for good.

Of the Mansion and its hounds recollection now stirs
I was the servant boy, shining shoes, chopping logs, replenishing coal.
Mine the joy before breakfast of feeding and grooming those
       loathsome curs,
Unleashing their lusts, giving them a hand to lick, taking them for a
       stroll.
To be a lackey to a dog is something most men would rather not,
But set aside the gentry and the stench, and that's exactly the lackey's
       lot.

By dogs I was surrounded from the day that I first saw the light –
Wil Ty-Cwrdd's dog and Tomos the Shop's, Gran's dog and the dog
       next door;
And when there'd seem not a hair of the wild menagerie in sight
Suddenly there'd come a woof-beneath-the-bed or an under-the-
       sofa scratching of floor.
A dog might seem a priceless creation, but the truth is, though
       some may find it odd,
That it has in abundance the virtues of Man, the Devil's devisings
       and the omnipresence of God.

The old fellowship by now has more or less come to an end:
Of pedigree companions all that's left to me is just this one.
A lop-eared, amusing dandy of a boy, whom I never have to reprehend,
With his back and his legs like hedges and his bark like the blast
       from a gun.
In an hour or so we'll go out, him and me, have a walkies powwow.
The pedigree sign of a bow tie marking the higher-nosed one as a
       bow-wow.

[NJ]

Mountain Streams

(extracts)

For the children of the Welsh School at Ynys-wen in the Rhondda
Valley and in memory of three of their champions
John Robert Williams, collier and poet
Robert Griffiths, pastor and preacher
James Kitchener Davies, teacher, patriot, writer

Listen.
The rejoicing of waters fills my ears this evening:
Ynys-wen, Ynys-feio, Ynys-hir,
All the way to Eglwys Ilan
And the small spring on Pen Rhys
As lovely as a jewel on the breast,
Still praising Mary –
The mountain springs are alive!

     Stranger in these parts?
     Yes.

He was sitting on a bench at the foot of Moel Cadwgan.
Cap. Stick. Cigarette.
I seemed to remember his face, or what was left of it.
     Lleteca? They've pulled the old place down.
     He was a poet.
     And the best collier from y Bwllfa to Maerdy.
     A craftsman at the *englyn*, he was.
     And none were as good as 'im in an 'ard 'eadin'.
Cutting coal with a mandrel and writing verse,
Chalking the *cynghanedd* on the coal face.
He was this mountain's first poet.

Walk on. Ask at the chapel.
     Only women left now, like the few on the Third Day.
Open the door. Go inside. Stand and stare.
     This plaque's in memory of the old minister.
     'Prophet, shepherd, and friend to all.'
     There are a few left who remember 'im.
     Spent a lifetime 'ere, he did.

The grave of Robert Griffiths is on the high hill above Treorci –
As if he couldn't let Moriah out of his sight.

177

Walk on. Gelliwastad and Tyntala, Llwynypia and Trealaw,
And Brithweunydd. (There were Welsh poets there once.)
Is there a poet in Aeron nowadays?
>   He died young.
>   Some said, for Wales.
>   Black hair, large eyes, and a smile.
>   'Andled a spade like he 'andled words.
>   Nationalist, but a real gentleman!
>   Dramatist, poet, Calvinist and contented sinner.
>   Fine voice for the loudspeaker,
>   Soap-box and pulpit, too.
>   Corduroys and a clay pipe.
>   Theomemphus and a pint of beer.
When they laid him to rest in Rhondda earth one afternoon,
The Llethr-ddu had a seam richer than coal.

Listen. I was born here. The Valley's mark
Is on me like on a sheep. Accent. Memories. Creed.
The Great War was part of my birthright. Like cutting teeth,
>   And whooping cough.
The General Strike was part of my growing up. Like marbles,
>   And girls.
I was brought up tenderly in the Sunday School and on the coal tip,
School cap and hobnailed boots on weekdays, velvet and pearl
>   buttons on Sundays;
I was familiar with foundry, cinema, football pitch, bandroom and
>   singing festival,
A chubby Welsh cherub learning verses from the Bible and how to
>   swear.
I remember…
>   lunatic hooters frightening the innocent birds,
Wheels, engines, trams clanging night after night,
And the shameless pit stretched by the river,
Its tips like the teats of an old sow in the water,
Farting in the face of heaven,
And the cowed womenfolk, their men naked in the tub before the
>   fire…
>   Shut the bloody door!
>   Come an' wash my back!
And the children aping their parents in the street…

Listen.
Can you see now, here, the day of the red squirrel,

And the wild pigeon and pheasant and fine partridge,
The clear mountain streams always to hand
For the industrious people, when there was only water and the
         good earth
To ease the hunger in their kindly eyes?
Can you see in that country light,
A man as patient as his beast,
Spending his life in two fields,
His mind as narrow as his hedges.
And Welsh gushing from his lips like a mountain spring?
Can you hear in the perfect silence,
Stars as loquacious as birds
And hands that steered the plough
Tuning a harp like Orpheus once in a surging song?
Innocence was as common as the dew
On these mountains in those days,
And the goodness of men's hearts in the all-purpose kitchen –
Hens, cats, dogs and meddlesome sheep –
As warm as a new-laid egg in its nest.

It was a world of trees,
Multitudes of tall trees as far as the horizon,
One lazy path to everywhere, scraped by boot and hoof and paw,
Leaves falling on it daily like green rain,
And only the sun and moon and stars and sometimes a drover
Calling – the sun come to tarry a while,
And the moon on its way to Hirwaun Fair for some fun and a quiet
         drink,
And the drover making for Bristol, his beasts groaning under their
         loaded skins.
Leaves of the tree, the scent of flowers and an eyeful of the sky's blue –
The limits of their world!

                    *   *   *

Listen.
Can you see now the ruined forests and fine trees like cadavers,
And the squirrels lost on the bereaved mountain,
And the dove bewildered in the sky,
And all the birds searching madly for their nests?

Can you hear now the hooters clamouring
In air that once trembled with the song of nightingale, linnet and
         dunnock?

179

And the waggons and carts and engines and steam and tumult
Mocking the tranquility that once was seamless and green?

Can you see the earth displaying its wounds to the sun
And the river dying on its bed and the trout on the surface of the water?
And the man who turned his harp once on a merry hearth
Having to go down like Orpheus into the black depths?

Listen.
(This song is made not of tears but of steel.)
The farm was bought for a price,
With the stable manure thrown in for luck!
(The stable's sewage was a real bargain.)
And from that moment on, the epileptic depths spewed forth into
      the streams,
Staining the estuary,
The river lost its virginity
And the streams were disgraced under the stars.
    I remember Rhosynnog comin' to Noddfa.
    I was there when Ben Bowen won 'is first chair.
    Did you see Joby Culverhouse fightin' in Scarrot's booth?
    Mabon came to my parents' weddin'.
    Siloh was packed for J.J.
    If you didn't 'ear Todd Jones, you don't know what a tenor is.
    Noah Ablett wore 'imself out for the people.
    There's a Northman opened a chipshop in Wattstown –
    What with the Northmen and the Irish, the Rhondda Valley –
    Who sent the police to Tonypandy?
    Before the English give in –
    Will John and Will Mainwaring are in clink –
    Mrs Clement is best at tellin' your fortune.
    I never saw anyone punch like Jimmy Wilde.
Can you feel a difference in the atmosphere?
Can you see the wheel turning?
Can you see the pattern changing?

Who's this coming down from Ynys-hir,
His blood up and blue with pneumoconiosis,
His banner aloft and his Bible under his arm,
And the Judgement and Armageddon and the Fire and Brimstone
      in his eyes?
    O Sweet Jesus, send the Holy Spirit to Ainon!
(Englishman, mind you. Fundamentalist. Military. Myth.)

Who's this, pale as the dawn
And lovely as the moon,
Tainted like one of the Dark Sisters,
Standing in a shop doorway in Cardiff?
     They say it's all *'is* fault.
     You can't afford to dress like that when you're on the dole.

What's the trumpet I hear sounding
From Blaen-cwm to Blaenllechau?
And who beats the drum for the jazz in Blaenclydach?
And who's the Carmen dancing with a red rose in her mouth?
     Her mother sang with Evan Roberts in the Revival.
     Her father died under a fall in the Cwtsh.

Our Welshness is not an ornament but a struggle.
It's no laughing matter, we carry a yoke on our shoulders.
(It's heavy. The struggle is not an armed struggle.)
The soup-kitchen aggravated our poverty,
Our dignity was purchased with the pittance of the dole.
We were uprooted by the hundred and transplanted all over the world –
Useless old weeds that grow on any dump under the sun!

     Our Morgan 'ave got 'is B.A.
     There's nice to see 'em gettin' on in the world.
     Our Megan 'ave got an 'eadship in Stoke.
     Always good with the kids in Saron, she was.
     Our Percy's now a curate in Stepney.
     'E'll suit the *crachach* to a t.
     Our Dyfrig's a male-nurse in Uttoxeter.
     Tommy Farr will be as good as Tom Thomas.
     If Jimmy Murphy gets a start with West Brom –
Who will be left on these mountains
To rust with the gear and the rails and the wheels,
And grow old with the Chapel and the Cymmrodorion and the Language
Like old hens scratching in the rubble of the years?

     I've got a new *englyn.*
     Now take it easy.
     Just let me have a sit down –
     Lean on my arm!
     I'll be all right –
     A new *englyn* to –
     If I can only sit down –
     There we are.

Death is a merciless sculptor – it cuts to the bone.
Passion. Muse. Soul. Where are they
Behind the big eyes filling that small yellow head?
He died. With only the *englyn* on his mind
And Welsh on his lips,
And the invincible dust bringing down his frail flesh.

> Must go to the service, just in case –
> But the doctor said –
> Sarah James and Annie Davies will be there.
> Rest is the only –
> *They* are still faithful –
> If you don't rest –

The faithful were there. He preached his sermon. His last.
He fell in the big seat. Robert Griffiths had delivered his message.
The funeral proceeded up the Valley. The main road was hushed.
> Children weeping.

Everyone knew this was a death the community could not afford.

> An open-air meeting in Trebanog!
> Are you in pain, butty?
> If only we had 'Ome Riwl –
> What about a drink?
> There's more Welsh spoken in Trebanog –
> Trebanog!
> There are *budgies* in Trebanog who speak Welsh!

One day more. Nobody could deceive him. Neither friend nor Death.
Teasing. Laughing. Arguing. Dreaming.
Till the Darkness embraced him…
Dear God! We put the pioneer of politics and poetry in the Valley's
> earth!

Can you see now where pit and lamp-room and siding once were,
And the prayers and hymns and blasphemies and curses at the coalface,
And the Hippodrome and the Gaiety and the Empire and the Tivoli,
And the strong man from Neath showing off his muscles for money?

Can you see where the black man from Merthyr swallowed fire and
> knives,
And the Nazareth Band of Hope put on *The Pirates of Penzance*,
And the Maiden from the East was sawn in half,
And the Pendyrus Choir sang the great anthem?

Can you see now the sarsaparilla machine on Giovanni's counter,
And *Das Kapital* discussed over tiffin and at the Prayer Meeting,
And the Grand Concert and jumble-sale and fair,
And the Morning Service and the Singing School?

Here, the wild pigeon and the pheasant make their nests once more,
And the revived trout return to the waters,
And there are new lovers in the heather up on Moel Cadwgan,
And the apples are ripe in the orchard of Pen-twyn.

Listen.
The rejoicing of waters fills my ears this evening.
Ynys-wen, Ynys-feio, Ynys-hir,
All the way to Eglwys Ilan,
And the small spring on Pen Rhys
As lovely as a jewel on the breast,
Still praising Mary.
The mountain streams are alive!

      Stranger in these parts?
      Yes.

He was sitting on a bench at the foot of Moel Cadwgan.
Cap. Stick. Cigarette.
I seemed to remember his face, or what was left of it.
      My daughter's children go to the Welsh School.
      A young man straight from college 'ave come to Nebo.
He made as if to go, challenging the Valley's woes,
His stick as firm as his faith.

[MS]

Dyfnallt Morgan

Dyfnallt Morgan (1917-94) was brought up near Merthyr Tydfil in Glamorgan, and became a popular and civilised radio broadcaster and producer. After his period at the BBC he became lecturer in the Extra-mural Deparment at the University of Wales Bangor. He published a number of volumes of literary criticism, was a prolific translator of plays and words set to music, and won the National Eisteddfod Crown for a verse play. He failed to win the Crown for his long poem in dialect which is anthologised here, although it was the poem favoured by one of the adjudicators, Saunders Lewis.

The Curtain

Aye, 'e was buried the day before last,
In the cemet'ry at Twynrotyn!
It's sure to be twenty-five years
Since we buried 'er:
I couldn't make out the 'eadstone
'Cos the earth
Was all piled up over it.
Did I go? Well, aye, mun,
Cos I 'appened to be down there stayin' with friends
From Friday night till today;
You know 'ow I do like
Goin' back to the old place now an' again!

This time,
I'd thought of going down to Cardiff
Saturday mornin', in time for the match in the afternoon,
But I 'eard about the funeral...
Aye, aye, just before twelve, see –
'Cos the gravediggers are all in the Union now
And won't do nothin' of a Saturday afternoon.

I just 'ad to go
To the old fella's funeral.
'E was very good to me years ago
When I went to work with him as a boy at the coalface
'An I used to talk with 'im a lot...
Was there many there?
What you mean, mun –
It's all private these days!
At 'leven o'clock there was nobody
By the cemet'ry gate, 'cept a 'earse,
Two cars an' me.
No, the children didn't 'ave a clue who I was,
Total stranger: but there,
They didn't know the minister either:
There 'aven't been a minister at 'is chapel
For years now,
And they 'ad to coax this 'un, see.

Dêr, 'ad a job to understand 'im, I did,
Sort of deep Welsh and all in 'is throat!

(I 'eard 'em sayin'
'Is 'eart's still up in north Wales,
But 'e do think 'e'll get some useful stuff
Down there in the south, like;
'E got a 'obby writin'
For the Welsh programmes on the wireless.)
I got a good grip on what 'e said, though,
When 'e prayed at the graveside: 'e
Gave thanks for religious 'omes in what 'e called a ''eathen age',
That's the words 'e used, I think, though I don' know what they mean).

I 'ad my eye on the children,
An' I was thinkin'!
There was Gladys and Susie,
An' their 'usbands they met in the A.T.S. –
An' they've 'ad jobs on the Tradin' Estate now;
An' Isaac an' 'is wife –
She's an Irish girl an' 'e've turned Cath'lic like 'er –
An' not one of 'em understands a word of Welsh.
But all credit to 'em for givin' 'im a Welsh funeral,
An' they kept the old boy tidy right to the end, too.
(It was 'is 'eart conked out sudden, like.)
Oh aye, did their duty all right, they did; after all,
'E was only their grandfather, and another thing,
'E wasn't really part of their world.
You an' me know all about that,
'Cos our children don' talk the old language, do they?

But boy!
I couldn't 'elp thinkin', too,
The old fella's no further off now
(From them!)
Than 'e was 'fore 'e passed away:
In fact, p'raps 'e's a bit closer,
'Cos Gladys and Susie are reg'lars with the Spooks, once a week,
An' 'avin' some funny experiences, so I 'ear.

Dêr, things 'ave changed!
I was up in the old chapel last night;
When 'e buried 'is wife
The whole fam'ly was there Sunday night
'Eads bowed and not gettin' up to sing –
Nobody in 'is pew last night!

An' the deacon that took the second service was blubbin' out loud
(But that's 'ow 'eve always been
– Since the Revival, anyway.
I 'ad a job not to laugh
When I remembered the fun us kids used to make of 'im),
An' 'im sayin' 'e didn't like to see a fam'ly dyin' out.
Aye, I says to myself, we do run down
The Paddies 'cos of their religion – but
Their fam'lies don' die out!

They 'ad some preacher from the country last night,
'E 'ad a bit of the old oil, too,
'Cept 'alf the chapel couldn't understand 'im
An' I dare say
They'd do better if they went over to English,
'Cos that's been the language of the Sunday School for years now.
But they're donkeys, see.
Oh, I know 'em alright! I remember Jones
Packin' it in twenty years ago.
'More money and eggs in the country,' the chapel said.
Aye, and more sense, too!
There's nothin' even a saint can do with a big seat full of donkeys.

But there it is!
It's me doin' the kickin' now. That's 'ow I do feel
After bein' there, see.
That's 'ow you'd feel, too in my place.
It was enough to make me sick seein' Dai Lump Coal at the pipe organ
Shigglin' 'is shoulders like 'e 'ad a sieve in 'is 'ands
An' pretendin' to play with 'is feet
As 'e tried to make a Volunt'ry out of a tune for the kiddies –
An' I knew 'e 'ad the Bass Coupler out all the time.
Poor dab!
'E don' fool nobody 'cept 'imself –
An' anyway.
Who else can they get for ten quid a year?

But it was singin' Moab that put the kaibosh on it for me –
In mem'ry of the old boy, see.
Dêr, better to let it alone, mun.
I remember the time
When 'earin' the gall'ry sing the third verse
Made you think
You was in 'eaven already, mun...

There wasn't a livin' soul
In the gall'ry last night,
An' the screechin' downstairs was like the noise
Them wogs made in Egypt!
Talk about the zeal of singin'! It's worse without it believe you me!

But this is what I was goin' to say –
It's a wonder
They've kept the cause goin' at all;
After losin' so many members
The collections went right down
An' the money they 'ad from sellin' the Manse didn't come to much,
either.
I tell you what saved 'em –
The War!
All the men, and quite a few of the women, 'ad work
In that new fact'ry:
And a lot came back who 'ad kept away 'cos they was so shabby!
Shabby, indeed! It wasn't them who was shabby –
It was the lah-di-dahs who left like rats from a sinking ship!
Don't give me that, we don't want them back.
The likes of you an' me
'Ad to come up 'ere to England to look for work,
It was quite another thing
Movin' to a more sedate chapel in the same town.

The old stalwarts are just as sedate these days;
There's not many of 'em, but
They got money in their pocket and ev'ry one 'ave got Sunday clothes.
An' I'll tell you somethin' else –
They're goin' to 'ave a minister, no I don' know
'Is name, but 'e 'aven't got a degree,
They 'ad enough of those students
Durin' the war, an' the p'lice turnin' up to listen to 'em, an' now
The deacons think
It's be better to 'ave someone they can 'andle; matter of fact,
I agrees with 'em!
Don't you think some of these youngsters are apt to go all 'aywire?
That's 'ow the old donkeys see it,
(They're cute enough when it comes to the point)
An' all they want now
Is someone man enough to keep up the old traditions
'In a 'eathen age' – as milord puts it;

Ev'ry Sunday, anyway,
Even if 'e don't 'ave anyone
Comin' to meetins during the week. No use expectin' too much.

They're lucky
'E's not married, 'cos they 'aven't got a 'ouse for 'im;
An' they do tell me
It'll be 'ard enough to find 'im lodgins, too.
Anyway,
'E'll 'ave no bother with the ladies,
'Cos all the young women in the chapel are married.
But 'e won' be able to lodge with them
'Cos they nearly all lives with their parents –
Bar one or two who've married key workers.
But I did 'ear,
'Fore I left,
One of them lah-di-dahs I told you about 'ave got rooms to let.
They're comin' in
'Andy after all, that sort.

Well, best of luck to 'em.
I'd like to 'ave stayed for the Singing Festival tonight
(Mornin' an' afternoon, did you say? No, not for years now!
An' their conductor this year's only Tommy Sol-fa, a local boy,
An' 'e's on his last legs, mun!)
But I could never start work tomorrow
After travellin' all night.
P'raps I'll go down to the Induction Services in August:
They still 'ave somethin', see, these English 'aven't got!
I wouldn't bother up 'ere
Unless I 'ad to,
To show an example to the children sometimes,
An' the curate takes such an int'rest in 'em at the Youth Club.
But this year there was somethin' diff'rent down there, too.
I seen it 'appenin' for years now,
But this time it clicked in my 'ead, like...
You know
'Ow the curtains in the 'Ippodrome close...so slow, like...
At the end of the performance?
Well, it's like that down there!
I sees less of the old scen'ry ev'ry time...
An' I gets the feelin'
I'm bein' squeezed out with the crowd.

An' now the last old stager 'ave gone;
I'd 'ave liked to see 'im 'fore 'e went,
'Cos 'e knew a lot about days gone by, see.
('E missed the meetins of the Cymreigyddion somethin' awful
When they came to an end.)
'E told me all about life in the country
When 'e was a lad – 'fore 'e came to the works.
'E used to go back there for a week
Ev'ry summer, year after year –
Till the old fam'ly sold up an' went to live in London...

Aye, buried the day before last 'e was,
But some'ow I can't 'elp feelin'
'E was dead...months ago.

By the way, mun, I saw in the paper today
Things are lookin' up in Russia!
'Bout time, too!
There's no sense in one 'alf of the world not knowin'
'Ow the other 'alf lives.

Aye,well! Back to the grind tomorrow...

Hoy, we'll meet at the match on Saturday...
...If we're still alive.

[MS]

J Eirian Davies

J Eirian Davies (1918-98) was born in Carmarthenshire, and spent his life as a
Presbyterian minister – albeit a somewhat colourful and unconventional one. His
son, Siôn Eirian, is also a poet, dramatist and scriptwriter, and is represented in
this anthology in his own right, and is the translator of his father's poems here.

Bafflement

My Bethel is a house of God between slagheap and factory
Where the language's vein with every knock grows weaker;
Our religion and old traditions are now perfunctory;
Soon new moulds will replace them with something sleeker.

In my blood I feel the butting ram of past generations
As I heave against the tide on behalf of my flock
To resist this metamorphosis into childish configurations
In some quaint picture book depiction of our ancient stock.
And yet it's at me that the parents direct the torrent
Of blows from their whips, twisted with spites and snubs;
Parents who have made no mark themselves, except the indent
Of their fat buttocks on the seats of cinemas and pubs.
And I've learnt that life is a bafflement to those who seek
To keep as a nation this society that's starting to crack and to creak.

[SE]

The Black Thorn

This twisted and bitter figure
    A thorn in the side of our field,
Is now leaving its lonely station:
    To its final call it must yield.

The locality hardly notices
    As it's lowered into the earth;
It has only one solitary mourner
    Weeping for all she's worth.

For who would recall, but a mother,
    As the tears come down in showers,
That this old black thorn in its season
    Was a breathtaking whiteness of flowers?

[SE]

Hard Song

This is the first time I've seen a song
That's become hard.

A daybreak song that should vibrate the dawn
And dewdrop the arid ground
In years to come
– Is now here, hard underfoot.

It's fallen from somewhere.

Not from the sky
A spiralling scansion of assonance
Nor a warbling trill
From an open beak.

It's dropped,
A scrawny heap
From a roof to a hard floor.

Without a sound
The downy feathers fluttered
As if touched by the breath of a breeze.

No spurting spring of blood
No splitting of flesh
No fracturing of bone.

I daresay the death was no more than a gentle subduing.

Some blame lies with the popular sun
Which kissed these remains for many days
With its fierce lips
Until the smudge was sucked dry.

And then, those feet had to walk –
Women, men, children –
That did not select their path,
Flattening with sole and heel.

The cars swept by
Like rich old ladies,
Their bloated tyres
Steamrollering over a life already extinguished.

I'd never seen this before –
A song that's become hard.

Stubs of small wings
A dried gnarl of skin like the rind of a farm cheese,
A tiny arrow-point of a beak
Which should be piping notes in months to come
– Here now underfoot
Shrivelled hard.

A nocturne's nightingale to light tomorrow's darkness?

One of Rhiannon's birds for our charmless future?

A starling to spread word of our emancipation?

Whatever, it now matters not.

Underfoot it lies,
A song that's made hard
By a fall.

[SE]

Emyr Humphreys

Emyr Humphreys (*b.* 1919) was born at Prestatyn, Flintshire, and read history at Aberystwyth. He has been a schoolteacher, a BBC drama producer, and a university lecturer in Drama before becoming a full-time writer. He is first and foremost a novelist who writes about Wales in English from a native viewpoint. Apart from over 20 novels, he has written short stories and volumes of poetry in English, and is also a prolific television dramatist in Welsh. Despite using English as his main medium, he has written poems in Welsh.

On the Guincho

In a restaurant at the sea's edge
I saw muscular lobsters eating people
They praised the bleached linen tablecloths
Admiring the sea, blue in the sun,
The mincing metre of the baby waves.

They praised, too the red meat, the white meat,
Said how convenient it was to keep them, live, in cages
Between the rocks and the tide
Until ready to be boiled and pulled to pieces.

The wine of long friendship lent the gathering flavour
A source of puzzlement, of wonderment,
'What if we were this dish upon its bed of leaves,
What if these humans were quadrilling all around us
In evening clothes, to their cacophonous instruments?

192

Thank God we have investments in the sand
Property lent out at highest interest, unconditional
Rights to the produce of labour from the world's gold beaches.

We, inheritors of the culture of the ages
Let us savour the choicest portions of these powerless dishes
In this endless feast between the sun and wine.'

[EaH]

Poughkeepsie

A keepsake to treasure?
His great-great-grandfather came from Wales –
Everyone comes from somewhere –
And at some point, before or after the voyage
Wrote his name in an unpractised hand
On the title-page of this Bible.
Bold gougings under Peter Williams'
Respectable, red-lettered name;
His great-great-grandson from Poughkeepsie
Understands that much.

Diffidently, he asked the value
Of one thousand, one hundred and ninety-two pages
He couldn't read
For in America everything has its price
Except for water and constitutional rights
Even a bulky old book
Gathering dust in the apple-loft.

'Its weight in gold,' I told him.
That untroubled creature, his face and belly
Gleaming with plenty and sweet ignorance
And shamed, I remembered then,
How a university principal's wife in faraway Wales
Offered a pile of old Welsh Bibles to an experimental artist
To be charred, hacked to bits and sprayed
With glue and paint…
While I said nothing of value.

The great-great-grandson was readier to take my word
Than I was. What are they worth,
Clogwyn Du'r Arddu, the croak of a raven
The reddening glow of far windows, the gap
Between the stirrup and the dust
And that luminous moment when Williams
And the great-great-grandfather were saved?

Our job is to gather the evidence
The medium is not the message, or this world
Would be dust and ashes by now.
But how to glean proofs when it's the other side
That really makes things happen?
Maybe they could be shared about a bit
Like TV soap commercials?

Viewers of the fifth monarchy
A piece of the meaning of existence, a piece of Wales
Gathers dust like a mystery in far Poughkeepsie.

[EaH]

John Roderick Rees

John Roderick Rees (*b.* 1920) was born in Pen-uwch, Ceredigion, and still lives and farms there today. He is a man of *y filltir sgwâr* (the square mile), deeply rooted in his own community. He graduated at Aberystwyth, and taught for 20 years in Ceredigion, before going back to work on the land, and to look after his foster-mother who was suffering from Alzheimer's disease. In both 1984 and 1985 he won the National Eisteddfod Crown. One of the winning poems, 'Glannau' ('Shores'), is based on his experience of caring for his foster-mother. He is independent-minded, and has the ability to see the merits of opposing viewpoints.

Brenin Gwalia
(Song for a Welsh cob stallion)

Your coat, beer-and-milk, with crowns on velvet,
Sickle of the nape like a bow of lightning
And bone, flat as a board, beneath the knee.

Silken feather above graceful pastern,
Rich symmetry of a noble topline
And both ends restless as flying flags.

Balanced behind and with sloping shoulder,
Arc of the ribs, so full and pleasing,
Trace the blood-lines whence you are sprung.

Light-footed you enter the ring like a lyric,
Stepping-high-as-your-belly, with a noble gait,
Upturned hooves like cups that would catch the rain.

Fire of your forefathers, a rhythmic spur,
Placing you always at the head of the row,
Show after show a leader apart.

Remember, your hooves echoed in a London stadium,
At the International Horse Show, leading the throng
And you richly upheld the glory of your line.

Eighty thousand clapping their enthusiasm
And, by my side, every move at your noble best,
The people's king from the distant hills.

[AUTHOR]

Gareth Alban Davies

Gareth Alban Davies (*b.* 1926) was born in the Rhondda, and spent three years as a 'Bevin boy' in the coalmining industry before going to Oxford to read French and Spanish. In 1975 he was appointed Professor of Spanish at Leeds University, where he remained until his retirement to Llangwyryfon in Ceredigion. Apart from his academic publications, he has written extensively in Welsh, including travel books, criticism and poetry.

The Wild Geese
(to the miners)

Their cry may be heard at eventide.
Under the heavy oppression of their wings
anguish mingles with faith,
and hope turns to wildness
as they challenge the fury of the dark.
I do not know
from where they came,
nor their mysterious, distant destination.

195

But I know their grief:
they bear a burden beyond their means,
recognise journey's end
in journey's pain,
and turn a clumsy softness
into an arrow of obedience and violence.

(Written during the great Miners' Strike.)

[AUTHOR]

The Chilean People
(September 1972)

Starvation was their legacy.
The bountiful acres,
under their bending bodies,
flowed away like the waters of Tantalus
to a horizon of landlords
and drunken capitalism.
Allende offered markets, roads,
and farming methods
that were like fairy magic.
He handed out the lands,
sharing them slice by slice,
like a father sharing the bread
among the gathered family.

And he died. What difference
whether he or his enemies held the gun
that broke into a thousand pieces
the head that held a dream?
And he was buried. Secretly
they bore his coffin to Valparaiso,
and there placed it in a niche,
with only the grieving widow
to give the dead a name.
And as she placed a wreath of flowers
on the coffin, she said:
'We leave you here, Salvador Allende,
you the President of the Republic,
whose family was forbidden
to follow you to this place.'

While in the South
the gathered family mourned,
before taking up again their fragile implements
and under their bending bodies
watched their lands flow
towards a horizon
of utter despair.

[AUTHOR]

Christmas Card to a Friend Who Might Be Dead

Do you remember, I wonder,
that journey on the Southern line,
from Puerto Montt's *bourgeois* aspirations
to power's centre in green Santiago,
where Allende captained his ship of despair?

You got on the train half-way,
when we were tired out
after twenty hours and more
of putting on weight, and chewing the cud.
The snail-like, grubby train
blew its smoky threats
in the snow-white teeth of the volcanoes.
A green land offered
its chest of wealth to all,
to all except its scabby, poverty-stricken serfs.

The train was all puffed up,
and between us
lay a miasma of sweat and words.
In struggling for a place
you came to us quite by chance,
and started reading Cronin's *Citadel*,
and I told you I was a Rhondda boy.

A sentence sparked off talk,
till a fire of enthusiasm burned,
brought once again to life
by jolt or question,

only to be banked up
by the frequent stops
when we would get down
in search of coffee or a piece of cake
in station canteens
on this line to nowhere.

You spoke of a peasantry
receiving this slice of land,
of the need to teach them
how to keep house,
how, after the centuries,
to harvest for their own sakes.
You spoke also of justice,
of oppression by Anaconda, of the deceit and violence.
You were a proud, confident man.

What cowardly instinct in you
directed us afterwards
to the *Hôtel Crillon*,
to rebellion's nursery,
the museum of the *Ancien Régime*,
where rape stood
in the aspidistra's shadow?

Did you already know,
beneath your skin,
that a conflagration
was what awaited you?
Was it some ironic sprite
put you up to it?
Some conviction
that we were the enemies,
made rotten by our liberalism,
and our flighty faith
in the power of the vote,
and in the goodness of man?

[MJ/AUTHOR]

Death in Venice

(Robert Browning in San Barnaba)

The minotaur lived
in the labyrinth of canals,
his bellow louder than the lion of St Mark,
his mystery deeper
than the iridescent waters,
his tenderness like a woman's.

The poet was in his cell.
A bond stretched between him
and distant England,
his eyes uncovered skin by skin
every April he ever saw,
every woman that drew her body's bow
between him and the wall,
every good left undone,
every hate to which he yielded
unwillingly.

And when the minotaur placed
a death mask on the poet's face
like some carnival disguise,
a lively youth sat in the corner,
listening to the weakening heartbeats,
gazing on the sinister struggle
between the man and the beast
with that intense unconcern
that marks the act of creation
in the disorder of centuries.
His name without name
is Pasternak, or Tolstoy,
or Titian whose linen cloth is red
with the blood of the sacrifice.

*(It appears that Boris Pasternak was present when
his father made a mask of Tolstoy's face on his deathbed.)*

[AUTHOR]

Time's Muteness

Not in time's inches or blood's whispering
do I measure time,
but by the tongue's silent bell
and the stillness of a lip's shuttle.
I spell time in mute sentences,
the praise uncomposed,
the rebuke unvoiced,
the death that climbed to the mind's windows
and shattered them on the palate.
And I listen to a town's muteness
after the Welsh that drove its wheel
has failed, and rusted on another generation's axle.
I measure time in dead Welsh.

[JPC]

Incomers

'We didn't appreciate it!'
clipped the woman:
my crime of writing in Welsh.
No use my explanation:
their son who brought the load of firewood
had an inkling of the tongue.

Her mind still walled in:
Welsh not even an extension!
Refugees from a Midlands city, perhaps,
or smallholders
looking for a better place.

Pleasant, hardworking people,
but with high walls about them
to keep Wales out.
By looking over the parapet
they could catch a glimpse of London,
and between them and the city
spread the undifferentiated acres
of an English culture.

Without thinking
I lit a fire underneath the tower,
with one word's heavy hammer-blow
I split open the gate,
daring to show them
that the language was alive.

And bugger it, if I don't carry on
making them feel uncomfortable,
upsetting their assumptions,
poking fun at their narrow mind-set.
But I shall never win their appreciation:
if I'd had that, Wales would be free.

[MJ/AUTHOR]

T Glynne Davies

T Glynne Davies (1926-88) was born in Llanrwst, Denbighshire, and had a chequered career, working for a period in a laboratory, then as a 'Bevin boy' in Gwent, and after a stint in the army, he turned his hand to journalism, and eventually became a radio journalist and producer with the BBC. He was a popular and gifted broadcaster. In 1951 he won the National Eisteddfod Crown for his long poem in *vers libre*, 'Adfeilion' ('Ruins'). He published two novels and a volume of short stories as well as poetry.

The Bailiff

(in hospital)

Someone is shutting out the stars and the buttercups,
Someone killing the toad in the grass,
And the bristled barley is vanishing.

The old man in his cradle dozing
And the gorse fire going out
On the mountain of his mind.

He lingers, a pippin of a lad,
Loitering in the pudding-fields,
Brown eyes watching the lark
Climbing its hurdy-gurdy stairs to the sun.

201

Someone is shutting out the stars, the dung and the chaff,
Scattering the lapwings' nests in the fallow field.

An old man in his antiseptic upper room,
An old man, his pot of years
Boiling dry,
His sixty years shrivelling under their eyes.

Now he's holding the head of the gnat-plagued mare
In the peat-bog like a graveyard,
But some freezing fingers are squeezing
His small red hand,
Ripping soul from body by the bones.

Who is shutting out the stars and the buttercups,
Scattering the ever-and-ever stones of the well-spring,
Crunching the grain in the granary,
Scorching the seed in the ground?

The old man in his upstairs moon
Seen the gorse fire going out
On the mountain of his mind.

What do *they* know of the pippin of a lad
Who lingers loitering in the pudding-fields?

They are lost in their clouds of concrete,
They are poking about the thicket of wires
Under the white hair.

They are squeaking with their stethoscopes
Along the slippery wooden floors
Tending the meadow of his mind
With their rigmarole of pills.

The old man in his upstairs moon
Sees the gorse fire going out
On the mountain of his mind.

[JPC]

Ruins

(extracts)

I

I sat on the steel stile the other day
And watched the pageant, eternally sad:
Hats courteously greeting hats,
Smiles baring teeth on the street,
Sorry old maids searching in the mist
For the holes of their homes
Like black beetles
Forecasting rain;
Young lads gnashing their puny bones
At the mist's barren sinewy lasses,
With me watching.

I watched the day turning grey across the land
And the night shyly making itself at home
In the street's rocky armpit around me,
And I heard the mumble
Of the bones' procession,
Every face wax to its roots,
Every eye still stagnant water.

Night came to hide the heap of stones
We christened home because it remained.

II

The birds are speckled and tame tonight
In my darling's stony room.
Darling!
The birds are speckled and tame
In the skeleton of your house.

Where your eyes would flash a promise
That they'd burn eternally,
The earthworm pushes its long snout
Under the hearth's russet leaves.

My sweetheart's room
Is dark tonight,
And the stones of her dwelling are a jumble.
They're not tidy by now
In your house, Rhiannon:

Through the mouths of the walls every evening
Abominable children come running,
They drive the spears of their harsh cries
Through the night that's rotting around them.

And I in coat and specs
Shiver with cold in the silence.
They point their fingers at me,
All the people:
'There he is! There he is!' they say,
'Have you seen the moth round the neck of the candle?
That's Jo defying the dead.
Hey Jo! How is she, your corpse of a sweetheart?
Has she finally bred new bones?'

And the children laugh from the ragged pavements:
'Poor old Jo, lost his wits,
Second-hand coat and crooked specs.'

And they rush into the belly of the night.

*　*　*

VI

On the twenty-fifth of October
A frail little woman left the hayloft,
Stepping cautiously on the stone stairs.

Old hands curdling,
Old fingers like twigs,
Her little black cap
A knot on her head

The eighty years of her eyes were gazing
At Pen Nant's yearning
Sun as it set,
Enticing the sky behind it
Into the unwinding mountain's
Heather bed.

She'd once been a restless
Whole-hearted little lass,
And the light of the sun would nest
In her hair.

Now there was long white hair
On her scarred forehead
Like a tuft of wool
On the hedgerows' thorns,
Her veins rusting red
In the close graveyard of her tiny bones.

Old, like a reddish-brown wheelbarrow
Rotting near the mountain gate,
The little fragile body
Watching Pen Nant's
Yearning sun as it set,
The old years
Ill at ease.

She grasped the farmyard's wooden rail
And remembered the shy touch of the sun
On the white silk of her breasts,
And the stream binding waves of water
Round the stubborn crests of the banks
Long ago.

Old sweat, old straw,
Angry old eyes in the mist,
The old voices' faint old laughter,
A little old woman in an old farmyard
Scratching the fiery scab
Where the blood gathers into a lake.

On the twenty-fifth of October
The mist of the mountain-top was
A white apron
Round the source of the distant rivers,
And the tremors of the breezes gave
A thrust
To the castles of the transient hours.

[JPC]

Caernarfon, July 2, 1969

Castle to castle –
Is there peace?

Those who came for a song
In Lloyd George's parlour
And for a hooray on the field have gone.

The cheer and the boo have gone,
And the proper hats of all the Prince's aunts,
Everyone who said 'lovely, 'love', and 'thanks'.
The velvet cushions have gone:
Five guineas' worth of memories.

The policemen have gone,
And Scotland Yard's file of suspicious names
And pictures and fingerprints.

The cameras and the microphones have gone,
And the cavalry and the battalion of dragons
And the clamour about American tourists
And the cost of the plainclothesmen's Bed and Breakfast
And all the rush for the special stamps
Gone.

On the quay, the soldier has gone
In a fiery chariot like some chapter from the Old Testament,
And the cry of Llywelyn has gone
And of Owain Glyndŵr and status and 1282.

The sober dignified benches
Have become a hundred thousand planks,
What they were before yesterday and long days before.

Another Prince has started on his journey:

Castle to castle:
Is there peace?

[JPC]

Einion Evans

Einion Evans (*b.* 1926) is a miner's son from Flintshire who worked as a coal-miner himself before becoming a librarian. In 1983 he won the National Eisteddfod Chair for his poem 'Yr Ynys' ('The Island') which is a kind of elegy on the death of his daughter Ennis (the title itself alliterating with her name), a talented fiction writer who died at the age of 29.

Gadafi's Little Daughter

Her eighteen months shattered,
our own leaders to blame,
their lethal playing
stopped dead her game.

Hate figure, her dear father
stoops over his buried flower,
red blossoms deep under sand –
blood falls here in showers.

[MJ]

John FitzGerald

John FitzGerald (*b.* 1927) is an Irishman by family (though born in England), and was taught Welsh by Saunders Lewis at Aberystwyth. He was ordained a Catholic priest and has been practising in Wales since 1956. For a number of years he was a lecturer in Philosophy at the University of Wales Aberystwyth, and has published learned articles in his specialist field. His fairly small output shows a meditative mind and a fertile imagination.

The House Beyond

I was joyful when I was told,
    'Let us go to the house of God.'
And then, on the threshold, we were told:
        'Take off your words and leave them in the porch,
        and come through to hear the resounding silence;
        shut your eyes, shut them tight,
        and come through to see the iridescent darkness;

proffer your empty hands, your withered hearts,
to be filled with what eye has not seen and ear has not heard.'

We entered the house, and then we were told:
'Come share the bread of the pain and the loss,
drink of this bitter cup.
'Eat, for there is still a way to go.
'Drink, so that you have within you a living spring.'

We were promised in the gloom a way to his many dwellings,
and that he was the way, but we did not see him.
And yet, here he was, within us and around us in his own expanse.
'Blessed are they who have not seen and have believed.'
'Blessed are they who have not heard and have listened.'

[JPC]

God in Hiding, God of Faith

I GROPE for your cold trail
though my hands' nostrils are reeling drunk
from the bubbling of the damp green swoon in the memory
that rises like vapour round the world's every motion
and flares like silk with shimmers of a gracious presence,
fainting still at every feat of splendour
that can satisfy the eye for the moment
before slipping away with the stream leaving only the odoriferous moss
to encrust the rocks of the ford.

I LISTEN HARD for the course of your swift-moving light
though I'm blind of hearing
from the pricking ticks of the clock hard at it always
pounding wild gold into memory's honeycombs,
sprinkling the song of the dawn, come summer, aslant
the length and breadth of the trees' hidden waterfalls;
plucking the song of the wood, come autumn, from its sunset flush,
and flaying them overnight, every string, except the deaf pines;
the speech of the river, come winter, will not be stilled.
There's no silencing of the iridescent voices
that glitter scattered beneath your white unity's presence.

BY THE SKIN OF MY FINGERS I am a pendulum
on the rock of your face, without seeing you.
I cling to you with all my might,
a leaf beneath the fickle pressure of the wind
slipping, clutching, slipping.

[JPC]

There Is But One True Friend

Come in, friend, if I may be so bold,
    and make yourself at home.
I'll gladly do so, friend, but I hope
    you won't find me a burden.

I can't say; or take the chance that the house would be
    dreadfully empty without your company.
Remember you'll have me with you, me, who'll yet claim
    your house, your whole self, your gear.

But that's dreadful too! So you'll wish to be brother, parents, sister,
    home and sweetheart, to fill my mind?
    What else? Yes, all of them.

[JPC]

Great Little One

In your bosom
the vast rotation is at rest;
in you
the stars run a steady course; and look, a cradle rocks,
a snug shell to hold your first sleep.

      (I'm tongue-tied, Lord; and my best words
      – scarcely do they touch the hem of truth.)

Tonight,
new-born,
you are older than the oldest light, that came

swiftly through the infinite night of deep space
till men saw, at last, the yesterday of the stars;
you are in the beginning, with the Father.

Tonight,
the word of your power filling every place, every time,
you are silent,
after falling asleep in the hay of your bed
for the first time, and beginning to learn
to know your mother.

(Christmas 1960)

[JPC]

Being (Human)

'Only one person lives
       Within my body.'
'Where is he, and who,
       Within your skin?'
'In my heart, in my head, in my brain,
       In my feet;
In my belly, and last of all,
       In my blood:
               Only one.'
'Are you sure that you exist
On your own?'

[JPC]

James Nicholas

James Nicholas (*b.* 1928) was born in St David's, Pembrokeshire, and graduated
in Mathematics before becoming a comprehensive school teacher in Merioneth
and Pembrokeshire. He was then appointed headmaster of Ysgol y Preseli in
Crymych in his native county. From 1975 he was a schools inspector, but has
now retired to Tal-y-bont near Bangor. He won the National Eisteddfod Chair
in 1969, and was Archdruid of the Gorsedd of Bards in the early 80s. A friend
of Waldo Williams, he has edited a volume of critical essays on his work, and
written a study of him for the *Writers of Wales* series.

The Bush

(to Hazel)

I celebrate a bush that belongs
To the ancient line of sunshine and woods.

In the pure earth she puts forth her roots,
And like one whose hand holds her in place
She is firm, a power rises,
A secret from the soil to enlighten the wood.

I saw fire, – her leaves' green was
Open for its arriving;
The flames rose from the roots, creating
A great stir in the twigs and causing thereafter
Blossoming in the branches, –
Because the green growth was not consumed,
But throve, flourished in the fire;
The powers of life purified the bush
And before the wonder of blossoms,
The blossoms of fire that burgeoned
A brilliant miracle over the bush,
I marvelled, I stood amazed.
The fire freshened the land,
A fire of every growth's vitality
And a fire of vision:
It enlightened the bush, it brightened the world.

I celebrate the bush, her beauty's flame
Entices the wind, and ignites the song,
Sustains strength, enkindles night
And day an ecstatic fire;
I celebrate the bush that bonfires
Her splendour's spring
High to the sky and scatters the breeze
And brings summer's life to the face of the land.
I see her henceforth lighting my world,
And her vision's lofty crest will be
A praise to the Lord forever.

I climb through the fire undying –
Because her fire bestows her growth;
And there I gather her fruit, and her ripeness is full,

So unblemished is the bush's season –
And I will have her harvest to stave off hunger
By storing her wealth in the heart.

[JPC]

Bobi Jones (Robert Maynard Jones)

Bobi Jones (*b.* 1929) was brought up on an English-speaking hearth in Cardiff,
and only began learning Welsh – almost accidentally – at Cardiff High School,
but he graduated in the subject and has had a distinguished academic career
culminating in his appointment as Professor of Welsh at Aberystwyth in 1980.
His published output is prodigious, and his work includes scholarship which
takes in the whole sweep of Welsh literature from the 6th century to the present
day, practical criticism and literary theory, studies in education, linguistics,
theology, novels and short stories, an autobiography, and he is the most prolific
Welsh-language poet of the second half of the 20th century. His epic poem
Hunllef Arthur (Arthur's Nightmare) is one of the longest poems in any language.
Bobi Jones is a nationalist and an evangelical Christian, and yet he is one of the
most controversial and unconventional figures in Welsh literature.

Having Our Tea

There's something religious in the way we sit
At the tea table, a tidy family of three.
You, my love, slicing the bread and butter, and she,
The red-cheeked tot a smear of blackberry jam, and me.
Apart from the marvellous doting
Of a world's interchange with each other…there's tea.
Stupid, they say, to think of the thing as an ordinance,
And yet all the elements are found to change in our hands.
Because we sit and share them with each other
There's a miracle. There's a binding of unmerited graces
By the cheese, and through the apples and the milk
A new creation of life is established, a true presence.
And talking to each other, breaking words over food
Is somehow different from customary chatting.
I know perfectly well that generations must,
Of necessity, have performed this petty action.
And surely their pattern has long since burrowed
As part of our consciousness. Then too, back beyond the epochs
Is depending, turning back to the fountainhead,

And listening on the connecting wires to a Voice
That is at the same time food – He expresses
Himself here from the beginning. All would acknowledge
That the food in itself is a pleasure:
The spirit grows stronger too in its wake.
Still tea is not worship…But it overcomes
Things so the spirit may happily hop
In our hearts. Assimilating heaven's carol
Into our constitutions, we are a choir, our throats
Blending calories and words together in the presence
Of the unseen Conductor who laid the table.

[JPC]

Pregnant Woman

(in bed)

Like a hippopotamus in a river's sultriness you wallow
In a fold of sheets, I a wooden crocodile
Beside you. You meditate behind your flesh-buttresses
Deep in the current's slowness, turning your head above
Cautiously from side to side, and sink once more
Into the full waters. Interesting, to watch all the back's
Efforts when you try to climb from the river, as though the mire
Of the bottom enmeshed your feet, and the water were stocks.
There's a landful of you. You ought to depopulate.

Like mother-earth with your other, set in place
With its swellings for a day of harvest, in broad contemplation
You breed a close society all by yourself: I catch you,
Locked away in island introversion, conversing
Without a mouth, connecting with no one, listening intently at times
To a distant voice in an existence that makes no utterance.
Another world is near by: you know it
For its own sake, the separate one, the besides of the self
In a secret dungeon you carry. And the heaven in the blood of each limb
Is throughout you, your meaning. There is point and purpose in you
That's in growth. To be will be the secret of all your contents –
To be in the flow of time's mud, dear beautiful old hippopotamus.

[JPC]

The South Shore (Aberystwyth)

Bones I can understand. One after another
It's peeled them, turned them white as soapsuds
In the mad muscles of its belly. And even
Stumps of rare driftwood: to gnaw the elasticity
Of their grip, in the teeth of some of these nights,
Would savour of vegetables. I can understand
What moves it to digest those, and then toss
The remains on the beach. But shoes! Dozens of them,
One after another, every form, size and make –
What quality was in them? Was it the sea
Or (horrors!) some apparition of the sea bottom
That wore these leathers, and lorded it there?
Oh what dancing! What a show of feet!
Or was there one wave – as a rule so shy –
In the midst of lobsters, the mob of crabs, and that crew,
A wave which showed the glint of her heels, that kicked
For gladness in the face of deep seaweed?
To think in this way of the great sea
Putting on such teeny shoes, venturing out
In the gloom to prance – it is a portent
Of a gaiety at the bottom of grief: in labyrinths
That flow with blue and so transparent tears,
You'd see shoes awkward, not in pairs, tap the floor.
But what did happen last night? For here, in a bucketful
Of stars, behind the brows of the moon, the water
Shook the shoes off its feet; and then barefoot
Bounced out, wholly sure of itself, striking the beach.
There was much chanting, there was stretching
And much shaking of locks. Among grey stones
Like a squirrel come into a graveyard, full-drunken
(And wasn't it around here that Cantre'r Gwaelod waltzed?)
It was a night of ecstasy, when were flung up
Among the tyres, tin cans and bones – these shoes.

[TC]

The Women at the Pit-head

I find it difficult to not see the women
at the pit-head when I pass a closed pit.
The pit itself is waiting for men
to come up. And the job of these spectres
is waiting and waiting to garner some leavings,
so I cannot look at the mouth of the shaft without
them furnishing the ground around it with their shawls.

They are helpless doubly, helpless
because of not being men, because of failing to go
down with them, and helpless together
with the men in the elemental way they scrape a crust.
Dab hands at washing bodies and dressing them for coffins,
well-versed widows and all of it not for the sake
of some fossilised principles, precious culture,
but to survive in the flesh for the following day.

They are my mothers. There is nothing of me
that hasn't come from this row. Since waiting, waiting,
without anything they could do, was their labour of watching
for the wheel to turn, for the cage to rise, and for
stretchers racing towards the gate to the unavoidable
meeting. A row of women was taught about waiting,
because, out of their own painful pits and their waiting,
was drawn, against or in accordance with their will,
a joy inconvenient, a little rapture costly
to the agonising world price of subjugation. Then,
the after-birth and the after-birth's blood from the depths. Keep
your heroism, you romantics. This row is only
a mechanism for giving birth that will go on waiting
through gap-in-the-bed nights for children who might
sometimes have a bit of schooling to tune a talent
for crying plague on capitalists. Waiting
for the coming some day – from the bottom of their hope's pit –
of a little less despair, that will stumble out
to the light…with ousting in its fists.

[JPC]

The Conversation of the Deaf

When one deaf person meets another,
    the door that shuts
the ear will be, close at hand,
    flung wide.

Hand will listen to hand,
    and these hands are
the thoughts that free them. Through the supple fingers
    the hard-of-hearing play piano.

The bars of the song, for so long iron,
    will be bent,
like branches boys swing on. They're the ping-pong balls
    on jets of water.

Theirs is a dance inheritance,
    an identity that
unites them as their hands waltz together,
    all ears.

Through these strings of flesh
    they pluck a tune.
The bone staves and the spaces between them are chords,
    an ancient language so lively

that's piercing, when one sees through them,
    better than sound.
Their culture's well-stocked by the alternative speech
    of the dullard's hands,

the comely hands that construct a bridge
    between solitudes.
We feel pity, we do, but in their story
    every gesture's a handshake.

In a wind outstretched the prodigal twigs
    caper warmly
on the kiss of their leaves, and they're drawn, a nation, to be tuned
    into knowing each other truly.

And in a trunk they'll become a community by bearing fruit,
    a tongue's petals.
And through boughs that accentuate the earth
    they'll listen to seeing.

[JPC]

Portrait of an Overpopulated Woman

You'll hear her all the time on the street, talking quite sociably
To the wall. That insists, in its unyielding way,
On answering her with silence, if not with sheer astonishment:
Everyone knows her as odd, without anyone knowing her really.

She waves her arms in front of her, mills of handy electricity.
Without anything, no light anywhere, she's a dramatist of the absurd
Enacting her own universe that's so gloriously giddy,
Rushing home to an audience of tableful absence.

I do the same thing myself, but I'm respectably careful
First that no ear is dawdling within my hearing.
But she goes at it like addressing a public meeting.
She's a traveller with her jaw raised to the wind

Who fills every yard of the path with a drove of turkeys
Screeching through her megaphone, denouncing the rain
And telling the world and his wife without mincing words
What she'd do if she were in charge of such filthy weather.

She doesn't need anyone. Ignores all the gossiping
By sensible audiences around her. She has plenty always
Of garrulous company inside her own large head.
And such a head! They whisper (between you and me) that maybe

The skin oddity and her stoop betray the true situation,
And that she was the result of incest. She loiters now within
The complexity of a tribe of one, and guards her feeble fellowship.
I've seen her for twenty autumns spewing her immanent

Concoction, uttering outward syllables to every breath of the Unknown.
But today, amazingly, close by, she restrains herself for now;
Look at her sitting on a bench near a sorrowful old man
For a time, a minute of communication. A tiny syllable or two

Is all I've ever spoken to him. Though I knew a bit
About the grindstone of his experience, I didn't dare
Linger there to sympathise: my reserve was so stubborn
And independence shyness so amply easy for me.

But across my awkward ditherings and bunglings
I see the beautiful peace of two: this madwoman stays
To settle down near him, and he smiles quietly
In her lax company. They're so richly cheerful a duet.

Two of the disabled, one not exactly all there,
Two apparently lonely, but quite conscious of a world
Around them, that speaks of jumbled numbers on a balance sheet
As broken dishes that can't be put completely together.

And I stumble ahead knowing that I have experienced,
For a time, the grandeur that's ocean wide, the woundedness of praise,
And the Hand that's upon the moon. I've seen two of the pretty
Dishes that were placed in the three-piece cupboard of being.

Though her rags are impoverished, though her dignity's dreadfully frail,
Though the dailiness of her spree is blathering to the void,
(Indeed, because blathering to the overflowing void is her spree),
Madness comes marching among us to sober us up.

[JPC]

The Chestnut Tree Deciding to Fly in May

The chestnut tree's fearful. It stirs
nervously, refraining from shouting or shifting
its whisper along the day's metres,
Slowly the white roof
is born without a scream.
The tree, it appears, is sleeping, snoring as well
some naked evenings.

Hear its gossamer closing its eyelids.
The chestnut tree's hard at it pretending to doze
above its heavy engines,
while it mass produces
air for the sky to breathe

and become more air. It's at work
as secretly as snow.

The breath of its fair-and-Guenevere
existence shies from the fleeing and head-over-heels
horizons. The chestnut tree's growth
is a mole in a grave,
though its streams of pearl
anoint the heavens, and the rooms of the highest
boughs, through the roots,

penetrate its cellars, where
the white wine is stored. Therefore this nuclear
chestnut tree's a reeling palace
for silence to open
through its shoots: even in
the firewood's pensive pool it readies
the mushroom explosion of blossoms

without raising an uproar. This is how
it forms its decision in its feather bed, as quietly
as closing...
Here, however, is a district's home
for a flight of crows. And so,
though the inside's yearning, blossoms
wishing to be sky, the peace upon the tree
is complex, since its guests

are a riot. Like people who do not know
how holy it is to touch the hem of the lake-shapely
serenity's garment, the scarecrows
of crows fire
their idiotic guns
on a morningful of branches dreaming their
twenty years into a party.

There where stillness lingered
invisible, and as oppressive as milk, look,
the black noises flit across it
(as if it rained
cats and dogs), to crowify for hours
air with their cloud bubbles, a thunderous
shower of chicks

through the sun's negation, hunting
and rolling in a carnival of hounds'
crowish curses. The tree,
as slowly as
solitude, remains content
to be a silent explosion, saying
nothing, refraining,

as taciturn as its candid
ageing. And of course, our crows grow weary.
Then, from within itself
the tree comes
back with the sound of its light,
regaining confidence and the single-legged resolution
of a church taking

triumphant shape in the midst
of corpses on the field of battle. But it can only,
unlike the crows and their fleshy beaks,
intensify,
as the branches kindle
tiny lights high up on its sacred
crest. The chestnut tree

shows that it too,
because of the negation, can fly, a dazzling brightness,
over them. It runs through existence a while
before spreading its years
of knowledge of the crows above
the murk of their harsh croak, and on it flies
with its chandeliers to floodlight

the refraining. Silently it spreads
its white wings across their desolation,
a demented dome, and onwards
it flies, a full-branched
abundantly greened white
angel, till the light flames in flakes,
illuming its faith to the skies.

The chestnut tree is a guest-house
that shelters us (its sleep a deceit) from a flight of crows,
having drawn into itself the sunshine
that on each branch provides

another party for the squirrels,
but which invests it in its radiance
with every wounded thing.

Having climbed a tower, the blossoms
are so high that they, in gazing back
at the crows below, shoot fire specks
unsaddened and soundless.
(Seeing is light's true guest.) And the blossoms
fly for the whiteness to aim from on high
and spread – against the multitude of noise – a single silence.

[JPC]

Emrys Roberts

Emrys Roberts (*b.* 1929) was born in Liverpool but brought up in Penrhyn-deudraeth, and was trained as a teacher at the Normal College, Bangor. He has taught in schools in Anglesey, Oswestry and Montgomeryshire and now lives in retirement at Llanerfyl. He won the National Eisteddfod Chair twice (1967 and 1971), and served a term as Archdruid of the Gorsedd of Bards. Twelve volumes of his poems have appeared to date, including four for children.

Primo Levi

After a night of boozing and praying,
was black morning to the writer like the approach of a train,
the scream of a plane above mothers washing their children
before taking them with their toys by rail to their deaths?

And was there a ghostly weeping from the novelist who'd lost
        everything?
The weeping of a man stripped naked of pictures of his loved ones,
        his name;
crying in the yard as he crumbled, a black
number on the blank paper of a puppet.

And was despair to the poet like the march
of exhausted men, stumbling to drum and bugle's beat?
Creeping to the demonic music of the Germans with their cymbals
and the contempt that whipped bones out to their work from the
        swamp of the camp.

And was returning dumb to fresh groans and screams
from the furnaces and the gas, and to an agonised longing for sleep,
a brief respite from torment and hunger;
only to slip back into hell's cold mist before a wet awakening?

Wasn't bleeding on ice after battling to seize the sun
to the wordsmith a winter, and long?
The snowdrift's harsh colour was a clump of shapeless shivers,
and a *danse macabre* the writer's approach for soup.

Wasn't bearing the same cross to a Jew through the ages with his
             offspring
a steady knell to his extinction as a man?
The craving of a wretch to strangle the candle of his reason
before erasing an entire race from memory?

The surge of spring through stripped bones held him together –
a glimpse of new growth from afar, a tune from a bush
maintained him in his right mind;
the sunlight on a shrub's white lace as it opened itself in colour
like the gates of Auschwitz at last.

[RP]

Dafydd Rowlands

Dafydd Rowlands (1931-2001) was a native of Pontardawe in the Swansea Valley, and was a minister with the Independents before becoming a teacher, and later a lecturer in Welsh at Trinity College, Carmarthen, and thereafter a freelance scriptwriter and television producer. He was twice winner of the National Eisteddfod Crown, and also won the Prose Medal for a volume of essays entitled *Ysgrifau yr Hanner Bardd* ('Essays of the Semi-poet'). He described his only novel as both a novel and a poem.

The Little Boots

    Tell us the story about the little boots...

The Llandeilo boots, because that is probably where
they were made
a long time ago.
Two small black boots gathering dust for your mother.

Uncle John's boots, Mam's brother…

Mam is old
and the boots are very small…

John died when he was a baby,
he died when he was two years old.

It's odd that a man in his forties
calls a two-year-old child
Uncle John…

Uncle John was Mam's brother,
he died when he was two years old.

It was John who wore the Llandeilo boots
when helping his father in the garden;
and my grandfather was a big man –
he worked in the steelworks
and played rugby in the scrum.

John worked with his father in the garden.

He died suddenly,
leaving his footprints
in the garden's soil.

Uncle John was two years old when he died in the soil.

After burying Uncle John,
my grandfather would work in the garden;
there was one small square patch
he could not bring himself to dig.
And my grandfather was a big man –
he worked in the steelworks,
and played rugby in the scrum.
But there was one small square patch
he could not bring himself to dig.

John died when he was two years old,
leaving his footprints
in the garden's soil.

And these are the black boots that were pressed into the soil –
the Llandeilo boots,
because that is probably where they were made
a long time ago.

[MS]

Schutzstaffeln 45326

*Today, in the language of figures, the number 45326 must from now
on be accepted as the ultimate in the definition of cold horror and evil.
For that was the SS number bestowed upon Adolf Eichmann...the smaller
children usually cried, but when their mothers comforted them, they
became calm and entered the gas chambers carrying their toys...*
        – COMER CLARK, The Savage Truth

Let the number be learnt like a verse from Scripture:
        not out of revenge
        and the anger that arises from the vomit
        in the memory;
let the cold number be learnt
        so that we see in Buchenwald
        the living skeletons
        that were conceived in a man's mind.

Let the number be learnt in pleasant summer
        when children catch the sun
        on their flesh by the seaside;
let the number be learnt,
        so that we see in Auschwitz
        the toys destroyed in the gas chambers.

Let the number be taught in autumn
        when the scent of leaves decaying
        reminds us of rides in the twilight of the woods;
let the number be learnt,
        so that we see in Belsen
        the layers of corpses rotting in the mud.

Let the number be learnt in white winter,
        in the clean laughter of the snow
        between the bare branches;

let the number be learnt,
>so that we see the small bones in Dachau
>raw in the breeze.

Let the number be learnt in the joy of Spring
>when the faultless gambolling of the lambs
>animates the green fields;
let the number be learnt,
>so that we see the finger-prints
>of the beast that is within us.

Let the number be learnt like a verse from Scripture:
>four, five, three, two, six;
>and in the salty repentance of its ugly saying
>let us see
>the toys destroyed in the gas chambers.

[MS]

The Village

*'I was born in Pontardawe in the Swansea Valley...It was this village
made the deepest impression on us as children and young people.'*
— GWENALLT

And on me.
But the place has changed.
You wouldn't know the place now.
No hooters, no furnaces, no smoke;
poison from the chemical works killing the primroses;
the Tarenni Gleision tips a pyramid of pine trees;
a super-market where the steelworks was –
and no one remembers, as they fill their trolleys between the shelves,
that it was here your father was burnt to a cinder.
The old sad things have been forgotten.

Yes, the place has been spruced up.
No one spews his 'dirty red' guts up into a bucket any more –
except perhaps for some old man from a byegone age,
the shadow of a worker that no one notices,
a doddering apparition, short of wind,
the pale glow of a guttering candle under his skin.

But his sort are fast dying out,
just like 'Utopia on the summit of Gellionnen'.
No one drowns cats and dogs in the canal;
people feed their Rottweilers well,
every bit as well as the pampered creatures up at the Big House;
and the unemployed who live in council houses
seem just as well-off as the old ironmasters,
if a satellite saucer is a sign of wealth.

And the old Public Hall.
It was there you heard Adelina sing;
Ellis yr Ysgwrn won his chair there
two years before he was killed.
And it was there I saw Tommy Davies of Cwm-gors
floored by a black man
in a square ring full of blood and sweat and Vaseline.
The place looks hellish rundown now;
perhaps they'll demolish it soon,
and plant a tidy grove where visitors can sit
among flowers in the sun.
Just as well, seeing how few today
know who Patti and Hedd Wyn were.
(Or Tommy Davies if it comes to that.)
Anyway, we now have a Leisure Centre
and it's packed out whenever George Melly performs there.

You know, of course, about the Leisure Centre;
there, on its outside wall,
on a grey-blue slate set in a fountain
is your name –
poet 'of this mechanised and industrial life'.
Don't worry about the Coke cans and the empty condom packets
that float silently like leaves of the water-lily
on the calm surface of the immortals' pool;
it's no insult to you and your kind
that kids piss into the water.
As they say round here – 'Boys will be boys!'
And as I've said, the place has changed.
The old village has been spruced up.
The smoke has gone and the air is clean.
The place has been improved, so they say.

[MS]

Cricket

Today at Lord's the second test began
between England and Pakistan,
and the magic names sweeten the summer once again:
Salim Malik and Mushtaq, Javed and Wasim Akram,
names that drip from the tongue like honey.

Cricket.
Was there ever a game so romantic and civilised?
Those long ago Saturdays will never be forgotten
that we spent with bat and ball,
slow and leisurely,
till the sun went down beyond the horizon
on the summit of Gellionnen.

And in the year One Thousand Nine Hundred and Forty-six
we went to London on holiday with Mam.
Mam was civilised:
she took her son to Lord's to see the test match
between England and India.
A double century for Joe Hardstaff,
wickets galore for a young Bedser,
and the magic names that dripped from the tongue
like honey:
Amarnath and Mushtaq, Mankad and Merchant.

I kept the score-card for many years thereafter,
but it was lost somewhere between the sunsets
beyond the horizon
on the summit of Gellionnen.

And we lost Mam, too,
she who had sat in the sun all day,
watching a game she didn't understand,
because her son's happiness was important to her.

[MS]

Archipelago

(to Euros on his 21st birthday)

It is not a fissure.
A gap, more likely; or gaps
between the scattered parts.
And the scattered parts are legion;
I know that from experience,
for I am one who is just so.

Difficult to understand the self.
It is not a continent where the land is all of a piece;
more like an archipelago –
a group of islands where the land seems to be unconnected.
But there is a connection:
the sea, that ebbs and flows
between the islands' beaches and rocks
in the sun and under the moon,
in a whirlwind and in the hidden currents.

To know the sea is to make the self whole.
And to swim gloriously in it from one island to the next.
Not only life is a journey;
the self, too, is a voyage.
Knowing that is important;
as important as learning to swim
between the islands of your mind.
It is swimming that keeps you from drowning.
Swimming, and knowing the sea.

[MS]

Sawing His Wife in Half

That's what he did, on a stage and in public;
and not only sawed her in half.
He separated the parts, burnt them,
pummelled them.
I saw him with my own eyes;
I was there, I saw it all.

228

And then, because he loved his wife, I suppose,
he put her back together again.
She leapt nimbly out of the box,
smiling at everyone. And they all clapped
their hands. So did I.

Was the woman split in two?
Of course she was split in two.
Is not every one of us split
when we lose ourselves in the difference
between what is and what appears
to be?

The sawing, the splitting, and the separating
is quite common in life;
it happens time and time again.
Things are not as they seem.

[MS]

Bryan Martin Davies

Bryan Martin Davies (*b.* 1933), originally from Brynaman in Carmarthenshire, graduated in Welsh at Aberystwyth, and taught at a sixth-form college in north-east Wales until his retirement in 1985. He won the National Eisteddfod Crown twice in succession, and has published a number of volumes of poems, as well as prose works and translations from English.

Blue

When Saturdays were blue,
and the sea at Swansea lolled, laughing, on the beach,
boats and castles and the floral clock
filled our day;
and with luck
off we'd go in the red-pencil train
marking its half moon of track
around the blue rim of the bay
to Mumbles Point.

We sat on the warm sand
drinking the blueness
our hungering eyes gazing with desire
at the sea's table
we followed the gulls' restless white darts
as they played target practice with rocks,
stared in wonder
at yellow banana boats from the West
skating slowly over the blue glass,
then berthing under the tall cranes
that scraped a clear sky
above Glandore.

These were our Saturdays of wonder,
the blue days of youth,
when we were one-day, burning fugitives
and on our tongue, our shortlived freedom
from the black valley,
the totalitarian coal.

[EaH]

Widow

Twenty years have fled before your bitterness
like clouds in March sliding over Penllerfedwen's peak,
the cruel, black clouds of winter.
Twenty years
since your flesh sang in your white bed.

In the picture,
you're sitting by the fire in the back kitchen
in a grey woollen dress, a black and white bibbed apron,
your face a web of worry,
your hands busy with the duster and candlestick in your lap.
You worked hard
with the scouring, the brushing, the dusting and tidying,
throwing your energy into it all,
the energy that, in the evening,
pooled in your reservoir of loneliness,
whipped into waves of longing
by your storm of wanting.

Springs were the worst;
spring, when you felt the warm breeze from Gower
walking beside you like a lover in the park,
saw young couples arm in arm on Hewl y Cwm,
woke from an odd dream of children, warm as wool
to the cry of lambs on Rhosfa slopes.
Spring, with its Easter Sunday,
the funeral scent of the dearest lilies
whittling the nib of your longing, which wrote once more
the tragic story on your heart's page.
Spring, when in April rain fell,
rain from the Black Mountain,
the symbolic rain that wet your lips twenty years ago
on death's acre at the top of Hewl Cwar.
Yes, the springs were the worst.

Today,
in the picture,
you're one of the valley's 'brave, silent women',
they still send you cheap coal,
a few pennies of blood-money each week
to warm and coddle you through winter
till springtime should come again.

[EaH]

Snow in Wrexham

Yesterday,
snow lay thick on our town,
acres of snow, shivering
on the roofs and chimneys of houses,
waterfalls of snow
freezing
on walls and shop windows,
streams of snow
flowing
over glass and concrete and stone.
Yesterday,
snow lay thick over the town.

Like the mother tongue from the uplands,
it came to us on a day trip,
not syllable by powdery syllable on a sunny Saturday,
nor a snowflake of a saying on market day,
it came instead
as a bright shoal of silvery words,
a shiny weight of pure syntax.

It came,
and subtly conquered
for one day, anyway,
the town's bruised and mangled pidgin.

Yesterday,
snow lay thick on the town,
like a shiver of Welshness
from the hard uplands,
like a stream of whiteness from Bwlchgwyn and Gwynfryn
until, today, the thaw
exiled it to its lair in the hills,
where it squats, stubbornly,
above the sad town.

[EaH]

Berne

(Switzerland's legislative capital: from the sequence 'Yn y Swistir' – 'In Switzerland')

'Look at the bears;
we keep them here
because the bear is symbol of our city,
look at their cute tricks,'
said the proud, patriotic *frau*
in Berne.

In the treelined park at the city's edge,
obediently, we watched the bears.

Canny old senator-like creatures,
self-satisfied, luxuriant, in their coats of fur,
living well on children's treats.

They lie down, they get up, they shamble around,
then suddenly, they snatch

232

the bread and meat
the fruit and nuts
into their greedy mouths.
And having eaten, they sleep,
dreaming shivery nightmares
of the crags' cold dangers,
the white hunger of the forests
in their far homeland.
Then they wake, sighing their relief,
to give thanks for safety and comfort,
by dancing enthusiastically before the crowd,
smiling at that woman, winking at this man,
rolling here, stretching out over there,
these hairy senators of Berne,
masters of the canny politics of compromise.

[EaH]

Consideration

(on a February night, 1986)

When, in these gardens, in February
night slides suddenly
spreading its darkness over the grove of trees
sweetening the Dyke soil;
then, my stirring doubts
beat about my mind with their dark wings,
trying to trick me to unbelief
in the blessed Welshness
which has, until this night
claimed its small place in the sun
in the empire of my longing.

**

Where, truly, in this neighbourhood
is the language hidden?

**

She is, it seems, wrapped up
in papers;
documents;

wills;
intentions;
the withered roses of the past,
yesterday's sepia petals
lying in the lower drawers
of a handful of valuable pieces of oaken furniture
in Rhosymedre, Acre-fair, Cefnbychan,
Pentrebychan, Pen-y-cae and Rhos,
their petals tightly folded
against the rapine shining
in the greedy eyes of today's grandchildren and great-grandchildren.

She is also, I should think,
sunk in beds,
in the wet slops of memories
of rosy little old ladies
in the area's old people's homes,
those who faff about their penny pensions
to nervous nurses, in an alien tongue,
in Rhosymedre, Acre-fair, Cefnbychan,
Pentrebychan, Pen-y-cae and Rhos.

This, perhaps, is where the language is hidden
in this neighbourhood
for this,
I am afraid,
on a narcotic February night
is what Wrexham says to the Welsh language:
scram.

[EaH]

Dic Jones

Dic Jones (*b.* 1934) became proficient at writing *cynghanedd* at an early age, mainly under the influence of Alun Cilie and the country poets of lower Ceredigion, and won the Chair at the Urdd National Eisteddfod five times in succession. In 1966 he won the National Eisteddfod Chair for his ode 'Y Cynhaeaf' ('Harvest'), a poem reflecting his own meditation on nature as a farmer in Blaenannerch, Ceredigion. Dic Jones himself seems the most natural of poets and his work performs the social function of praising, satirising and elegising, as well as meditating on universal themes. In his own rendition of extracts from the poems 'Harvest' and 'Spring' below, he has tried to mirror the metres of the original, including elements of *cynghanedd*.

234

Reaping

Yellow ears' rustle of praise
Weaves through the valley meadows;
Grain dances in summer haze;
They bow to the wind's power
From ridge to ridge, the patterns
Of rust and gold interlaced.

To Cae'r Nant's gold-grained furrows
At morning with his machine
A brisk man comes, the dale's heir,
On his cheek the sun's imprint,
Through violets and clover
Seeks a prize for April's sweat.

He hems the yellow waves,
His pomp makes the field tremble;
Shredding peace, his contraption,
Spark-spitting ugliness there:
Spears of oats where it attacks
Cannot withstand its challenge.
Where yellow flourished, a swath
Of stubble attests its passing.
A lofty pile in the lane,
Flood-tide of swollen sackfuls.

Once horns would invite our strong
Elders to the same battle,
Early scything's fearless men,
Forefathers of his fathers,
Old fellowship, unselfish,
Cheerful reaping's peerless troop.
Oppression had made it strong,
Hardship had made it wealthy.

Mother and children turned out,
And sweetheart, to the cornfield,
In autumn perseverance,
To tie its top-heavy gold,
And an unmatched battalion
Of craft-bound ricks clothed a ridge.

They have not, today's farmers,
One-third of the old crew's craft;
His field will hold tomorrow
Of its long gold drooping ears
Merely the battle's stubble,
And a lustreless clipped mane.

[JPC]

Lamentation

I know this chapter of misery – must bring
    The two of us some mercy
  Soon, but evermore for me
  A valley of grief's Glangwili.

Grief we have for each other – our new dawn
    Dark and clouded over,
  Grief flees the day we lost her,
  Grief, and our shame together.

Our frail Esyllt is taken away – where's no
    Lap for her, or kisses:
  What more poignant than Tristan
  Trying to comfort Siân?

The hurt in her face, and the woe – of an
    Unanswerable question,
  And most, in her cry to us
  A dearness of dependance.

A heaven and a hurt her birth – a kind
    Anguish the losing her,
  And a remorseless mercy
  Her end in its endlessness.

Shroud white, like a madonna – in the storm
    Of the utmost silence,
  On her breast emissaries of summer,
  Her cold cheek a garden of snow.

And tonight, under the flowers – summer's
    Ancient truth is working,
  And comfort's new-budding, where
  Her ashes keep the memory.

She'll be in the tears of dew, – in the sun
    Long after our passing,
  For ever, here in the earth,
  Her dust makes the flowers lovely.

Tomorrow shall never unmake longing.
We get no braver at negating death.
As long as we've memory, the loss shall last.
Humanity's worth is its power to weep.

[TC]

On Seeing a Dead Lamb

Like the time of her birth away from the world's face
The mother moves to the edge to birth her lamb,
We stand, all of us, close to the fording-place
To hide our pain from the flock, our hour come.

There is no leading us on our journey's way
And before we come, no showing us the road
Nor is there guidance on our leaving day,
And once we're here, no sign on the road we trod.

In the afterbirth, the winding cloths of death
Bind life's two ends together, tightening,
And captured on the hedge the blood of birth
Declares the certainty of suffering.

Being March, the length of day and night are equal
All one, bed of the grave, bed of the cradle.

[GC]

Harvest and Spring

(extracts from two poems)

When the birds of spring again are singing
Their long lost arias to set me stirring,
When dries the furrow a warm breeze blowing,
The boughs in colour, and lambs are calling,
I again will go sowing as of yore,
The age-old cycle once more completing.

And when in a fortnight's time I linger
At the gate of evening gazing yonder,
The budding corn will lace each acre
With on each sprout a dewdrop tear,
And I shall see draw near in the rows
Of the dragging barrows the dreams of summer.

I see the sweep of a squad of reapers
And the bending backs of busy neighbours
Building the stacks of their age-old labours
From the waist-tied sheaves of their endeavours,
With this old tongue of ours on each lip
In its workday strip, for it knew no others.

I see again the hunchback stacker
Kneeling the rustling sheaves together,
Circling tier upon careful tier,
Shaping and tying his oat-sheaf tower
That he might be secure in his haunt
From the ageless want of the joyless winter.

The urgent tractor will roar tomorrow
In the fragrant swathes of a distant meadow, –
A sun-dried breeze, a whisp'ring windrow,
And the whitening slopes with bales will billow
In row after iron row, awaiting
The waggon, shedding an evening shadow.

When the milk of the oat shall August harden
To see its beauty my soul will gladden,
The gate of hope shall open: a vibrant
Four-wheel giant will claim the garden.

Around and around on its wide-mouthed journey
Roaring its hunger across the country,
Pouring the golden bounty of the soil,
And April's toil into streams of plenty.

And the barn shall be full to overflowing
With autumn's riches in fine tomes reaching,
And when the tempests of March are blowing
And the forest giants themselves are creaking,
What joy will be in seeing this treasure trove,
This golden cove of my well-being.

The dross of barnyard gossip
Now is loud on every lip,
Talking a stirring story
With a snack upon its knee.

Yet again is the grainstore
Heaving to its flowing floor,
The gold-dust of the headlands
Running free through horny hands.

Let the north winds blow and the blizzards roar,
The pangs of want shall not pass the door.
Let the fields be locked in a frosty hoar,
The herd will lie as the herds of yore.
Their hunger the summer's store will allay
Till it be May in the land once more.

While lives mankind shall live the farmer,
And an ancient breed succeed its sire,
While winters weep shall live the reaper
And a living beast shall dung its pasture.
While sun shall follow shower, yet again
Shall bloom the grain, lest we should hunger.

[AUTHOR]

R Gerallt Jones

R Gerallt Jones (1933-99) was the son of an Anglican priest in Llŷn, and was educated at public schools in England, and read English at Bangor, before becoming a teacher, a lecturer in Education, the First Principal of a College of Education in Jamaica, the warden of Llandovery College, an extra-mural lecturer and warden of the University of Wales's residential centre at Gregynog in Powys. A prolific writer in both Welsh and English, he published literary criticism, novels and short stories as well as poetry. He also wrote plays and scripts for radio and TV.

For Ewan McLachlan

(A memorial to a Gaelic poet stands in a graveyard in Fort William. He was buried, according to the inscription in English and Gaelic, in Ardgour.)

Ewan McLachlan, the rickety footbridge
between us and your singing is long down;
it's Ewan now, not Eobhan, even in Welsh
for the remnant who speak it.

You lie, so it says, in Ardgour.
But what is left now that is yours
in Ardgour, or here in Duncan's town
or anywhere? Where are the poet's songs?

Nearby a girl sits on a tombstone
reading verse; she and her dog and I
own the tipsy graveyard, thighdeep, thistled.
She reads verse, but Eobhan, not yours.
Has she heard that your bones and the bones
of all civilised living lie in treeless Ardgour,
watched by the sentry hillsides? No.
Not a word. Not a grieving word ever.

The chasm yawns uncrossed, not between us
so much, the Welsh, and the Gael,
but between this grey tomb and every yesterday,
between this dark afternoon and mornings of simpler light.

Words, words remain; ruins of houses squat on Mull;
ghosts of Eobhan Maclachlan, your father's father
and MacDonnell of Keppoch, fierce at Culloden,
walk where each sunset weeps on Ardgour, nightly raw and red.

[AUTHOR]

Geese at Gregynog

The geese have gone. No lack
of bustle on the lake's surface; coarse
and boastful coot about his black
affairs, busy fuss on the quiet grey;

wild duck ascending in fear,
circling, *cwaa*, *cwaa*, whipping the rushes,
creating commotion in the island jungle;
one ominous buzzard watching the summer night.

No lack. But the fleet I have watched
nightly this year once more, sailing in rank,
an orderly progress through reeds at sunset,
it took wing and went. The world's bereft.

Without their dignity, the lake
is stripped of gentility; the stereotype
of geese – how false! Their flow was fluent
on the lake's mirror, it was calm and easeful.

They would proceed at evening, a careful
company, from tall grass grazing
to their true home in the bulrush forest,
and become one with their dwelling –

six bundles, brown and vulnerable, proud father
leading, and one, long-necked, at the rear,
sharp-nosed in her concern for her chicks,
an organic family, a cellular nursery.

Over months of business on a lake – crows harsh,
jays malicious, man's heavy tread,
they were its civil order, their perseverance,
their daily upbringing willing perpetuity.

But tonight, at summer's end, winter seems near,
its sudden, untimely chill a certain portent
that I shall know, perhaps next year, a spring
when the geese will return no more to the lake.

[AUTHOR]

Yasnaya Polyana

I never went to Yasnaya Polyana
but I had the chance. There the apple trees
stand as they did when Tolstoy walked his private Eden, tilting in
        his own way
at this world's windmills. For such red apples, such sweet
immemorial apples, grow in Yasnaya Polyana.
But when I heard the weasel, the red-eyed alleycat was dead,
I was back home again listening to the mouthing off
of the proletariat's own boss class,
searching for excuses to keep the people on their knees.
And then his papery face came up on the screen.
There was the orator, the acrobat of words,
whom I had once seen touch a cradle with the lullaby of his hands.

I never went to Yasnaya Polyana
but when I heard he was dead I could imagine it there
and I knew the apple trees in the orchard
in Yasnaya Polyana, and the pear trees in my own garden
were the only possible beauty
and that the creation in which we find our peace
is a gift we must give back.

Maybe he didn't agree. His was an exquisite rage,
a wormwood wisdom where laughter lived.
He was a bantam swollen on scorn,
and ah, how he sucked his cigarettes
as if he knew there was nourishment there,
each fiery point the spark of a ferret's eye.

For such a quiet Quixote, he did well.
If battles were lost his understanding grew
unstoppably – until on his deathbed
the world's madness was too ridiculous to condemn.

I never went to Yasnaya Polyana.
Instead I wasted my time in libraries and galleries,
with poets and translators in the usual toasts
to Wales and Russia and mankind. But I was drowning
in a stagnant world. Like a draft of cold air
it took that man's death to bring me back to life.

So so-long, to the light-carrier.
To the featherweight who was a colossus of words
and whose echoes are exultant everywhere.

[RM]

To Derek Walcott
(on reading his poems)

It churns;
longing for the sun
unsettles me.

Your words sear black
into every white page.

Thighs chant,
narrow, smooth,
and the hands huge and slack.
Palm trees
bend obediently.
Old men like monkeys
ride in their sleep
patient mules
towards the sea.
Dark sand, ragged shacks
mango leaves, well-proportioned,
banana leaves, awkward ragged leaves,
great leaves dangling high,
taste of orange, sweet taste of corruption,
taste of fish and the nets a spider's web
between me and the red sun.

It's a river
a flood that I cannot tame,
it leaps through the great gloom
and slays it.

[AUTHOR]

243

The Nurse

It's a miracle, waking every morning
in this graveyard, in these marble aisles
where each man makes a white dune of his bed,
emaciated men who stare through frosted panes
at the world. It's a miracle unasked.

And arriving with the light, there she is,
hair a glimpsed gold under the starched cap,
and those eyes that last night flashed
in some quiet corner (over whose shoulder?)
are a schoolmarm's eyes today.
Those just-so eyes have perjured her passion.

From patient to patient
she pours herself like antiseptic,
each one receiving the measured dose
of her totalitarian smile.
She's a conundrum in her camouflage
as she moves through our broken ranks.

She's able to leave her other self behind
like yesterday's paper, or that nightclub dress
thrown across the white atrocity of her bed.
Real life's lived over the way
in the rendezvous of all the city bars.
Love's knotted under her apron now
and her hair balled tight beneath her cap,
this one whose smile could frost the glass,
on guard in our graveyard.

[RM]

T James Jones

T James Jones (*b.* 1934) is one of three brothers born and bred on the farm of
Parc Nest in Carmarthenshire, all of whom have won the National Eisteddfod
Chair or Crown. Jim Jones, who began his career as a minister of religion, has
been a lecturer at Trinity College, Carmarthen and a BBC script editor. He has
also written plays for television and theatre. *Dan y Wenallt* is his Welsh trans-
lation of Dylan Thomas' *Under Milk Wood*. A freelance writer, he lives in Cardiff.

Dylan

He strode young into the landscape of old age,
the locust not yet come to weight his shoulders,
innocent of mourners loitering in the road
and of the withering of the flesh's desire.
The rare child scarce had leapt the brooks of morning
before Death clasped him by the hand,
and like a solemn father, had him home.
The summons came so sudden as to not allow
a glimpse, a wave, a smile, farewell,
there was only the old turning
of dust into dust, and the iron sound
the cell-door makes when locking for the night.

We will not see the humour
in the drunken clothes again,
or hear the keen voice hew the word.
The small wood cross stands rooted
in the consequence of bone, and only
the cold kissings of the memory remain.

I do not linger in the burial-ground
of longing because he sang the metres
in his mother's tongue; he did not care
that it was dying, docile as the sparrow,
in the countryside around him, muting
with each new stone in Bethesda's yard,
and he was blind to that death also, down
the funerals, all his days. He searched instead
for scripture in the seething tavern,
contended with the schoolmen of the smoke-filled room,
had sport with words, and with what gods
that lurked the corners, there in Laugharne.

I linger in the burial-ground of longing
because a poet's soul, among the graves,
cries vibrant as a red babe in an ancient bed.

[JD]

245

Dyfed Devastated?

Dyfed a somed, symud – ei mawrair
Am eryr bro yr hud...
(Dyfed is devastated by the death
of a great leader of the enchanted land.)
– from the elegy of Dafydd ap Gwilym for his uncle,
Llywelyn ap Gwilym, constable of Newcastle Emlyn.
Dafydd was acknowledging his debt to this learned man.

The east wind, moving with a chillness
in its edge, prepares the ferns
for winter on the hill above Cwm-bach...

I think of how I lay there as a lad,
the ferns scorched by high summer sun,
every field a friend, familiar –
Parc Llwyncelyn, Parc y Plain,
Cwm Mora, Bariwns Coch, y Llain...
And then Parc Nest, the pond well-sheltered
by its yard, the willow yielding down
its branches, like long strands of tears, to water...

Those were summers of cricket and laughter,
father at bat on harvest evenings,
the rick-yard neat, and full, behind him.

The game was over when
the ball went in the pond...

Turned into a son-come-home,
I walk the place where I once ran,
morning's schoolboy, book in hand.
Though I recognise some faces,
nine of ten resist a name...
The clock is striking the eleventh hour...

The magic land is large with strangers.

The Englishmen eye me like a brace
of stunned goats when I mention
the old tutor's school at Dôl Goch.

'The school did you say?
It's Category A.
But our kids are OK
with Education First down the valley...'

The son-gone-from-home
let gates stand ajar,
left the goats to strip the fields at will,
the ferns to root unchallenged in the rick-yard,
and the willow, one bent griever,
to weep constant as deep rain...

Is the ball in the pond?

[JD]

Thursday

FROM *Janus Poems*

Everything closes in. The wind from sea
whips the rain across the fields and down
the grey corridors and pavements of the town.
In the tawdry café, I am close
to my people and the smell of wet wool.
They are like wet sheep. In the morning,
before the rain came, I saw horses
in the fields, solitary, heads erect,
immobile in the wind. They were grand,
and for a moment seemed of stone.
The rain must ripple down their brawn
and sinew now. Here the people
smell of wet wool. I must not dwell on it.
Peoples have been great with sheep,
and had the horse as well. These people
smell like sheep. I cannot help it.
They are sheep. They bleat. The café owner,
an Italian, does not notice. He drags
on his cigar. I rise and go out.
The street is rained vacant. I force
myself to think of horses, strain
to hear the clean thunder of hooves.
The rain streaks my glasses. The soft wet
houses huddle together. I hear them,
I swear it. I hear the huddled houses bleat.

[JD]

Face to Face

(the tenth poem from the series of the same name)

He did enjoy the evening, gracious daughters,
keen young men, though all, at times, spoke
bitterly of war. At the stroke of ten,
the General rose, went round the windows, closed
the shutters, and made no move to sit again.
The young men, promptly, took respectful leave.
A daughter showed him to an upper room,
and soon the house went dark, and still. Strong light
woke him; there was no cloud. He heard soft voices
in the rooms below. He rose, went down, and found
the General waiting, dressed in a gray uniform
of finest cut, with all the signs of rank
removed. They walked from breakfast out to morning,
strolled by soaring columns, hailed young men.
It was clear and cool, the sun still rising,
a clean breeze lifted through the green-leaved trees,
and looking up, he saw, beyond the town,
the western ridges washed with light. They took
ease, later, in the genial parlour, talked
again of all their lives. It was going noon
when the General sent to have the horses brought
around. Traveller, gray as dawn, was grand.
They rode together to the edge of town,
to where the Shenandoah swept before them,
and then reined. The General, turning to him
in the saddle, gripped him by the forearm, met
his eyes, and then, without a word, let go,
wheeled his great horse sharply, and rode south.
Glyndŵr glanced back, then turned his face to home,
towards legend stirred. He stiffened, and spurred on.

[JD]

T Arfon Williams

T Arfon Williams (1935-98) was born in Treherbert in the Rhondda, trained
as a dentist in London, and was Dental Officer for the Welsh Office in Cardiff
for a number of years, and later in Gwynedd, where he retired. He learnt the

bardic craft from 1974 onwards, and became a master of the *englyn* metre. His work is almost exclusively in this metre, and he wrote a book about the craftsmanship of the *englyn*. Below we print two alternative translations, the first closer to the form and literal meaning of the original, and the second conveying the impression of the original, though less literal.

Quarry

I

I opened a stone volume – but only
    a unique Geologist
  knows how to decipher it true
  since, in each sentence, it's earth.

II

A stone book opening:
only Professor Exceptional
really gets it, because
the words are earth-clogged.

[EL]

Foam

I

When a gust from above plays – with the sea
    the ancient beasts of the deep
  come to the surface to be
  born again as seagulls.

II

A gust tickles
the top of the sea, and then
the old monsters
from down deep
come up re-born
seagulls.

[EL]

249

May

I

Mortality shrinks back – because
    the bounteous Virgin May
    generously gives her milk
    to fill humanity's bowl.

II

Mortality takes a hike because
Virgin May delivers her milk
for free to fill up mankind's bowl.

[EL]

One-day Snow

I

Impossible it is fully to sense – the artist's
    torture, who coloured
    yesterday our fields with his brush,
    today that they're vandalised.

On the beauty of his creation – below
    was poured uniformity;
    the great rainbow from the canvas gone
    interfered with.

But villainy will be vanquished – the bad turn
    will spur on the artist;
    full of fun tomorrow
    restoring the elegant picture.

II

It is impossible fully to know
how the artist has suffered who was colouring
yesterday with his brush the fields of the land
today that they have been vandalised.

Over the beauty of his creation below
uniformity has been poured;
the great rainbow from the canvas has gone
by reason of the meddlesomeness.

But the work of the villain shall be vanquished
the bad turn shall spur on the artist
who full of humour tomorrow shall
restore its elegance to the picture.

[EL]

Eirwyn George

Eirwyn George (*b.* 1936) was born at Tufton, Pembrokeshire. He won the Crown
at the National Eisteddfod in 1982 and 1993.

Family

From the Foel Eryr ridge the Wicklow Hills are pale
but I remember them in brightness,
melding the setting sun with its rays,
throwing its blood
at the horizon's sea bed.
There's a Celtic memory here
a lonely farmhouse
and a long yellow summer.

>		*We like the Cymry.*
>		*We are at peace, asleep in Erin.*
>		*These trees, fields and rivers,*
>		*these crosses on hewn stone,*
>		*aren't they all one?*

As a nation the temperament roars,
how they hate the Lion
who ate their flesh at the Easter rising
and their bones in the darkness of the Maze.

>		*We like the Cymry.*

Mary holds her son in a frame above the bed
and the shamrock which spreads its arms in the porch
in its pot of clay
grows from the depth of their hearts.

251

Breakfast is sweet.
      We like the Cymry.
We shake hands
so passionately
as we leave.

How else?
It's our common blood.

[PF]

Gwyn Thomas

Gwyn Thomas (*b.* 1936) was brought up in Blaenau Ffestiniog and studied at
Bangor and Oxford, eventually becoming Professor of Welsh at Bangor. As a
scholar he has published a major study of Ellis Wynne, the 18th century 'Sleep-
ing Bard', but he was never prone to lock himself in an ivory tower, and he has
done much to popularise medieval literature. His *Tales from the Mabinogion*
(in collaboration with Kevin Crossley-Holland) appeared in 1984, and he pub-
lished an English translation of the work of Dafydd ap Gwilym in 2001. It was
he who coined the word *llunyddiaeth*, a kind of pun on the word *llenyddiaeth*,
where the element *llên* (literature) has been superseded by *llun* (picture). He
believed fervently that poetry should not be limited to the printed page, but that
it can hold its own on radio and television, and he himself has written poetry for
the media. His own poetry is direct and down-to-earth, and yet it is basically
serious.

Killer Dog

Night, and part of the world locked in silence.
Moon, a veined, slovenly eye
Scratched from the skull of darkness
Glaring through its death at the earth.
Far off the stares of the stars. By night
Fears will run through the fields.

Ewes with lambs are uneasy,
Sniffing the moonlight for killers.
Flock of hooves,
                  stirrings,
Stances
      on the still earth of night.

And the urge that breaks sweet buds from the boughs
Looses instincts deep down, draws Mot from his chain of tameness
To the darkness that is dripping with blood.

Corpses of sheep in the pallor of dawn
Woolly, bloody,
Stiffened, hideous
          and pregnant, cold with death.

Grass turning green and lambs waiting for birth:
Slaughter too is at large in the spring.

[JPC]

Microscope

Through lenses the world opens,
Disclosing movement, restlessness and ravening;
A look at the other side of stillness.

Strangeness.

The small things amplify their being,
And armour is bred of brittleness;
Fierceness is born of frailty,
And the weak organs grow strong.

The caterpillar is metamorphosed to a hustle of shields
And its belly becomes like an army, living by moving.
It obliterates the leaves with the machines of its head.

The grasshopper develops complexity –
Legs' links, links legs,
Links legs, legs' links,
     Agonised iron.

A fly leaps into largeness.
Its multiplied eyes a lattice.
Its body turns metal, black, in layers.
     Glass and steel.

The other side of stillness:
Hardness.
The world, beneath its surface:
Harshness.

[JPC]

Horses

Suddenly there were forms there:
Heads bright of eye
Leapt out of the alien dark,
Out of the night into the headlights' gleam.

The twentieth century braked
And in the tousled manes before us
Pieces out of the past were
Gazing at us brightly.

Neighing and snorting nostrils,
Legs teeming with terror;
Scattering then. After the hooves
Stopped threshing the darkness: stillness.

After the nerves of seeing
Stopped twitching with the imprint of the flurry
Of the forms that came before our faces
Like a fist, the light was full of quietness.

Shifting into gear and moving
On a road that wound along the face of the world
In a wide night where time was untied
And let loose in a fearful roaming.

[JPC]

The Nativity Play

It is a Christmas rite that
The children of the vestry
Present in our chapel
The drama of the nativity.

Some adults will have been
Stitching Christmas into old shirts,
Old sheets, old curtains
To clothe that gang of thespians.

'The Gifts', too, will be throwaways:
An old biscuit tin, gilded and adorned,
Will become a casket of 'Myrrh';
An old carton of tea will be 'Frankincense';
And a lump of something coloured and wrapped
Will become 'Gold'.
And there will be, always, a star that's electric.

Other adults will have been coaching Angels,
Attempting to show Wise Men how things are done,
Trying to prod into the unruly
The decorum of 'Shepherds',
And struggling to keep Herod and his Men
From wild and perfidious insubordination –
For this there's among them a strong inclination.
Mary and Joseph will be somewhat older
Than the rest and, so, easier to manage.
Baby Jesus is always a dolly.
From time to time in the rehearsals there will be
Unseemly bickering between Wise Men and Shepherds,
And, sometimes, loud arguments there among Angels,
And the walloping of heads will be an unmajestic
Temptation for Herod's Men with their swords made of plastic.
And when the sombreness of Gift-giving is rudely shattered
When one of the Wise Men drops the biscuit tin, with great clattering,
There is need of grace to stop our Reverend from swearing.

But in the love that is there within those walls
On the night itself, all there are a family.
There the white innocence of those who are acting
Makes, miraculously, a birth out of ordinary things,
And in our night the electric star will lighten the darkness
And will point back to that very first Christmas,
And show us the light that can't ever be buried.
And in the midst of the horror of a world ruled over by Herod
It is said once again that God does not die.

[AUTHOR]

The Welsh-speaking Welsh

Those of us still left,
Aren't we like piranha
In a bowl here
Intent on devouring each other?

[AUTHOR]

The Last Things
*(A young woman suffering from cancer who was, in the
end, taken abruptly from her home to a hospital to die.)*

On the wrist a watch
Coldly ticking, ticking
As if there were no eternity.

Cancer here has been, like a black crow,
Inside her scavenging,
Pecking her life out of her.

In the house, in a tin,
There's a cake, whole
Except for one slice.

The bed's not been made
And the shape of her sleep's still there,
That and Bruno, her old teddy bear.

There are clothes with signs of life in them
Hanging heavily, like longing;
Skirts, frocks, death.

A note to her husband: 'The milkman,
Remember to pay, money cupboard,
The drawer on the left.'

In the face of these things
And as they see her harrowed husband
People find that they are
Compelled to be kind.

And in the midst of all this trouble
A man finds himself wondering
Whether life has cankered
Or, some way, somehow, conquered.

[AUTHOR]

For

For Marxist dialectic: spouting, spouting;
For decaffeinated coffee: trying, trying;
For an unprivileged proletariat: shouting, shouting;
For dogs with the shits: imploring, imploring;
For the peace of all nations: warring, warring;
For the freedom of canaries: chirping, chirping;
For uninspired art: asserting, asserting;
For the passions of the gay: tolerating, tolerating;
For fish without lifebelts: enquiring, enquiring;
For the rights of coloured people: politicising, politicising;
For moles without glasses: daring, daring;
For the man nextdoor:
                    Zero. 'Sorry and all that palaver,
                    But I mean to say,
                    Am I my brother's keeper?'

[AUTHOR]

Greetings

Congratulations. Well done.
Twelve dead;
Two men burnt
To black cinders;
Ten more persons mutilated –
Fragments of them
Over fifty yards of the street
Are being gathered into plastic bags;
A girl's leg blasted off –
And that, as it happened,
Two days before her wedding;

One child lost an eye;
A baby's arm was burnt raw.
Three houses shattered,
Two shops, and ten cars.
Forward, forward still.
Well done. Congratulations.

[AUTHOR]

Gwynne Williams

Gwynne Williams (*b.* 1937) was brought up at Ponciau near Rhosllannerchrugog in north-east Wales. He graduated in Welsh at Aberystwyth and was then a teacher at Ysgol Dinas Brân, Llangollen.

Oak Tree

Not summer
but winter

is when to see
an oak

after snow
and hoar
have bitten her

her leaves
thrown
and nothing
nothing
but her black boughs
and her core
are
rearing
from old rock

I do not know
who said this

but know
no truer word
ever
was said
of tree

or of a poem

[CM]

Winemaking

Once
only
did I make wine –
and elder wine it was.

Despite the kick
of seeing
the ugly lumps
from my father's
garden
of pressing
and pressing them
long
through fine muslin
turning
in a miracle
into wine,
tonight,
there's nothing
not even
a red
stain
on the glass of memory
to recall it,
but I still
press
press the
word
to get

the poem
pure
    as rain
red
    as blood.

[CM]

After the Exam

No collier comes from the belly of earth
into the alien light
as happy as we –
the last exam done
and the sunlight laving the dust
from our skins.

No monk ever comes from his cell
out to the free prayerless dawn
as merry as we –
the last exam done
and no more to learn
but the unfinished book of the fields
and its green annotations.

No mechanic comes from the shell of his workshop
out of the ungreased breeze
as fit as we –
the last exam done
and only hilarious wheels of the trees
to turn and to tick
on the axle of sunlight.

No voyager comes from the skin of his capsule
onto the shoreless sand
and jumps down as lightly as we –
the last exam done
and all the long summer
opened before us,
a moon made of silver.

[CM]

Gilbert Ruddock

Gilbert Ruddock (1938-98) learnt Welsh as a second language at Cathays High School in Cardiff, and went on to graduate in Welsh at University College, Cardiff. There followed teaching posts at University College, Dublin and the University College of North Wales, Bangor, and a post as researcher with the Board of Celtic Studies of the University of Wales, before being appointed lecturer in Welsh at University College, Cardiff, where he remained until his retirement in 1990.

To a Blind Mother

In God's name, mam, don't mention
those days of seeing,
because I'm full of shame
in the shadow of your visions:
how full of colour, how ardent
those scenes you paint
where there are suns
I never dreamed existed.
My light's a mere boast
beside your shaded depths
and slant of rays captured
by the sweep of words.

If blindness is an island, apart,
then I hear stirrings at dusk
in the skirting breeze
of graves you etched
with fine floral patterns.
They remain in morning's glass,
two points like lighthouses.

If blindness is being isolated,
the cave I inhabit
can be blocked with foolish stone
and all your light cannot remove
its shame of the fumbling stick,
sad realisation no Lazarus
will rise up, re-born.

But on the tideline I touch
and comb for your sense of perspective,

feel in the tangle of seaweed
a moist canvas forming forgiveness.

[MJ]

Double-decker

Tread-mighty monster, fearsome and ferocious.
High like a mountain.
His shadow's scowl swiftly blacks the ground
Like an eagle's shadow on the fold.
His life's breath is poison-smoke,
His nostril quivering and deformed
With fury's fire.
His intestines snarl together like two continents colliding.

There is none who can oppose
Him who bears sixty and more people
In his paunch.
Who is there can oust him,
Militant dictator of countryside and town?
His kingdom is extensive, and fearful are his subjects.
In defying him,
You'd be spread like cheese across the road
Or thrown like a balloon into the air above.
Let his governance be not doubted.

Hear his roaring!
See now the flash of armour on his lengthy flank!
Awesome his irresistible charging –
Inevitable as the assaults of Fate itself.

[AUTHOR]

Donald Evans

Donald Evans (*b.* 1940) is a farmer's son from Banc Siôn Cwilt in Ceredigion, who graduated at the University of Wales Aberystwyth, and taught Welsh as a second language at Penglais Comprehensive School in Aberystwyth. He now lives in Talgarreg near his home area. He won both the Chair and Crown at the

National Eisteddfod in 1977 and 1980, and is a prolific poet, a master of the traditional metres, but also fond of fusing *cynghanedd* and *vers libre*. He has also made a substantial contribution as a critic.

Wales '99

(in memory of Ted Hughes)

You once asked, it's said,
your beloved mother-earth,
to consider the quiet hour
when you skulked in a speck of dust.
You stitched your mother tongue
to the power of the black moors,
soldered it in a restless century
to the spirit of the hawk,
fish of the alder, creatures of the wind,
ancient offspring of the loved one.
Lady of earth and bright water,
she so much in the day's emptiness
must be left alone now
to bind again her people to herself,
and to psalm in praise
in the Devon summer night and the Pennine mist.

Tonight, January fog
was like a mirage, blessing
the blue bay with its fingers
from the ravines of Cilie to the headland of Cilan.
This year wet from the start,
with a half smile
forewarning Wales with the thrill
of the swallow and bustle of lambs.
Soft rain from an acid sky
brought the power of crocus,
buttons of buds
over the land of the long cairns.
Then her ice and the nails of the moor
fall from the sunset to the bone
of the bog in the bitter night
to release her earth.

[GC]

The Rubbish Tip
(modernity)

At dusk we listened too much to the rats' cry,
at dawn we stared too long into putrefaction,
so for aeons we failed to hear the earth's blood sigh
like the sea, for fear of the stink of corruption.

And we never noticed above us the sun's prayer
or the stars' understanding, or saw their meaning there,
just their chemistry and mass, and the smoke of war
on the light of wisdom, its mindlessness and fear.

And poison snaked down to the aquifers below,
killing the heart of valleys where rivers flow
till an old song darkened the marsh, water on stone,
and the spirited joy of the stream is dead and gone.

But, as about us confusion descends into chaos,
we see again the unflinching Christ on the cross.

[GC]

Pig Killing Day

Two or three men would go
about ten o'clock to rope the pig;
driven and dragged from his sty
into January light,
dancing and dodging in the icy wind,
squealing, fear in his marrow.

The tether tightened, his jaw jerked up
for the butcher to plunge the knife,
burying the blade
in billowing fat.
A red bellow of agony burst
from deep in his throat;
everywhere blood,
the unstaunchable heart blood
till suddenly he faltered,
staggering…staggering in the grass.

264

Then, watching the men
pour scalding water
over his back and belly,
and the scritch-scratch of the hedge
in the wind, the steam and the blood.
Left to his nakedness, turning and turning
all afternoon. We'd glimpse
sometimes the gash in his throat
agape and moist with meat
to the fat of the breast,
and catch under the scraper
the grunt of flayed flesh
in the folds of his chin.

I remember the cattle
at tea-time, come home for milking.
Even they were uneasy
the moment they stepped in the yard.
They sniffed the bushes and dirt,
eyeing the close,
wondered at water and blood.

That night I was afraid
to pass the shed
by the stable.
A child's fear...and the great pig
hanging, astonished...the sound
of droplets dripping from his head
into the cask in the dark.
Even then, a child, I knew
the creature must be killed
to keep us in meat and lard,
and the winter ahead.

[GC]

The People

They're no heroes,
magnanimous as the giants of the old days.
I see them in the pub,

in the street, in the shop, at the fair;
ordinary men, the sly, the good;
the cruel, the simple;
by turn cunning and courageous.
Just the same old crowd
their lives shaped by goodness and sin.

They cleck in the old tongue;
a gabble of gut-talk
in the old blood-words, about work, and play;
the power and speed of machines;
of drinking, women, prices in the mart
and the rest of it something and nothing…
They cleck in the old, old tongue;
older than ancient kings,
newer than the latest scandal.
They're no heroes,
magnanimous as the giants of the old days.

The couldn't-care-less, the don't-give-a-damn;
tough, unbelievers in
cultural matter, weighty and grave;
not passionate, not defenders of a language
and a way of life, it's easy to despise them.
They're no heroes,
magnanimous as the giants of the old days.

But should they stop living,
become extinct, somehow, in the future,
their nature grow languid,
their kind disappear from the land,
the old red tongue of their blood
would diminish to a language for study and debate,
would dwindle and die,
grown grey as a cultural relic;
a skeleton of cold words
torn between the hounds and the crows.
They're no heroes,
magnanimous as the giants of the old days.

[GC]

Creation

Listening to Siôn Onwy
breathing steadily...steadily in his sleep,
I'm struck to the heart by the clean beat of the sea;
by the river's tender rhythm over the stones;
by a shower caressing a green tree;
by the voice of the blackbird in morning mist;
by evening sunlight on the bushes of the moor;
by the ewe's steady love for her lamb;
by Jesus blessing the children under the cloak of heaven.
Then I think of winter that is not winter that threatens us out of the night;
of icy death over a land of ashes;
and nothing breathing.

[GC]

Dewi Stephen Jones

Dewi Stephen Jones (*b.* 1940) is a native of Ponciau near Rhosllannerchrugog,
who was educated at Ruabon Grammar School and the University of Wales
Aberystwyth. He still lives in Ponciau, and contributes regularly to the poetry
journal, *Barddas*, not only poems, but also critical articles.

Diptych

1 *Houses at Night*

Their roofs and floors unstaved, the houses
are down below, underneath their tranquil sea,
boats
        on the bottom.
Where did their white paint go?
How faint their red tints were.

The sun turned in its course over there
to its costly setting and its consummation
        with no visible afterglow,
                no flush on the sides of the houses,

but once it set
          its heat lingered
in the black cradle of the planks
and the curvature of rafters,
a seed within the descent,
a hope in every framework
          despite the floodtide's depth.

They wear their sun-shadow.
I sense the warmth of many a year
of coal fires and their golden chit-chat's
persistent stain on slumber's wall.

With not a pane retaining the noise of company,
with not a porthole lit,
they make themselves at home
in their furrow of slowness,
boats
          on the bottom
                    with their cargo of wine.

2 The Temperature of the Rock

By day, by day,
          with the sun like a bell on fire,
there are traces,
          beyond their shape, in the bare hills,
of their builder's hand, the glaciers.

A network was left
          (Oh goodbye to ice's old rags on the summit!),
lighter than a spider-web:

in the grain and on the surface
of the smooth stone
and in the grey rock's body
the temperature is colder
by a mere fraction
          but it clearly bears in mind
                    the weight of the giant long gone.

In the season of our fever
I happen on the trail's bright shadow

and from the granite's nesting-place
to lowland
and the valley's wound,
it's held in store,
        an elixir
                on hand.

[JPC]

The Coat

With no tear-marks between the shoulders,
why! you're almost as new,
without frostbite tingling the sleeve,
without a pocket ravelling,
but somewhat hunched, perhaps,
like the curve of the hill.

Between one pace and another, somewhere,
a button was lost, the colour
of horn or the tallow candle
(now burnt-out)
leaving its black wick
like scorched stubble in one corner of the field.

Thread by thread
the loosening,
like the leaves of the forest in the stillness:
one by one
each glowing lamp is darkened,
the taste,
the sight.

Coming closer,
from the holes of a ruin
I hear the sea
call the foamrags of all rivers
home.

[AUTHOR]

The House

(words in memory of Jane Charles, 1959-1980)

Turn away from the noise of light
and peace shall come with the day.

In the night each one of us is alone.
Man. Woman. Boy. Girl.
Each one is alone in the night.
After a night lit by lightning,
dawn broke to the crack of thunder
        and you were going,
and each night, like last night,
we sit beyond the warmth of the fire.

On a fine morning, how frail the house
and pain its window,
a window where the summer flourishes,
dark the plaster, low the wall.

Beyond its ground and without towers
lies a ruined city;
to the archaeologist's eye,
there are layers upon layers of hours there –
the shapes of a history wrinkle the surface
like a wall and its corners above an old hearth,
the world as it was over the rooms of hell,
a still boat where there is no rowing
floating above the chills of a river.

A table with its shadow rises from the dust,
(an excavation of moments from a lost time)
a room in its entirety
as homely as in a cottage
and our perception is of a door, opening
to let in the sun:
a fire in the grate and you,
yourself, are there,
the book still rests in the palm of your hand
and its print on the white page
like a speckled egg in the clays of the nest,
until your sudden smile lingers and holds
above words.

'O house in the weather
shall summer come to your beams?'

'The shining ash tree is here a window,
a green house unlocked.'

[AUTHOR]

Last Window

In your frail loft
(a fortress of shadows)
before desire is trimmed,
before the soundest sleep,
stark and symmetrical,
(without the freshness of twigs)
from the sorrows of the frame
not the hubbub in its glass,
grace comes
from the dawn
of the black cross.

[AUTHOR]

In the Beautiful Glass

And what (extraordinary)
        ordinance
            is forming
in the corner of the French window,
its axis near the topmost panes?
The blind scraps are interweaving
(isn't the chimney ablaze?)
a Black Mass above earth's muzzle.

Crows?
        They come (like the day's burden)
to the blue to twirl an hour
and swim air in their numbers:

soar like a shoal of fish
from the depths of the salt acres
and swirl in a circle, professors of blood,
the blood on the face of the grass.

Readily they ignore
everyone and everything
in their chosen world.
They frolic till a breeze's sister
warm and unswerving
(not a goblin's spinning-wheel
but the heart's thermal)
lifts them in their linkage
aloft,
      above the globe's commotion,
higher than the gull and the bite of the brine,
distant as the skylark's notes,
up there in the beautiful glass,
out of sight,
      one with the light.

[JPC]

Meic Stevens

Meic Stevens (*b.* 1942) is a singer-poet who was born in Solfach, Pembroke-
shire. He is one of the foremost singers of his generation, and has flirted with
jazz, blues, folk music as well as other musical genres. He has sung with various
groups, especially with Geraint Jarman and Heather Jones, and has recorded a
number of albums in both Welsh and English. His most memorble recordings
are his solos which can be alternately romantic, poignant, haunting and reflective.
They are often based on personal experience.

Sylvia

My lover was a wonderer,
Travelled by herself,
Her spirit has flown
Her corpse entombed on the borderline.

Love turned to tears
Flows like sewin to the sea.

Wherever she was wandering,
Lonely and so sad,
Searching for a saviour,
Budha, Bach or Jesus Christ.

Silver harpists of the moon,
The golden orchestras of sun,
Have planted blades of poison
The curse of fungus midst the leaves.

Love turned to tears
Flows like sewin to the sea.

Her eyes are frightful
Hysterias in her voice.
But she nurtures dark and nightmares,
Binds her art in a black shroud.

Love turned to tears
Flows like sewin to the sea.

Too late to grab her hand,
Pluck her from the lair,
Where demons snare her soul,
Blinding the green beauty
Of her eyes.

[AUTHOR]

Dafydd Iwan

Dafydd Iwan (*b.* 1943) was born in Brynaman, Carmarthenshire, and is from
the Cilie family stock. He studied Architecture at Cardiff, but has made a career
as a folk-singer, director of a recording company, Sain, and organiser of a housing
association. He has been a leading language activist, and his songs are strongly
nationalistic. His satirical songs, 'Carlo' and 'Croeso 69', made a great impact
(pro and con) at the time of the investiture of Charles as Prince of Wales. He
has produced many records and collections of his songs.

Why Snow Is White

When the sun's on the mountain,
when the wind's on the sea,
when the field's full of flowers
and birds fill the tree;
when the tears of my beloved
are like gossamer dew,
I know in that one instant
that this is what is true.

 REFRAIN:
I know what freedom is now,
and truth, I understand,
and love, I know what that is,
for a people and a land;
so your stupid questions will have to wait,
you can look dumbfounded all night;
only fools need to question
why snow is white.

When the words of my comrades
are mellow like fine wine,
and old familiar phrases
trip from these lips of mine.
When I hear the sweet notes
of an age-old melody,
I know what 'belonging'
and 'living' mean to me.

I know what freedom is now...

When I see the scarred miner
and the bloodstains on the slate,
when the haystacks all remind me
of the tired crofter's fate,
when I see the humble schoolboy
branded with the old Welsh Not,
I know I've got to stand up
for my brother and his lot.

I know what freedom is now...

[GL]

Derec Llwyd Morgan

Derec Llwyd Morgan (*b*. 1943) was brought up in the village of Cefnbryn-brain in Carmarthenshire, and educated at Bangor and Oxford. His academic career has taken him from the Welsh Department at Aberystwyth to its sister Department at Bangor and back again to Aberystwyth as Professor of Welsh, and later Vice-Chancellor. He is a distinguished critic and literary historian, specialising on the literature of the Methodist Revival.

Bow and Arrow

On feeling, blue blaze of noon,
the sun's strong spell like passion's
parched kiss suck, dance of power
in the sky's corner, my skin,
I thought of a slim darling
who nakedly loves heaven's squire.
He leaps in bliss like a buck
to know her well in Niwbwrch.
For a kiss, he makes lips a summerhouse;
there I'd be, in her summer.

Ache under a brown silk sun,
disgrace of brown-skinned lovers,
from Sir Gâr, our apartness,
up to the land's edge in Môn.
Two sides we are, two covers,
of summer's wall, immense book.

Will something toss me tonight
across houses to Menai?
What science-inspired piston,
what train, what copter, what cart,
what plane that splits the heavens
upon wild electric's wings,
what nuclear ship will bear
me there, exile of summer?
A modern hell with no tools
to oil, forcing defiance!

Sun sobered; a respite came
to tame a heart that's starving.

I go, I negate the song,
bridled, down Dyffryn Aman.

Then in a stag's leap cross
the mountain in a minute
he tore, – he stands supported
on night's brink, heavenly bow.

'Hurl swiftly, sun, and expel,
drive far before it arches,
passion's arrow, the mass of
these pangs, yearning's foster-son.'

How lovely would be the stint
of bleeding the sky, leaving
a trail of sunny trembling,
world-roofing winnowing-sheet!

'Fulfil, my sun, friend she loves,
my command's hasty challenge:
now – before night, like Eros,
shoot me straight and true to Môn.'

[JPC]

Registering the Little One

White girl
of Gwynfor's year,
cradle-gift, daughter for his choir.
I was drunk with joy
I tell you,
as there surged
(shattering independence!)
quivering and rushing from the closing womb,
into Carmarthen
Elin's radiance.

Elin?
Denied kindly by each startled wretch of an Englishman.
'No such name,'
says the lively bloke,

belly-full of law,
'believe me. More
like a weapon.
Don't load the lassie as she grows
with the lumber of a sick tongue.'

Oh I had trouble
– a hell-quest
without doubt,
and God will judge him –
with this fellow, big with the glow
of the crown's glitter,
making a case for this little one
till in the end, late,
Somerset House
sent the delicately scribed certificate.

But for Elin, what nonsense
of her right to both tongues.
What price a name for her, belonging
– Miss Existence –
to the cosmos, anonymous?

From the womb, unfair
for the fair one
to be eighteen months nameless,
a non-Elin of the Hosts,
daughter of punishment,
as there as a cuckoo's nest.
One day,
'Dafydd Iwan,' she said, 'that's me. And Japan.'
(Missionary miss
to these grey courts of exile.)
Solid as a shield-boss,
merry as music
when not hiding and seeking;
she's the dance
of time's patience
round the Maypole of my being.
Flings paint like it was just invented,
flamboyant as Picasso.
She's a pretend-mum,
stirrer of messes;

she's the fluster at every feast,
flash
of a brilliant dynamo,
witch of restlessness.
'I'm a train now.'
She's Venus,
the saint that polishes stars,
a pope of divination,
last night arrayed
in her magic nightgown
fooling love, a bridesmaid.

That afternoon
after baptism,
all the wrong way up, sudden,
she went crazy on the carpet
happy and fervent
(oh, the racket)
as gentle Jesus.

What price a name for her, who belongs,
Miss Existence,
to the cosmos, anonymous?
Priceless, that from a seed's centre
such a world has burst
and entered mine.

[CF]

Meirion Pennar

Meirion Pennar (*b.* 1944) is the son of the distinguished poet Pennar Davies, and was born in Cardiff, and graduated at Swansea and Oxford. He was a lecturer at University College, Dublin before taking up a post at the Welsh Department at St David's University College, Lampeter, but he retired in 1994 due to ill health. His poetry was influenced by certain German and French streams of Modernism of the inter-war years.

Reading Croce

Feeling
   if you ever sleep in a grave
   having chafed down the years
   with knowing – stone dead – and doing
   if someone re-erects some limb or other
   which we don't recognise
      because of your cock's jerking
      to the summons of eager fingers
      and the burning of your feverish skin
      you will be the first to wake
      at the dawn we did not see
      after the night we did not sleep
      with your scorching clarion
      you will wake your friends
      burning cheeks puffing out your perpetuity
      another awakening – not an alternative wakening
      already your nimble buttock-kneading hands
      at work beneath the sheets
      already your blood whipped to a frenzy
      in your loins
      a shuddering along your back

   through the commitment of your arousal
   the perfection of your anguish
   he knows that the oomph will be there once more
   under the eternal fingers
   the soul
   will have its own strengths

[MD]

Ecce Homo

On the threshold of the black cave
– for a minute – I stopped being
from my flesh hobbled bits
of rotten bone
ecce homo – I said
to prevent the tears – I laughed

it is I [me?] who is the digger of my grave
with my own busy hands
I am the author of my undoing
my poetic inspiration – my craft
a constant pounding of the rock
from which I was carved

dust to dust
ashes to ashes
son of adam
you are a man
behold the dust in your hand

your puny magnitude

[MD]

Lovers

I

as a blind man
    fingering a child's face
    in the dark
       you and I

II

your kisses
    like three shaken apples
    they know their law
    and the deep, dark earth
for ever am I

III

Your luscious velvet
    your thighs come to meet me
    I place my ear to your womb
    and her an ancient energy
like the whispering sea in a shell
    held fast by the moon

IV

there you are
here am I
curse the course
the finite land
        and yet
this is what makes
our soil, soil
our living, living

V

like the sower
    I too sowed
                kisses
    in good faith
without my knowing
        an end
        or beginning

[MD]

Branches of a Mabinogi

I

Ecce homunculus   c'est moi   'tis I
rhiannon and teyrnon take a firm hold   and here
I am   the self-kissing narcissus

the little panegyrist   the mabinogistic youngster
bawling in childhood tongue

where's that little scamp   coo-ee nana   coo-ee
nana   *come out from there you rogue*   now
he's scratching his head over books

twixt the thighs of a world war two mother I was born
at christmas as it happens while everyone was
expecting the Messiah   out I popped   the little monkey
emerging the wrong way up   and the forcep's immediate grip
on the threshold of the hiatus of soil to soil
dust to dust navel to navel redressing
the initial injustice

II

As an adolescent in the prison of his manhood he felt the bars
of the martyr and the saint   on the sand of the arena the sinew
against those of the lion   he placed his faith
in the seed nestling in the rotten apple of the cold war

as an adolescent embroiled in the flesh   he
felt the freedom of blood
he sang that night a plague on its full moon
of luscious lips and full breasts   and then he
had no need of any sun

as an adolescent in the thrall of his nation   he
felt the primitive rhythm
of birth pains beneath the monotone elegy
of its funeral   he saw the splendour of the phoenix
rising from the flames and ashes

III

Between romance and lust down the years
a bee came to sting me in a tender spot
and to itch   its wings were the colour of
petrol petrol on water   and ever since that
time what ails him
bee's wings if I had them I would fly along the borders
of Annwn to snatch Ceridwen's cauldron   with the
white dogs howling away in the woods the homely
pigs snorting away at the foot of the
oaks   with Gwydion and Gilfaethwy as
deer in the brushwood   and
gloomy Manawydan through his manhood
bewitching the Grey of the misty fields   and so let
my typewriter sound forth in the heads of mothers

[MD]

Gerallt Lloyd Owen

Gerallt Lloyd Owen (*b.* 1944) was born in Rhos-y-gwaliau and grew up in
nearby Sarnau, Merioneth. Educated at Normal College, Bangor, he had a short
career as a primary school teacher before establishing Gwasg Gwynedd which
has grown into one of the most prominent publishing houses in Wales. In his

Cerddi'r Cywilydd ('Poems of the Shame', 1972) he lashed out at the somnolence of Welsh people for their toadying attitudes in the year of the investiture of Prince Charles as Prince of Wales at Caernarfon (1969). He has won the National Eisteddfod Chair twice, and is well-known as adjudicator of the popular radio bardic contest *Talwrn y Beirdd* (Bards' Cockpit).

The Shame of Llanfaes

History? Here's an end of that.
And Llanfaes? There was no such place.
Yesterday is today's dirt in Mona,
yesterday's values today's shit.
God's yesterday is today's muck
and Llanfaes liquid manure.

Is this an old insult at work,
Edward's vengeance at it again?
Demanding his place, demanding court,
lording it over the island's keepsakes.
Did he buy men for a fat sum
to wait on him in a chamber?

This was an act of old malice.
This threw down the gauntlet again.
here our nation is deep in swill,
here shame's effluent daily increases;
and the shame is the use of this shrine
for the processing of English sewage.

[RST]

Cilmeri

At nightfall, in this place
Llywelyn was killed.
Never will I forget this.

The stream I see in this place
Llywelyn saw.
He stepped on these stones.

283

At nightfall, in this place
Out of sight the enemy neared.
All was completed in this place.

Now I am in this place
Where his hair was on the grass
And drops of his blood in this place.

In this place is our memory.
In this place our life's breath.
In this place just now our birth.

[JPC]

The Man on the Horizon

Not frail, while's man, all frailty,
Not a speck of dust all dust.
And therefore, Wales, keep in view
The man on the horizon,
The one whose brain is keen-edged,
The fool of infinite faith.

On his face a dream's traces,
The grey distance in his voice;
But his calm coming, his lore,
Have gained no recognition,
Like the ancient Extremist
Who died for them on a beam.

The hero loves a country
Whose folk have no wish for love.
He hewed his heart for her sake,
A cell the thanks she gave him.
For a true act of Welshness
Her blade, not her praise, his prize.

Unconcerned Wales, the day comes
When you see your dishonour.
Sound cannot win a senate,
Never without a new grave.
And therefore, Wales, keep in view
The man on the horizon.

[JPC]

284

Inheritance

We had a country to keep,
a piece of land as witness
to our will to survive.

We had a nation from generation
to generation, and we breathed
the history of our selves.

We had a language, unsought,
its soul in the very soil,
its restless force in the hills.

We turned the soil, lit fires on the hearths,
planted trees and pylons of power
where there was no lake.
We turned our nation to engender
strangers, strange to her history;
humanity like seadrift left
by turning tides.
And we turned our ancient tongue
to a language too shy to speak up.

Consider; is there a proverb
that says here is the truth:
to value profit is a nation's shame,
her passivity her death.

[GC]

To the Death

We offer the prince a smile,
In return get the smile of a royal,
The smile of our self-betrayal.

We run where royalty treads
On the red carpets we spread,
Paths where our future lies dead.

We wave our arms in the air,
We all smile, our world debonair,
Close the day without a care.

We make souvenirs, trinkets, gestures,
To remember the royal fest,
Never counting the cost.

We go on without will to survive
To a night that won't need us alive.
We went willingly, all, every breath
In a race to the death.

[GC]

Nesta Wyn Jones

Nesta Wyn Jones (*b.* 1946) was brought up on a farm in Abergeirw near Dol-
gellau, and after graduating at Bangor she worked for the Welsh Theatre Company,
the Schools Council and the Welsh Books Council, before returning to her
childhood home to farm with her husband. As well as four volumes of poems,
she has published a diary written when she was living on a kibbutz in Israel.

Voices

Yes, this is my voice –
Voice of deft speech
Responding to eyes' knot
And rhetoric of hands.
A chain of words spoken –
Voice that asserts
One thing or the other.
This is my voice.

But, in a silence
When my eyes go dark,
Another, more importunate
Voice I hear –
A voice torturing every wire in my brain,
Lipped like a hooter at midnight
To shatter the dark of my being.

It's a voice lonely
Beyond expression
Where a wolf moans for ever its grief
At the wilderness moon –
A voice that would pace up and down
The bereft cells of my memory
In utter lack of rest.

O then, how terrible to look up and notice
You did not hear this agony –
The voice that stains silence with its shriek:
My dumb voice.

[TC]

Poppies

August, in Brittany,
And in the breeze sways and pirouettes
A red ballerina.

Brittany
As if someone
Had thrown tiny pieces of red
Tissue paper
Over the hedges
And they'd all unfolded
Flaming
In the sun.

August
And my hand itched to gather them,
But I knew, if I did,
There'd only be the stain
Of red
On my fingers
When the dew lifted.

Twilight, August in Brittany.
Into the dark staring and staring
I see their purple bruises

In every corner
Quaking
To the rumpus of crickets.

Here,
There's a wreath of plastic in the rain…
It's not that flower that's plaited in it.

[TC]

Shadows

The two World Wars – no, we never saw those days.
We were born when the dust was clearing
From the remains of slaughter and burning.
Our voices had no reason to crack
As we prayed for 'daily bread'.
Our dear ones did not vanish
So that we never knew
The when or the how
Precisely…

We'd come at a soft time
Into a world middling blest,
But sometimes a savour of guilt
Will maybe start
In the harsh wake of shock
When we see, when we hear
Fragments of what was
In the dark days –
Fragments searing into our consciousness,
Experiences too alien to comprehend.

That woman once, in Belsen,
Her sanity in ribbons in the shambles around her,
Who still insisted on nursing on the memory of an arm
Her dead child.

That body, so amusingly contorted,
Like a scarecrow that's finished its work
On the barbed wire…
A skull, all teeth, under a steel helmet.

The tenacious multitudes, dead, dead,
Ribs like washboards,
Stomachs empty troughs –
The terrible remainders
Of the gas ovens.

The orderly rows of white crosses
Fiendishly quiet, and so numerous
We cannot credit
That such a huge reckoning
Lies there.

No, we know nothing of those days
– Only we sometimes hear
Of incidents, before our time,
Beyond our understanding.
But as, from the slaughter and the burning
Slowly the dust rises,
Maybe we do feel a tightness,
An echo of a scream,
As the old, never-satisfied eagle
To the horizon flies,
The shadow of his wing
Perishing us with cold
For a moment
Before it passes.

[TC]

Scream!

Tonight
I will have to search
For the missing me.

They are making
A machine out of my self,
All modern
Mindless mechanics
Measuring my life
Without owning the right;
An engine

Endless under the semaphore of a clock
That screams at me
Before waking, before breakfast
            before dinner
            before supper
                before sleeping
All day
Deafening my eyes
And blinding my ears…

That machine,
That silent one,
That one that moves so quietly
Is me.

But tonight
I have to stop it.
I will hide and ambush myself
Watching
And watching
Fearful
   So fearful
That it's the real me that's walking past.

[RM]

Beaches
*(after seeing a picture of Hiawatha in his canoe paddling
to the sunset and his death)*

Autumn was ripe,
its berries dripping in water,
blood-red pools between me and the sun,
and the melting ocean
a honeycomb of gold, curled at the corners.
Rain came sudden, soft
mountain drizzle on the sea.
   I watched her a while before launching her on the deep,
comforted in oak,
her hands unoccupied, bright hair unbraided
in waves;
around us the gulls keening their tribal woes,
crack and slither of boots on blue slate,

blistered bladderwrack.
Knowing I'd see the oak's slenderness
long after, rocking down the flames' wake,
setting like the kin's joy into darkness.
That was Nain.

Spring was fragile; crystalline
dew on webs through the dirty slats;
sun too weak to slant in the caves,
frozen ruts in the sand.
I noticed a narrow crack in the sea-wall,
how the small grains trickled down.
    I watched her a while before launching her on the deep,
gentle in cambric
white as butterflies on limestone
lifting in the breeze,
heard the tinkling question the sand asked
as her cradle rocked on the surf,
why a sliver of sun should return so surely
after such endless winter?
The sea was fogged, blurred,
rainbows on my eyelids
despite April's early smile.
Mist closed over her.
That was Bethan.

Summer was tumult,
a roar of dragons after atrocities of rain,
beach sandblasted by storms
as we stood astonished.
    I watched her a while before launching her on the deep,
in a bitterness of pine,
saw the daisies' purity blood-edged,
parent's brief hopes flattened
by the ravages of rain.
It took a long time to let her go,
for her to disappear into the dark;
on the cusp of summer
grey shadows will come and cloud me
pine-drenched, salt-smelling.
Wouldn't it be treason to deny
her twenty years of dreams?
That was Eurwen.

I gave each of them dignity and the ocean
of memory to enfold them;
melting into yesterday's loss,
hands outstretched to the sun's hunting,
not any sodden weeping of soil,
crooked stone's skewed words
under a scornful yew.
Three boats on the lap of the careful sea,
acorn cups in rings of ripples,
lingering,
three stars on the horizon
going out, one by one,
while I watch from these beaches,
that wide water.

[CF]

D Cyril Jones

D Cyril Jones (*b.* 1947) is a native of Ceredigion, and was educated at Trinity College, Carmarthen and the University College of North Wales, Bangor. He taught in mid-Wales for some years before being appointed tutor-organiser for the Workers' Educational Association in north Powys. He is now part-time tutor in the University of Glamorgan. His Crown poems at the 1992 National Eisteddfod allude to a visit he made to Kenya.

Letters to a Kenyan Friend

I *Julius*

Hitchhiker of the ivory smile,
do you remember us gambling a journey
between Borgaghoi and South Horr?

Travelling the earth where you'd been young
shepherding goats, dreaming of stars...
The two of us, on the safari truck roof,
half dressed, a morning of
language and race jangling between us –
sentences spider threaded

into a web
much older than we were.

It's still there, that web,
shivering, half-hidden
in the corner of my heart.

Hitchhiker of the ivory smile
do you still gamble away your life
rattling between Borgaghoi and South Horr?
Or did you escape from that skeleton
burning sun of yours,
to sip, in Nairobi Uni,
the cool learning of the West?

*　　*　　*

Fly
from your southern skies to our northern winter.
Arrive where everyone wraps thick
in wool and glove
frowning, just
to keep the warmth in
and the welcome out.

II *Imagine*

imagine a blue country, a pure country,
imagine a half-moon of bare land
embracing Turkana, the lake of your childhood,
under water,
all waves.

imagine
the gulls flying up off its blueness,
from the place where
as a boy your home stood and hedges told tales
and religion had claws.

imagine escaping then
and seeing the whole world an ocean
and the place you flew from so small:

crossing the cobalt
rounding the estuaries
to the right;
tracking the facelike coast
which swells into the mountains,
like dough in the oven of day.
Then turning
to read backwards
the long sentence of land
which rushes towards the dot of an island
sitting
at its
head.

imagine hearing it, the ocean,
snarling, threatening,
a gull's wing away.

imagine the storms, many of them,
and the boy in his jail of a school,
language and alien lesson
hitting hard the bars of his mind.
imagine looking out
at the lashing sea,
each wave a wall-breaking white shower,
a storm of meaning,
and him, the boy, deaf to it,
hearing nothing.

imagine,
the earth buckling roar, heaving on its bed,
two boys night walking
a road filled with fantasy;
their new voices breaking in the darkness,
erotically groping, rubbing, trying,
while far away from this ink of a bay,
the provocative wink
of the lighthouse on the tiny island.

imagine tonight that boy, that man,
half the country on the move,
among the long fences and snaking borders
where the harsh eastern wind is thin
and the language thinner still.

imagine him
between the cold, empty pages of a country
far from blue sea
trying hard, pencil clutched,
to catch the colour, the breeze and the mood,
crafting his word-shell
for you.

[PF]

Robat Powell

Robat Powell (*b.* 1948) was born and brought up in Tredegar in the largely
English-speaking county of Monmouthshire, and learnt Welsh as a second lan-
guage. After graduating in German at University College London, he taught
German and French at Ystalyfera, and is now research officer with the National
Foundation for Educational Research. His Chair-winning poem at the 1985
National Eisteddfod was ground-breaking in its depiction of the industrial
scene of his own background in the strict metres, and he was the first Welsh-
learner to win the National Eisteddfod Chair.

For Jurij Koch
(leading author of the Sorbs in the Lausitz, Saxony)

The line of the willows is old,
As old as the river of mists
Where dusk and frost
Gnawed at the seed of the rye.

Old is the stream between the trees,
And its primitive, charged voice;
But near the lonely waters
A language flits to and fro.

She too is old amongst the firs;
Her evensong drifting still
Through the heavy dark of the forest
And the fears of the cottage hearth.

In her derided innocence
She limped through the land of her death

And bled in her shame,
Eyes fixed on the grave.

But where she lay wounded, there broke
The spring morning that painted
The colours of sound and word
Upon the fresh leaves of the wood.

Then you came, to the greening house,
And set without trembling
Your courage to be its door,
And wound your steel for its roof.

The honest iron in your ink
Arms language against the old scorn;
This is the force that marks
Its sinews and its champion.

[AUTHOR]

Heysel

Gentle sunlight of evening
Flows down the terraces of Heysel;
The light of spring caressing
The warm green of the field.

'Juve! Juve!', the simmering cry
In the throat of the youth,
Ignorant of the gathering rage
In the false sunset.

Out of the shadows glint the claws
Of dogs thirsting for flesh,
The feast hot in their nostrils,
Awaiting the hour of madness.

There is no flight from the baying
Of their night hunt;
And the cry of the youth fades
In pain beneath the wall.

His long hair sticky with blood
Across his cheek,
Crimson blood on black and white,
Soaking into the shoulder.

Sing them a Mass of peace.
And wrap them in our shame.
And the game which once we loved,
Broken, we bury with them.

[AUTHOR]

Alan Llwyd

Alan Llwyd (*b.* 1948) was brought up on a farm in Cilan on the Llŷn Peninsula, and graduated in Welsh at Bangor. He worked in a bookshop in Bala, then as an editor for a publishing firm and an editorial officer for the Welsh Joint Education Committee, before settling down in Swansea as full-time editor of *Barddas*, the poetry journal of the *Cerdd Dafod* Society (*cerdd dafod* meaning, roughly, poetic craft). He is a prolific and versatile poet, fluent in the traditional as well as the free metres, and often combining *cynghanedd* with *vers libre*. He was the second poet to win both the Chair and Crown in the same year at the National Eisteddfod on two occasions. His other voluminous contributions include books of criticism, biographies, an autobiography, poetry anthologies, and the screen-play for the film *Hedd Wyn* which was nominated for an Oscar.

The Hawk Above Felindre

Wheeling and wheeling above the woods
the hawk spinning in the invisible
whirlpool of his flight in the thin
sunshine's radiance
on a cold winter morning:
primeval rite,
the rhythmic movements of the hawk's
dance, round and around,
on the lines of his own horizons:
the day stock-still, and his fire-dance
one with the dance of all the planets,
one with the dance of the universe.

Every timorous heart beneath his wide
hovering, underneath his spirallings,
fills with terror and thumps through the silk
of the thin bosom. The world billows
within his wingspan:
animals, creatures and man
whirling about in his eyes,
in the vast vacancy that is the cleft
of his eyes, every living soul
held fast by the dance's motion.

He turns overhead on his axle,
his flight-path around his own
equator: he is the ripple in the middle
of the lake, that spreads
in waves around
the dint of a skipped stone.
The circle widens, widens as he hangs
on wings of fire,
and as he spirals he cuts an enormous
hole in the cosmos,
opens a hole through God's creation,
and through the gap our civilisation collapses,
falls through to its death.

[JPC]

The Bull of Bryncelyn

The geese goosestepping in terror, their hissing peevish from the sedges,
the hens scattering from the yard
helter-skelter like scraps of paper, his clomping from Riffli
resounding in the ears of the bitch, she too, like the hens, by now
crouching from fear of him behind the hay shed,
her heart thumping her ribs, and her blood pounding like a hammer.

They were fleeing from the bull of Bryncelyn
who was tugged on a tether, to be brought to the timid heifer:
a slobbering bull, the treacle trickling from his beard
a rope on his jaw as he struggled, his lustreless pelt
pitch-black, black as the darkest darkness,

the gnats lost in the folds of his double-chin's pillows;
the ring twisting through his nose, and his hooves, in crushing
and ripping up grass, leaving the meadow pockmarked,
while he groaned, grumbled, his breath like mist around him,
as though he were hauling the whole earth like a plough behind him.

His sound in approaching like the sound of troops marching together,
he's a clumsy drunken cohort, a woozy boozy company,
the armour of the months of coldness tight around him,
and the ding of the dung metallic, as if he were a battalion,
two horns like bayonets charging,
and his tail like a lash whipping his legion before it.

He nuzzled the heifer in ropes
of drivel, licking
and lipping her crotch, then hauled himself up to come to grips
with her flesh, snorting noisily in his lust,
the white heifer bending like a fern beneath a ton
of flesh, and the thrustings
of his flesh pressing her lower still:
the bull unsatisfied like a tractor revolving in place,
and the heifer's legs tottering as though the dome
above, in the heavens, had descended upon her,
the whole weight of the universe on flesh, and the flesh weakening,
and the labouring staving in the back,
her backbone on the brink of breaking before the clumsy rapist
freed her from his grip on completing the devilish ritual.

After the nine months,
the womb where he spilled his seed
ripe for birth, and the heifer
moaning in her labour
uttering a gutteral lowing, as the flood, the dam opening,
pushed her first-born in his blood forth from her womb:
a limp calf with his legs wobbling like wheels underneath him,
his wet coat glistening.

And he'd be the fierce beast's heir as his posterity increased.

[JPC]

The Scream: Edvard Munch (1893)

I hear an outcry in art,
a silent shriek across a wrinkled sea,
as the picture shrilly quivers.

The man on the bridge with the cry from his nightmare head's
agony sawing
sharp and cold through our nerves;
a shattered scream of violence and horror
shuddering in the molten landscape,
and loud and clear is the outcry of the white
skull of a head on the darkness of the bridge.

It is the outcry from the scraping
of a nerve with an instrument,
a yellow scream as though the tip of a wire were scraping a nerve
and the scraping of a nerve is the birth of the insuperable agony
of the old century's carcasses:
the red, inescapable birth;
it is a sharp cold cry in giving a new century birth,
and the discord of our anguish and our fears on the tormented strings
of our dim-witted century's shattered nerves.

It is the wail of Passchendaele and the uproar of the Belsens,
the cry of Nagasaki and the Somme;
it is a generation's death-rattle when the soil of France was blood-
        drenched,
and the clamour in the punishment cells;
it is an outcry in the hidden cell,
it is the cry of the black flesh as well
when torn to strips by the long-legged dogs.

With the shrill scream wholly red,
I see the outcry of art.

[JPC]

Our Godless Days

The silent, speechless God; the dead, uninterfering God;
the insubstantial being, the formless spiritual abstraction:

evil has been born in the rough shape of a monster,
and the Deity is not dwelling or strolling amongst us.

We walk, in our absurdity, our spiritual apathy's wasteland,
we grope for the ends of the tape in the den where the brute is lord;
we have tasted the animal's ordure, drinking its slime through the whole
century of worms and maggots that have rotted what's left of the Rood.

Our instruments are our idols, and our ideology's images;
our communion bread's the Machine, and the oil in its belly our wine,
and we hear not, naively clever, our technology's elegy and knell:
the oasis' spring is stagnant, and the soul a parched wilderness.

He hides himself from our presence, in his ancient heaven's far reaches,
with creation bereft of a God, but not bereft of a Devil.

[JPC]

The Welsh Language

Stand above the steep precipice, and cry out into the rift:
she is the peal of thunder in the stillness, the clamour in the cold void;
though the fugitives keep a tight grip on their fraying ropes,
she is the one who saves us from falling into the vast silence.

She is the rain that freshens the earth, she is the beautiful ruby;
the harvest breeze, as it wanders in the wheat and the corn;
she is the gem of light, she is the emerald in the green grass,
she is the barley's rustling, she is the precious sapphire.

It is she saves the people's honour from going astray,
she is the fort against every siege, she guards us from the silent
	cliffside;
she is the rope above the gaping abyss, and against our homestead's
	disorder,
she is the chain constrains us, it is she plaits our lineage together.

If the link break into bits, what destruction will follow? –
There on the precipice the rope is unravelling, strand by strand.

[JPC]

The Moons of Llŷn

(for R S Thomas)

The moon in Llŷn is pregnant,
like a womb on the verge of emptying:
the last quarter is already
spent, and from the bruised womb
language is thrusting itself,
language that isn't language unmaking
the language that has been language to us,
language that has been language to Mynytho,
Llanengan, Llangian, Rhoshirwaun, and Sarn,
and shy villages like Cilan.
The moon in Llŷn is filled with obliteration.

At the zenith of the obliteration's moon you came to Llŷn
as priest in its distress:
through the moons of the ages the first quarter's
zenith already was spent;
neither did you see
its second quarter washing the beach
with monolingual waves.
Your moon is obliterating's moon;
the last quarter's posterity's ebb.

I'm long acquainted with the moons in Llŷn:
in the lingering third quarter
the moon was the moon of creation
in Pen Llŷn to a muddled child:
the Welsh moon above Porth Neigwl
scattering sparks like words
through the pages of the water;
Porth Ceiriad's moon like wax
rubbing yellow against the night,
putting a shine on the golden
beads of stars above Abersoch,
and Bardsey's moon a consecrated
host above the bay's purple altar.

It isn't easy by now
to return to Llŷn: the darkness of a downcast moon
signifies the dying of a lineage,
foretells the end of this land.

If I take a step upon it
in memory, it is Tir na n-Og,
but when I return, come summer, to Llŷn
I am Osian hearing the mournful
music of the language dying in the sea.
Where the language with its chime once graced
my contemporaries' lips,
I am the last wave that breaks
on the beach of our identity.

Your moon is not the moon of creation
but an egg on the brink of hatching
obliteration: the moon in Llŷn
is giving birth, within a fragile
thin shell, to our death,
and the heedless feet of the summer strangers
trample, stamp surlily upon
our churlish elegy on the parchment of the sand.

[JPC]

Chaplin and Others

(from the sequence 'Farewell to a Century')

Heroism wasn't possible any longer
after the Somme and Arras and Passchendaele:
think of all those youngsters who went to war
to test their valour and their strength,
to test their manhood and their confidence.
They joined the Army as volunteers
for a chance to show their country and their sweethearts their courage:
the sturdy young men
who full of assurance swarmed
to the field of battle.

Most of them had no
chance, before their names were put
on a memorial tablet, to prove themselves
on the field of battle:
when they climbed over the wall of the trench
the machine-guns would spit bullets at them,
a shower of bullets harvesting

these boys, like a scythe cutting through a crop,
the swathes of young boys;
two would kill dozens in the mud of the Somme,
a single gun kill scores.

It wasn't an age for heroes.
All the excess of the War
proved that a man was insignificant,
and there came the age of the unheroic hero,
the age of the insignificant man.

The first was Chaplin,
Chaplin, the comical little man
who clowned his way into people's
hearts, making everyone laugh,
during the unhappy years
that followed the Great War.

Chaplin, the comical little man,
Chaplin, the sad little tramp.

Chaplin portrayed a sad little man,
an insignificant little man,
with a cane and a hat and a moustache like Hitler's
(before Hitler became famous, of course).

Chaplin challenged those bigger than himself,
the fat-bellied bully, the man in authority;
and he won all the girls
in spite of always tripping over his legs,
he was sometimes plaintive, he was sometimes cheerful
and he quarreled with everyone and he twirled his cane,
and the little man with his penguin walk
and the way he insisted on crossing people in power
won our hearts.

Chaplin, the comical little man,
Chaplin, the sad little tramp.

And others came after him,
unheroic heroes,
after Chaplin, the comical little man.

Take Heinrich Himmler, for example,
Heinrich, one of the century's heroes;
Heinrich was an insignificant little man,
a short man, a little man,
a mouse of a man, eyeing everyone like a mouse,
behind his little round glasses.

Himmler was an insignificant little clerk,
but he licked his way into favour,
and he became everyone's master,
everyone save Hitler himself,
Himmler, the unfeeling little man,
who disinfected, who cleansed his country
of the filth of the Jew.

Everything was black and white
to Himmler, the uncomplicated man:
he hated the Jews
because they were wholly evil,
but his own lineage
was pure and perfect.

Himmler, the uncomplicated little man,
Himmler, friend of Hitler and Hess.

And Himmler had no compassion:
he could look at his Gestapo
clubbing a man senseless
without giving a fig,
and because Himmler, the short little man,
was much too short, he had to stand on the dead,
walk on a carpet of corpses,
to extend his height.

And others came, others after
Chaplin, the comical little man,
and Himmler, the uncomplicated little man,
Himmler, friend of Hitler and Hess.

[JPC]

305

Gwynn ap Gwilym

Gwynn ap Gwilym (*b.* 1950) is the son of a Nonconformist minister at Machynlleth, and was educated at the University College of North Wales, Bangor, the University College of Ireland, Galway and Wycliffe Hall, Oxford, and spent a period as a lecturer at the University of Ireland in Cork. He has been a Church in Wales rector at Mallwyd, and a lecturer at the United Theological College at Aberystwyth. A winner of the National Eisteddfod Chair, he has published a novel, anthologies of poetry, collections of critical articles, translations from the Irish, as well as his own poetry collections.

Penyberth

'Beauty,' whispered the leaves to the night,
and the night to the moon, and the moon to the wind.
'Beauty,' cried the wind across the moor, –
'There's a fire in Llŷn.'

'Justice,' was the moor's verdict to the rock,
and the rock's to the rain, and the rain's to the sea.
'Justice,' moaned the sea to the strand, –
'There's a fire in Llŷn.'

'That's a crime,' said England to the jurors,
and the jurors to the judge.
'That's a crime,' said the judge, 'and the punishment's harsh
for a fire in Llŷn.'

'Not guilty,' murmured the sun to the dale,
and the dale to the stream, and the stream to the glen.
'Not guilty,' wept the glen to the dew,
'of a fire in Llŷn,'

'A vineyard was placed in my care,' he said, –
' I myself must tend it,
and a generation will rise like a phoenix from the ashes
of the fire in Llŷn.'

[JPC]

The Badger

The sunlit clouds navigated
slowly on the sky's waves;
so quietly they traversed,
trawling their shadows like nets across the hill's brow.
Apart from the sea-faring
of the soundless flowing fleet,
fishing the acres and the evening hours,
no breeze disturbed Bwlch Glyn Mynydd,
and no sound but the murmur of my motor going, going, going
through the mute stillness,
consuming minute and metre,
on one small journey under the great parade.

And he came on strange tread,
with his garbled jerk forcing the car to slow,
rambling from his retreat,
his whole body shaking.
He dragged behind him the long cords
of night's unclean banner,
and with his snout he swept the light from the valley road.

He was Annwn's ensign
routed reluctantly from the burrows of prehistory,
enchanted chieftain in his grey breastplate,
wizard of the ancient wisdom
none of our philosophers possess.

His body defiled the narrow road
between the groves and greenery of Bwlch Glyn Mynydd;
he trod before me on his certain journey,
like some relic from the temples of earth's old gods,
or some corrupt idol pregnant with sin,
and his grossness I could not comprehend.

In my swift vehicle I was Arthur,
hunting light's larcenist,
the old swallower of the sun.

The tribe's old drive was in me
to destroy what it cannot discern.

And the laughing clouds pulled away
slowly to their haven,
dragging us both in their nets
over the brow of the hill.

[GD]

Geraint Jarman

Geraint Jarman (*b.* 1950) was brought up in Cardiff and emerged in the late 60s as an enigmatic and whimsical poetic voice. By the mid-70s, having published two volumes of poetry, he channelled his creative energies into songwriting, and was the lead singer of *Geraint Jarman a'r Cynganeddwyr* (Geraint Jarman and the Harmonisers). Apart from recording several albums he was also instrumental in inspiring the creation of other bands with his independent television company *Criw Byw* (Live Group). He now works in the media industry mainly as a producer and actor, but is still considered the pioneer who shifted the Welsh rock scene into a cosmopolitan and sophisticated area.

Dad and Me

Christ!
the thing
was
hard
to take
mun

like
one minute
I was
making love
tidy like
on the
front room
sofa

and
the next
in comes
Mam
with

her head
under her
arm

shouting

Geraint!
get here
now
quick
Dad wants
to hear
you
say
your poem...

[PF]

The Wood
(a political poem)

Throughout the night the trees paraded
like blind druids across the town.

Their arms were thick with green prayers
and birds watered from their eyes like tears.
Their pink cheeks were damp
above their ragged sheets.

They sang so wailing drunk
as if angels had shit their hair
voices full of hymns like the 'steddfod's pubs.

And in the morning they stood naked in their
bits of gardens trying again to make the wind
rub their bodies with its caressing hands.

But there's no kissing and no licking
not in this world.
Here life runs with poetry
veins are stuffed with words, not with blood.

[PF]

Einir Jones

Einir Jones (*b.* 1950) was born and bred on Anglesey, and educated at the University College of North Wales, Bangor. She now lives with her Nonconformist minister husband in Rhydaman in Carmarthenshire, and teaches at Dyffryn Aman Comprehensive School. She won the National Eisteddfod Crown in 1991.

Shadows of Trees on the Lawn, January

The morning's early rime
gleaming,
shoots of light upon
the grass.

Sun
on the white hills,
the dead leaves
still
beneath the hoarfrost's dust.

The images of the trees
upon the ground.

They slowly creep
fashioning dark
branches and buds
upon the whiteness.

Steadily moving
they rise
along the lawn,
light's shadows fragile
bark and trunk.

They drip, and melt into solid
forms
for moments,

the lights of the drops
winking
where the grass
lay
within the shape
of the forests of their arms.

Gradual extinction
where the brightness was
and the darkness
of branches' shadows,

the lawn now
a barren blankness
under a sold
midday sun.

[JPC]

Ffynnon Grandis

Down under the surface
are the dark wellsprings,
slowly
trickling through rocks,
rising, gradually dripping.

Through the slit, the bubbles of its words
mount higher, rising spitefully
through the clear water.

Patterns
of nothing at all
creating beauty
quietly boasting.

Come high tides, the brine
overflowing the outflow.
And the fount's been choked
by the salt rushes and the wrack.
Time's laver, with no one bothering.

But the living spring
still there,

softly composing poems
beneath the seaweed
and creating strings
of unutterable words
that go slipping down
the empty beach.

[JPC]

Snowdonia after Chernobyl

The clouds of the earth
dissolved.
The heat of lava in the blood.
Hard bonfires
throbbing on the horizon,

and then the relaxing.
Their fires had coldly
taken shape.

Far down the centuries
there's the other melting.
The wind rising
and carrying,
and the rain from a distance washing
the stronghold's seams.

And springtime
tranquilly
descending.

Now
the hills burn blazing hot
but invisibly.
Heart's clicking is hard at it
electronically measuring
the consuming
rage.

A fearsome future
devouring the fruitless acres
in the perilous century,

the hills
on fire again
in the night's blackness.

[JPC]

The Picture

In the old picture
lost in the cubbyhole under the stairs,
worthless,
a moon rises
above the balcony
and two women there,
maybe three,
are reading sewing, reflecting,
I don't remember.

But the moon is like a pearl
in the night's dark
oyster shell,
and the curious light
casts a look upon a world
where I don't exist
and yet...

Perhaps I
am one of the three
sitting there,
as the moon's perfection
is drawn out of
the flesh of the night.

The body's clouds
spitefully hide it
but it's always there,
a white shimmer
in the soft darkness
and a round echo
in my memory's sky.

[JPC]

Cockles

Far from the brine
cockles open
in plastic buckets
and commonplace bowls
when the tide comes in.

On the kitchen table
moments before they're
boiled and eaten,
they respond
to the call of the moon
and the waters' power.

And we,
in hurrying to find a saucepan
big enough,
our ears shut
by ancient wax,
are deaf
to the clear and tranquil call
of the world's turn on its axle.

When the moon moves in the firmament,
and when the wind sighs above the sea,
and when the wave turns midway
we don't know
don't understand
don't feel.

We're not…

[JPC]

Grey
(Nant Ffrancon in the mist)

An old grey goat of a mountain
that's been chewing its cud
for an eternity,

the fleece of the clouds
rain's fur on rocks,
flecks on neck
and flanks,
under its horns' lonely pinnacles,

and the milk of the falls
flowing straight and white
from the teats of the mist,

striking the valley's pitcher,
a perpetual stream
and cold.

[JPC]

Menna Elfyn

Menna Elfyn (*b.* 1951) was brought up in Pontardawe in the Swansea Valley
and Peniel near Carmarthen, where her father was a Nonconformist minister,
and she graduated in Welsh at University College Swansea. Her many books
of poetry include three bilingual volumes: *Eucalyptus: Detholiad o Gerddi /
Selected Poems 1978-1994* from Gomer, and two later collections from Bloodaxe,
Cell Angel (1996) and *Cusan Dyn Dall / Blind Man's Kiss* (2001), and her poems
have been translated into a number of languages. According to Tony Conran,
she is 'the first Welsh poet in fifteen hundred years to make a serious attempt
to have her work known outside Wales', and she has travelled the world for
readings. Apart from poetry, she has written plays, libretti and children's novels.

Cell Angel

Grey cells either side of him
keep safe the bones that hide
for a second their weight of pain

yet weren't the angels mortal,
Greek and Persian soil joyous with vengeance,
the Bible quick with quarrels?

He led me from his cell, this angel, to the hall,
him and me and a grand piano,
the door-keys restless in my hand.

Locked, he began a concert for his patron –
twinkle, twinkle, then one violent tonc –
before failing to ascend the black slopes

an angel on the road, homeless, lost
and the sky drowned in the piano's depths.
How I wonder what you are.

The pause ends the solo. Keys locked sharp
in the black fist of the piano. Discord
an unplayed instrument in his face. Descending

angel and his passionate concerto
turn suddenly to notes reverberating
through this musicless place. To reach for one fine string.

*　　*　　*

I would give quotas on angels,
ban seraphic sopranos
from high-church places where stars play

their easy flutes in gilded choirs
of angelic boys, their voices clean as glass
between marble and echo. God's no more there

than here, in the angel cell
where chords ring without descant
where I rise to my feet of clay to applaud

encore to the dream of a cell angel
that he might fly bodiless
through walls, without shadow, light

winged to the great cathedral.
But behind this door the boy-gangs box
laughing through a chink in the brow of glass.

And for every Michael, Gabriel, Raphael,
there's a cell to keep him fallen
and the keeper of keys
is only a love song. A god without power to unlock.

[GC]

Driver

*(from a sequence of poems in memory of Gwyn A. Williams [1925-1995],
historian and people's remembrancer)*

> *'I was 54 yesterday. Everything I now do is a race against
> the undertaker. I can't waste any more time.'*
>   – GWYN A. WILLIAMS

Dear driver, you made every journey a joy ride
between deep stream and canyon. Everything a challenge
and the metal jumping round you…

assault on accelerator, squabble with brakes, friction
between lane and bushes. Every creature in flight
hearing you paddle gears to old age.

Moon retired to her convent, to her rosaries of grief
because you were highwayman every acre of the way,
a steel bull on the dogmas of tarmac.

Windscreen quaked, wiper blinked like an eyelid
to and fro, obedient to its thankless destiny –
more often than not, you made the hedge partner

closed with it – how humble the boundary dyke –
to avoid clash and crack of the stunned cars
that were, unwillingly, coming round you. A hair's breadth,

a labyrinth, between collision and earth. You diverted
every other helm; wheels scattered to exile,
slid on the black ice of your storm. Your lights flashed –

red ones always – delinquent, skidding, spinning –
your car, like a curfew of fireworks for creatures,
every night took part in a mountain rally.

But there's another screen shut fast tonight;
prostrate and battered, nothing thrills through him;
Wales has one less rash driver through the ages.

And you've gone on that last fine journey
through the Imagination's Portal, uncursingly quiet,
on the main road, stitch by stitch, in a spotless carriage,
silks all round you! A curtained limousine

driven so discreetly, so with the grain – safely –
never crossing white lines, or cutting a corner.

[TC]

The Theology of Hair
(from the sequence 'Secrets')

I came before you with simple plaits,
a long-legged maid, a lass who couldn't care less
that her sheaves were all bound up with ribbons,
for wasn't the hair on my head like the hair which foamed

over the hard pew-back with a rustle like rivers,
drops shivering as it arced and fell
over the communion shelf, and I ached to touch it,
to twine it in patterns, to fill up that hour by reaching out to a girlish
        wonder.

It made me think of summers full of imaginary ponies
galloping after me, taking my breath away
as I cantered over the hills, and the banditti-like bangs
outlawed their way over my cheeks. There were arguments,

but I loved my hair's energy. Golden moss
like maidenhair stroked my skin, longing to escape
and sometimes, obediently, regally, I would tease
a kiss-curl like honeysuckle over one cheek.

Why that fate for it? To this day, youth loves
the life-force of hair, the way it kinks a little.
Was it the secret forests in it which fuddled the ones above?
They called it a dark thicket.

318

And yet, O Holy Spirit, didn't you give us the gift
of praising it, this headful of hair. This full crown, these tresses,
to be prettily dressed? What harm could there be
in this crinkly, kissable harvest? They imagined it

tumbling over naked backs, charging desire. But cropping
– a full stop to lust's sentence? Locks tied back from breasts.
To leash passion, there was a hair-wreck.
I washed up on a deserted and sensuous strand.

[EaH]

Couplings

Life is a house in ruins. And we mean to fix it up
and make it snug. With our hands we knock it into shape

to the very top. Till beneath this we fasten a roofbeam
that will watch the coming and going of our skyless life,

two crooked segments. They are fitted together,
timbers in concord. Smooth beams, and wide.

Two in touch. That's the craft we nurture in folding
doubled flesh on a frame. Conjoining the smooth couplings

that sometimes arch into one. Aslant above a cold world,
hollow wood wafting passion. Then stock still for a time.

And how clear-cut the roof, creaking love at times,
as it chides the worm to keep off and await its turn.

[JPC]

Nothing but Curves
(having read about the underwear industry)

1

How wonderful the courtesan clothes
of our imagination. Diaphanous, flowing, they droop
over heavy counterpanes at the foot of the bed.

Having unlaced the memory
of grandmother's corsets blushing at me
– hanging ribs, like a human abattoir –

silky girls come to mind:
sliding in on memory's watercoloured canvas
– frameless, without hook or eye to hold them,

or a flannel hairshirt to flay and squeeze them,
no underwire to uplift them
to yet-unfettered heights.

The breast is the golden globe, whispering suggestions
to ruffled organza drifts,
serenely lanolined liberty bodices.

These things are full of calm,
their frail ribbons liberate
the motherland of the self,

making country a homeland all to herself:
where a woman is free of her pressure;
her self a blank sheet between her own hands.

2

– but by fluorescent light – this is hydraulics,
refined by forensic scientists, cantilevering
their brand-new way of getting

the rounded breast into bed. This is a lode to be mined:
thirty sections origami together
to create the other, the perfect orb.

Look. And you'll see that the stars of the screen
lie when they say they have hidden secrets:
their breasts push their facelifts up to their chins

and the body politic spurs on the scuba divers
as they bounce the buoys down in the bay.
There's no future these days in swimming alone.

3

'Nothing but curves' crows the ad –
but I return, barefoot, to the dark ages
to peer at a woman who stands in half-darkness

opening a hook and eye,
placing them in a drawer where they won't be disturbed
before slipping out of her soft fleece

by the candle's eye. Climbing the mattress
she slips into her fold, closing
with a 'good night' the gap
between herself and the bottomless pit
by sleeping on her front with scripture in mind,

putting tongue and flesh safe by for a while.

The night is a sinless sarcophagus –
rasping, hard like a blind man's kiss.

[EaH]

Rice Papers
(for Trinh, my interpreter in Vietnam)

I can see her now, gorging herself,
or gratefully picking at her teeth

with a splint, her mouth perhaps wide
with declaration, 'This is the best place

of its kind in the whole of Vietnam.'
And I'd ask in all innocence,

'How many times have you eaten here before?'
And always she'd say, 'This is the first,'

as she reached for a flaccid wad of dong.
She was my host, my voice,

my chancellor, my maid.
'Too expensive to eat in places like this

except with a foreigner paying.'
Then, through ginger, hoisin and Cha Gio,

all the flavours of the world on her dripping lips,
she'd loose a knotted, sickly laugh:

'You foreigners, so funny.'
And with tongue in cheek

I'd thank her kindly, as at it she went
with talons ten,

till not a smear bedimmed each gleaming bowl:
that I could keep her in restaurants

was as nourishing as any menu's boon.
And that's when she served up for me

the vicious war and how it robbed them
of their daily rice:

bread was their lot, as they starved
for their luxurious herbs – bone-dry baguettes.

The rest of the trip, with that hunger in mind,
I dined on the sight of her feasting for me.

[NJ]

Broadway Morning

In hurly burly Broadway
anticipation is the morning's name,
the breath of the city on glass,
lip on a straw
sipping the pitcher of the world.

I sing at the sight of the sky's skin,
a bowl of sharon tempting us
to the orchards of praise.

I set out in joy to my usual place,
here, nowhere at all,
between 47th Street
and 48th Street
where north and south meet
and west greets east
to share a cup of the day.

It'll be *'bore da'* of welcome
from the mouth of the Iraqi,
smiles succulent as olive
in early morning joy.
Then the answer in clumsy Arabic,
'thank you' over a cloud of coffee,
and the sound's thick scum
is beside me like a fury of swans.

I'll watch the sky again
holding human windows in its arms,
grateful to the belated city,
my homeground early with summer.
So we give and receive
the world's blessings in a cup,
till we're caught out, estranged.

Every eager morning it's easy
to believe that life's
the opening lines of a good story.
But I'm falling into ad-language,
knowing too well
of the lure of east to west,
that one slip of the tongue
can score the pages of flesh.

I sing, cut free from easy greeting,
that the firmament isn't an apricot sky overhead
but it comes to me, touching the ground.

[GC]

Siôn Eirian

Siôn Eirian (*b.* 1954) is the son of the poet Eirian Davies, and spent his forma-
tive years in Mold in north-east Wales, before graduating in Philosophy at
Aberystwyth. In 1978 he won the Crown at the National Eisteddfod. He is
now a full-time writer who has published a novel and one volume of poetry,
but writes mainly for the theatre and television, in both Welsh and English.

The Pain

my pain is not a generation's pain
nor a nation's pain:
it's a unique pain
like the symphony a lark leaves
in patterns over an empty sky
and its final note
like some arrow aimed at nothing.

who was it said the images of great wars
had flayed the conscience of my generation?
who was it said that Belsen and Buchenwald
were razor wire through every mind?
they're just stories.
okay, i sang about bayonets and napalm sweats
but singing for a Vietcong victory
was like supporting Cardiff City.

my own Belsen lies
under the lid of my skull
and the napalm burst over my soul
is simply living with the truth.

[RM]

My Dad versus Ginsberg

when I think that Allen Ginsberg (b. 1926)
is forty-eight years old this year,
only a little younger than my father,

i remember his beard

i remember his furious music

i remember a poet who himself has become a muse,
a daring prophet,

and between him and my respectable father from Wales,
the conservative, the predictable craftsman,

there's an ocean.

[RM]

Adolescent Experiences
(four poems from a sequence of nine)

Learning

i'm watching old films
about the sins of the fathers:

Hiroshima –
flesh melting and pouring
through the mind of a generation:
all that incinerated skin
like matches held up to the past.

pictures of Major Eatherly going crazy;
and his only reward
a decent pension and a nervous breakdown.

another film, showing
two lovers in their wet dreams:
flames sucking them off
until their double passion
is a single ghost.

I see them wake in the morning
and through the knots of their bodies
whisper together in Japanese
Hiroshima, Mon Amour.

turning away from the phoney screen
i stare in the mirror.

before sleep i read poetry
searching for the real me.
escape lies in the anarchy
of those pissed off English artists
instead of the small print regulations
of Welsh language craft.

so i walk in the shadow of Anfield
listening to the Kop sighing,
seeing the young Liverpool poets,
with fingers bloodied
from plucking out music
on the steel wires of their city.

there are things
we have never had words for
in Wales...

and every night before i sleep
instead of trusting myself to Jesus
i listen to John Peel on the radio
and Sounds of the Sixties.

a young stud
feeling the fire under his feet,
dismissing what he already knows
and heading for the exit.

Conquest

listen, i'm coming to get you,
roaring through the night's suburbs
on a Harley Davidson '74,
arriving in greasy black leathers
and stinking of that unholy world beyond.

there are stains of blood and Newcastle Brown
across my jacket
and studs that spell out verses from the Day of Judgement
and Wild Welshmen, and Eat the Rich, and your name.

and in your father's consecrated house
I fuck you on the best bed's quilt,
my filthy fingers kneading blood from your back.

it won't be long until you discover
that we are here to test every element,
or so says your fingernails' thrilling language across my scalp.

because isn't this the raw politic
that has vanished from our country?
invoke the body's anarchy
and we can stride like gods under the stars.

you're helping me live again,
your body's shining gutters of sweat
invite the mad ride
of our journey to that continent
spelt terra incognito on this civilisation's maps.

An Englishwoman

there's sanity in your scissored hair
and your measured clothes
and your winning smile.

your halves of lager
never drip on to your thighs
and your white armpits
don't even sweat when we fuck.

although your words are geometrical
your language is a shining hemisphere.

now there you lie, smiling up from the pillow,
and under its lingerie
your body the shape of a sacrament.

i go crazy sometimes
but never with you,
you are blameless as new laundry,
hardly knowing what it's like to lose control.

but sometimes I see madness
spit its oaths out of your eyes.
there's no ending to your appetite
once the bedroom door is closed.

at times like that
the only thing that works
is committing yourself
to my dark asylum.

Endsong

hands in a thorn bush
searching for a cricket ball
discover a blackbird's slick corpse.

i watch an old man cut his grass
and polish up the square of his lawn.
and i ask, how can dreams wither to this.

the streets of the city
are sombre for Sunday.
i'm buried under
a strata of grey geology.

like Christ in the desert
i have brought myself here
to ask questions and then refuse the answers,
a bastard messiah
who knows there is no god and no heaven.

i stagger sated
around the party of being young
and lie with the smoke in its poisonous vigils.

i saw my friends with their wrists slashed
and their blood dripping on blinded eyes
and their wounds smiling out of our sleep.

here, back with the living
i spend my time against bare walls
trapped in somebody else's civilisation.

a young prince
grows old
rattling bars
seeking a lost birdsong.

[RM]

Carmel Gahan

Carmel Gahan (*b.* 1954) is an Irishwoman born in Cork and educated at University College, Dublin. She married the poet Meirion Pennar, learnt Welsh and settled in Wales. She is now a business management consultant, and lives in Swansea. Her only collection of poems, *Lodes Fach Neis* ('Nice Little Lass'), projected a far from "nice" female image.

asking for it

you see them
erect in the distance,
innocent enough
during the day
but when night's on us
in some narrow thoroughfare
in the city
in the country
Wales is on her back
with an Englishman's tool
without any doubt
stuck up her

and if she screams
nobody hears
and even if they did
they would turn their heads
men and women alike
as they went past

in the courts
the description will be
that it's classic rape
'because a bottle couldn't do the job'
and conspiring still
the men will say
with a smile
that surely she
was gagging for it
while pitiless
in the gallery
women will look down

and they'll believe
that she was asking for it
asking for it

[RM]

Huw Jones

Huw Jones (*b.* 1955) was brought up in Welshpool, Montgomeryshire, and
graduated in Theology at Aberystwyth. He has been a secondary school teacher,
and later a Welsh tutor in the Department of Continuing Education at Bangor.
He taught in Botswana and Zimbabwe, but now lives and works in Salford. He
writes in Welsh and English, and has published volumes in both languages, as
well as one bilingual volume.

Mannyelanong
(where vultures defecate)

You visit our colony each year,
binoculars and zoom-lenses glinting below,
monkey up rock to poke our nests,
ring our chicks.

For centuries we have scoured the lands,
circled cattle-posts,
returning over Otse's tin roofs
to perch where wing and shadow meet.
We are poisoned
by goat meat left for jackals,
electrocuted on high-tension masts.
To find a carcass
we fly deeper into the desert –
when one of us descends
others close in.
We are scavengers of your dreams.

Yet, nothing compares to the rapacity
of your own species –
B52 bombers returning to base,
Desert Storm your latest video game.

You are dots between boulder and Bottle Bar,
this cliff-face, white with our droppings,
a mirror of your own survival.

[AUTHOR]

Geraint Løvgreen

Geraint Løvgreen (*b.* 1955) was born in Rosset in north-east Wales and was educated at schools in Wrexham and at the University of Wales Aberystwyth. While a student at Aberystwyth he made a name for himself as a composer and writer of satirical and political songs which he performed himself as well as with a band which he later formed called *Geraint Løvgreen a'r Enw Da* (Geraint Løvgreen and the Good Name). He is a regular perfomer and presenter of his work on various radio and TV programmes, and tours with his band or with other poets. His only volume of poetry to date is *Holl Stwff Geraint Løvgreen* (1997). His record albums include *Os Mêts...Mêts, Be Ddigwyddodd i Bulgaria* and *Geraint Løvgreen a'r Enw Da 1981-1998*.

The First Day

On that first day in history,
unless it's my mistake,
God created light, oh yeah,
then took a well-earned break.

Nothing else did God create
on that first ever day:
no weeds, no trees, no animals,
no water, stars or hay.

Okay, so God created light
but who was here to see it?
No one, so on the dresser
in a jar is where God put it.

God then sat on the sofa
to admire her masterpiece;
she really was exhausted –
making light was quite a feat.

She knew that when tomorrow came
she'd do some more creating,
but for tonight, she'd take a rest;
so she went back to her knitting.

[AUTHOR]

Life's Dovey Junctions

Life is just a journey, someone told me long ago,
well, I've been in Dovey Junction loads of times if that is so.
I've stood there hopefully in case a train comes down the track
to take me on from here, or take me back.

In life's Dovey Junctions you can wait and wait in vain,
and though everyone is very nice, you still won't see a train,
but just as hope is fading an express comes into view,
and you'd better pick your bags up right on cue.

I hit that Dovey Junction way back in '79,
on a dismal Friday morning, there were leaves along the line,
I slept there on the platform, I missed a train or three,
before long there was no one left but me.

From life's Dovey Junctions there is no escape, no way;
there's some who've been here for so long their hair is turning grey
but you get a lot less noise and smoke, in winter, spring or fall,
life's Dovey Junctions aren't so bad at all.

Life's Dovey Junctions are what keep us on the rails
despite the machinations of Plaid Cymru / Party of Wales,
old Labour turns New Labour in the politicians' game,
but life's Dovey Junctions always stay the same.

I like to go to Wrexham, to stand up on the Kop,
it isn't unforgettable, in fact it's not much cop,
but there you'll see us standing, young and old, out in the rain,
and somehow never quite catching that train.

Life's Dovey Junctions, here and there along the way,
they're islands of quiet solitude to pass the time away,
some people take the fast trains to avoid them, but not me:
life's Dovey Junctions are the place to be.

Of all the places in the world, life's Junctions are the best;
instead of moving, moving all the time, just take a rest;
in life's Dovey Junctions you can stop, enjoy the view,
but don't miss that last connection, whatever you do.

[AUTHOR]

Mihangel Morgan

Mihangel Morgan (*b.* 1955) is a native of Aberdare in the Cynon Valley of south
Wales. He first trained as a calligrapher, and then graduated in Welsh at Abery-
stwyth, where he also did his doctorate on the work of the dramatist John Gwilym
Jones. He now lectures at Aberystwyth. His novels and short stories have been highly
acclaimed as examples of post-modernist fiction, and have been widely translated.
Both his poetry and prose challenge fossilised attitudes, and his virulent opposition
to religion, and his gay sensibility bring a welcome freshness to Welsh literature.

Unidentified Flying Object on an Errand of Love

One cold and dismal night,
The fomenting cauldron of a troubled mind
Bubbling beneath his brow,
Emlyn went for an aimless stroll.

By chance,
He came upon the jet prairie of the park –
The night a layer of sleep,
The town a dark tomb.

The quietness possessed him,
The silence spread through him.
Enchanted by the night
He had an encounter of the Third Kind.

A flashy, lightspeed-busting UFO!

'Dream Saucer,' he blurted out,
'You came as a chariot of hope
You shot past the moon –
Radiant machine – as swift
As an idea – an arrow through Infinity
and the Milky Way.
You bade farewell to Venus

Scowling monsters
And planets fair and foul.

Great wingèd Saucer
Flying vessel
Unidentified Flying Object.
You are both gold and silver
And your motion silky and rapid.

O, Flashy, lightspeed-busting Saucer!

'Go now,' said Emlyn
'To my secret love, my heart's desire
To where he dwells in the city,
And give him a message –
My passion burns
It is he who is my dream
He who fills my thoughts
I have spun off my axis
I have become sickly
I swoon in my enfeebled state
As I think upon his face
Beyond compare –

'He lives in a garret
A hovel, perhaps,
There are many perils,
Criminals and policemen,
Thieves and murderers,
Who threaten the boy,
Ruins totter around him,
Whores and suspicious guys,
Cross-winds
The occasional drunk
And rampaging youths
And speeding cars
With careless drivers
And the worst danger – the religious types!

'Oh unknown flying object', implored Emlyn,
'Fly like a bird
Happy lightship
One thing I ask –
Convey my love to the sweet boy.'

Conversation

'I've got a talking chair.'

'I haven't heard a chair talk in years.'

'Come and have a chat with her. Her chair is very clear.'

'I'm not really fluent in chair – I can understand it OK but I can't speak chair as well as I do table.'

'I haven't got any talking tables.'

'The cupboard next door has learnt table as a second language.'

'Chair and cupboard are very similar.'

'Door is much the same too.'

'But door's a dead language.'

'It's a classical language like window – there's only a few left who
     speak it.'

'But the mirror language is spreading throughout the room.'

'These mirrors have got no roots.'

'Before long there'll be mirrors everywhere. On the floor, on the ceiling,
     even on the chairs.
You won't hear a word of chair after that.'

[MD]

Red High-heeled Shoes

High-heeled shoes
High
Red
New
Shiny
Toes squeezed into the little shoe
Squeezed to a pencil point
Forcing
A tippy-toed gait –
Walking on
Long
Nails –

Walking on
Tenterhooks –
Naked
Legs
Straight
Like
Upright
Poles.

High-heeled shoes
High
Red
Not made for walking
On pastures green
Nor dusty sidewalks
Nor arid tracks
Nor hard roads
But on soft
Human
Skin
Shoes made to draw blood
And for feet
That are not in chains.

High-heeled shoes
High
Red
Giving pleasure
To the welcoming living carpet
Beneath their tread

High-heeled shoes
High
Red
New
Shiny

The little man felt as a giant
A metamorphosis takes place
He is a new man, because
In the shoes
He is free.

[MD]

The Legend of the Baker and Her Daughter

When I 'ear my daughter scream in the night
I remember about our Saviour
And think
'Can He see 'er now?
Shooting to the ground
To kill the mice and rats?'

And I do rememberin' that mornin'
When Our Saviour came
To our bakery
And asked for bread.
I saw who it was straight off
And so I got 'old of a lump of dough
An' started 'neadin' it
To make bread for our Lord.

'Mam!' says my daughter,
'What on earth are you doin'?
Givin' all that dough to a stranger
Dressed in rags!
Can't you see, he ain't nothin' but a beggar?
'E'll just do a runner without payin' now.
But he's gotta pay like everyone else
We're poor enough as it is, don't forget.'

At that
The Meek and Mild throws a wobbler
And like a magician, his eyes all flashin' red like,
He did put a spell on my daughter where she stood
And turned 'er into an owl.

There's funny his anger was
Until he said
'Man does not live by bread alone'.

[MD]

Myrddin ap Dafydd

Myrddin ap Dafydd (*b.* 1956) was born in Llanrwst in Denbighshire, and graduated in Welsh at Aberystwyth. In 1980 he established his own press and publishing house, Gwasg Carreg Gwalch, which publishes a variety of materials, mainly in Welsh, including plays, poetry, folklore, novels and books of local interest. He himself is a great believer in making poetry accessible, and enjoys participating in live performances of poetry. Satire and humour intermingle with an underlying seriousness in most of his work. He has also written a great deal of poetry for children. He won the National Eisteddfod Chair in 1990 and 2002.

'A Language Is Only Words'
(*– Dafydd Elis Thomas*)

The mountain is only a moorland,
the rock is only a stone.

I shan't see the skull in the crags of Tryfan
nor in the peat the bones of names
nor high rings on fairy pasture
or hoof-prints from Catraeth in the reeds.
I shan't see the 'moon above the valley'.
White eagles won't come here to nest.

I shan't hear its depths sound in spring water
nor the twisting wind on the nape of the thorn.
There aren't any legends rising from lakes
nor hopelessness out of the marsh.
Neither shall I hear the owl in Cowlyd.

I shan't think of pipe notes in the sedges;
I shan't remember the tune lamenting a lark;
I'll not be reminded of tears by the name of a river.
Nor think of how giants have walked in this place,
raised walls, enclosed a homestead.

No, bogs don't sprout feathers.
There's no echo from the stone.
The mountain is only moorland.
Language is nothing but words.

[TC]

The Poet's Insurance Risk

Yes, it would be good to have boxes
on the car application form.
Tick which is applicable:
Do you hold a strict-metre licence?
YES.   NO.

I think a few prize bards
would find it tough living on their premium,
and one or two old rhymesters
would be hard pushed to get above
fire and theft, third party, poetry.

Because a poet's not fit
to be freed on the road,
travelling six stanzas an hour
in a thirty-syllable speed zone.

Scant grasp of the Highway Code,
worse record on the road than the *eisteddfod*;
more scared of the score in the contest
than concerned with his licence,
thinks more of the intricate lyric
than his weaving wheels,
tapping a rap on the windscreen,
keeping in mind all lines
but the white line.

He cuts corners between couplets,
sings for *Sain* on the Traws stretch.

His head in his pocket,
he pens a line in the snackbar lay-by.
He wavers as he wanders,
especially on long-haul.

He only spots a wall when he reaches a full stop
turning a metaphor on two wheels,
a danger to life at crossroads and connections,
and there he is
on imagination's heights
without brake-pads.

More often than driving under the influence
of John Morris-Jones' manual of metrics,
out of breath, short of wit,
one lemon over the limit,
on a journey to Mars,
mad, muddled, befuddled,
cruising with the muse
with a silly grin driving
drunk on rhyme and rhythm,
in his cups on couplets
and he won't bite his poet's tongue
if he's stopped by a cop.

But he packs a lot in a small space
as he parks in the High Street,
no middle-of-the-road song
is the ballad of the bard with a bite
in his belly and nobody
gambles on amber,
he doesn't see red, only the green light,
his everything evergreen.

[GC]

Gwenllian

(Llywelyn's only daughter, exiled all her life in captivity)

Sands do not weep on Lafan,
Even small pebbles are dumb.
Like a dead couple, the far pull
Of the waves has no language
For the ear. The clay's quiet.
A graveyard's Menai water.

No smile, no frown in Gwynedd,
No land for the ivy crown,
Neither white crests on the strait
Nor rock to catch its seashells –
No wailing of a baby
Known, no talk, no lullaby.

She, mothlike, this horizon's
Orphan, has no claim on land;
Uncradled are her words,
Homeless her entreaty.
She's no tomorrow, poor love –
Her nightmares are unspoken.

Behind her, like a shawl, here
Merciless is the silence.
There's no bosom gives comfort
At night for a lifetime's pain.
In her necessity her nation
Does not hear a single sigh.

But as I mourn, Lafan tide
In the brine's cry through shingle
Swells in flood, calls to her name
Praise, after all the malice –
And for that, from her ebbtide,
Over Menai sands she'll come.

[TC]

The War Cabinet

*(It was a pathetic piece of news during the Gulf War, but I confess to
cracking a smile on hearing a report of the behaviour of the war cabinet
in London when the IRA attacked their building. There they were, thou-
sands of miles away from the battlefield, planning the deaths of boys,
and they were frightened for their lives when they heard a bang in the
back yard. In a twinkling, the entire cabinet scuttled under the table.)*

Our ministers were a heroic faction,
Packing men off to the thick of the action.

Calling for sacrifice, calling for blood –
They rose up in war but not one of them stood.

It's great to be brave from a Whitehall pew
And to be an armchair general too.

It's easy to quantify smashed heads and thighs
When you won't see the blood in your brother's eyes;

To ask boys to die alongside their mates
And attend to the paperwork this creates;

To be at the front some noisy November
In red-poppied grief when people remember.

But they're on their arses now under the table –
For briefly hell has invaded their stable.

[RP]

Siôn Aled

Siôn Aled (*b.* 1957) was born at Bangor, and graduated in Welsh at Aberystwyth. He has been serving in the Christian ministry in various capacities, including a period as a minister in Melbourne, Australia. He won the Crown at the National Eisteddfod in 1981, and has published two volumes of poetry.

Weather Forecast

In Dublin
the rain falls softly,
lest it should disturb the captivity
of the lake in the concrete of the Garden.

In Dublin
the rain falls silently,
lest it should echo the violence
in the Post Office hall.

In Dublin
the rain falls warmly,
lest it should chill the grey veins
of a nation's heart.

In Dublin
the rain falls slowly,
lest it should empty the clouds
before they reach Wales tomorrow.

(The Memorial Garden, Dublin, May 1980)

[GD]

Tracks of Longing

If I had your smile awaiting me,
the journey would be longer
and the thrill of standing again
on the same land as you
would shake my heart.

If I had your smile awaiting me,
the train would recite, across the flat fields of Europe,
the syllables of your name.

If I had your smile awaiting me,
I would whisper your name to myself
amid the noisy queues
of unwilling returnees
and passionate foreign couples,
and would smile with self-satisfaction.

Or if I had your frown awaiting me,
reproaching me for failing to send a card,
or failing to return by the appointed day,
the trivial little complaints
that prove true love,
I would laugh at us both.

But I have nothing of you,
only the turn of your head
on the other side of the street
ashamed of ever having accepted me.
And foolish you were;
and I was more foolish yet,

captive to a longing across a thousand miles
as though only a street-breadth away.

(Ost-West Expres Poznan-Oostende, April 1981)

[GD]

Sunset Over Llŷn
(from Llandanwg)

The day assimilating to night
and the bloodstained gloom like Catraeth's field.

One day more,
and how many fewer
speak the language of Gwrtheyrn?

The words of romance are powerless
in the twillight of the black figures.

Night,
do not be gentle,
be terrifying, hag-ridden;
chill us
to the marrow of our fear.
Be Hell,
with your hounds scratching our doors.

Let the teeth of Yr Eifl still bite the darkness
and the waves of Porth Neigwl torment the silence.

Let there be sleeplessness in Nefyn
and disquiet in the woods of Cefnamlwch.

Let our fever seethe
in the bitterness of the last hours.

Parishes of Llŷn's heartland,
fear the darkness,
and disdain
the peace of an easy death.

[GD]

Dylan Iorwerth

Dylan Iorwerth (*b.* 1957) was born in Dolgellau and brought up in Waun-fawr near Caernarfon. He graduated in English and History at Aberystwyth, worked on the *Wrexham Leader* in north Wales and, for three years, was political correspondent for BBC Cymru, based at Westminster. He helped to establish the first-ever Welsh-language Sunday newspaper, *Sulyn*, which experimented with colloquial language but was unfortunately short-lived. In 1988, he helped set up the popular weekly magazine *Golwg*, of which he was editor for several years before becoming editorial director of *Golwg Cyf.*, which specialises in magazines, copywriting and design. He has edited volumes of journalism but, although proficient in the free and the strict metres, he had not written seriously as a poet until he won the Crown at the National Eisteddfod in 2000. He now lives at Llanwnnen in Ceredigion.

Sand

(A selection from a sequence of poems in remembrance of Dafydd Vernon Jones who died of cancer on April 12, 1999, aged 48.)

> *To remember Dafydd and Mayday holidays*

That first time;
the children a stream of colour
down the clifftop path
and a fresh new page of sand
waiting for feet to write stories.

Druidstone

Once a year
the sun would swing on its axis
to its ordained place.

A shaft of light
would slip past the blue of Preseli
over mysterious islands
to the place where sand is magic;
down between monolith cliffs
to an altar-beach.

And we were always drawn there
to our plot at the end of the earth.

Garden

There was a garden
and a tablecloth lawn
where picnics opened like flowers.

Around it, four walls
wrapping up the sun
like a present to be opened each year.

New Bottom

There's always a joke
that runs on from year to year.
And no joke is a joke
without bottoms.

Children aren't kids without punching
and, on the gorse-edged path,
the thought of an adult's bottom
filled the air with giggles.

'Ouch, ouch, ouch!'
You made a drama of shouting.
'I need a new bottom now!'

And there,
as gulls wheeled a black hole in the sky
and the sun spread stars in the wet sand,
the miracle cure happened.

A new bottom.
And the children were believers.

Horses

Even footballers had to stop,
when the horses came.
Watching the flurry of hooves in the spray
and listening to drumbeats of sand
chasing but never catching.

Then the game re-starts –
a ball spins like the earth
and Pelé, Eusebio and Best
live again in fathers' eyes.

Where the girls had been dancing
where Rhiannon's seabirds circled,
fairies had left their footprints.

The House of Teletubbies

Only an Englishman
would put up a house
by placing it underground.

It appeared suddenly,
a low cromlech,
like a beast from a primeval future
that crawled up from the beach.

'The Teletubbies' house!'
Six Dipsies sidled closer…
a half-turn and a peck…
then steps were strides
and droplet words a flood.
The baby in the sun was smiling.

All day, the house never moved;
it was only the teletubbies who vanished
to find the brand new wonder
of the waterfall's rainbow
and to follow the zig-zag footsteps
of waves.

But the beast remained –
one narrow window watching
under its eyelid of grass.
Watching,
ready to pounce.

Dafydd

You were caught for ever
in May's lens.
A flash of eyes,
crinkle hair,
a raised thumb,
a smile.

Three families' worth of children,
a weaving chorus about you,
the hero caught
in a beam of sun,

like a fly
under the blade of a knife.

Surf

Six little ones fighting the wind down the path
as brave as Gladiators,
as stooping as old men.

The sea was a cannon of foam
as if God had set out a fairground
for children from the land of soap.

But we could see drifting snow
on a desert of sand
as strange as a coffin in April.

Sea

Everyone knows
how cruel the sea can be.

You wrote your name meticulously on the beach
but it came by
with its scouring cloth.

Our photos of you are jetsam at high tide
the salt has gnawed at their edges
and burnt out holes in their centres.

But when feet start chattering again
and when the words start weaving,
rainbow rings
will sundance in the water.
And you'll be there,
thumb upraised.

[AUTHOR]

Iwan Llwyd

Iwan Llwyd (*b.* 1957) was brought up in Tal-y-bont, Conwy and Bangor, and graduated in Welsh at Aberystwyth. He has worked for Cenad, a public relations company based in Caernarfon, but is now self-employed. A member of the group *Steve Eaves a'i Driawd* (Steve Eaves and his Trio), he travels around Wales to give musical performances, much influenced by blues and jazz, and he has also participated in a number of poetry tours, often reading poems in the informal atmosphere of pubs. He has also travelled widely, reading his poems to audiences as far afield as Latin America, the United States and Canada. His poetry has also been performed on television, notably in the series *Eldorado*, in the company of his friend Twm Morys. He won the National Eisteddfod Crown in 1990.

Sure, you can ask me a personal question
(*'Sure you can ask me a personal question'* – *Diane Burns*)

How's it going?
  No, I'm not an Irishman.
No, not a Scandinavian.
  No, I'm a Welshman, a Welsh-speaking Welshman.
No, not from the Netherlands.
  No, not from Cumbria.
No, not from Cornwall.
  No, not an Englishman.
No, we're not extinct.
  Yes, a Welshman.
Oh?
  So that's where you got that accent.
Your great-great grandmother, huh?
  A Welsh princess, huh?
Hair like Nia Ben Aur?

Let me guess. From Anglesey?
Oh, so you had a friend who was a Welshman?
As close as that?
Oh, so you had a lover who was a Welshman?
As tight as that?
Oh, so you had a maid who was from Wales?
As much as that?
Yes, it was terrible what you did to us.
It's very kind of you to apologise.
No, I don't know where you can get leek soup.
No, I don't know where you can get Welsh cloth dirt cheap.
No, I didn't make this, I bought it in Next.
Thank you, I like your hair as well.
No, I don't know if the Edge is a real Welshman.
No, I didn't write *cynghanedd* before breakfast.
No, I can't sing *cerdd dant*.
No, I'm not in a male voice choir.
I never played rugby or worked in a coal mine.
Yeah, uh-huh, the muse.
Uh-huh, Yeah. The muse. Uh-huh. Mother
Earth. Yeah. Uh-huh. The muse.
No, I didn't do a degree in the works of Dylan Thomas.
Yes, some of us do drink too much.
Some of us can't drink enough.
This isn't a minority face.
It's my face.

[GD]

No Man's Land

Night never falls here,
you cannot see the stars
above Virgin and the St David's Centre neon signs,
above the plastic streets that freeze the marrow:

and someone is trying to sleep
under the automatic bank machine,
which pours its generous pieces of paper
in a heap on the sleeping youth:

and it's cold tonight in no man's land,
cold this close to the front,
where a man is alone as he turns for home,
and home is as far away as ever:

it's a weather of plague rats and thieves,
as the beggar begs for a shilling,
and the wind from the East cuts like a scythe
as you turn up the collar of your coat:

and it's cold tonight in no man's land,
cold this close to the front
where a man is alone as he turns for home,
and home is as far away as ever:

you turn into a tavern to seek comfort,
but the conversation is as synthetic as the music
as the great yellow night awaits you
in the company of cats and dogs:

and it's cold tonight in no man's land,
cold this close to the front,
where a man is alone as he turns for home,
and home is as far away as ever.

[AUTHOR]

The Disappeared

Augustin Ramirez (6.6.88)

On Sunday morning he'd be there
in the Barrio San Telmo
offering an improvised sketch
for twenty pesos
to the tourists who would idle past
with the freedom of some other country
heavy on their clothes.

And with their sparing dollars
he would go to search for rare books
on Libertad Avenue.

Miguel Bru *(13.8.93)*

Driving his way through the crowds
to curse Boca Juniors on Sunday afternoon,
his shirt bluer than the sky
and his voice flying
like fireworks through the terraces.

His little brother came home without him,
the afternoon full of sunshine
and victory banners.

On the Plaza de Mayo
the boys are learning their craft.

Maxi Maidana *(12.7.97)*

The smell of La Plata oil on their clothes
and the salt sea in their hair,
and every night Rosata
would scold them for coming home stinking:

she knew it wasn't playing cards
those nights,
when she couldn't sleep.

She can sleep fine now
with the scent of southern herbs
on her bedclothes.

Sergio Duran *(6.8.92)*

His friends pulled his leg
because he had chosen to dance the tango
instead of rock and roll:
every Friday night
he would wear his uniform with pride
to entertain the Americans in the Viejo Buzón,
then he'd dance home in the moonlight
through the shadows of the streets.
Somewhere, he's dancing still.

Damien Esquivel (29.1.07)

He looked like Dylan Thomas
serving in a café,
every menu reading,
a verbal presentation.

The afternoon shift suited him best:
then, the buskers
and the poets would come in for a cup
to plot the next raid
on the tourists' pockets.

He was at home in their company.

Painted names surrounding a memorial
are all that remain:
and where the lines of life
weaved a technicolour pattern on the city streets,
there's a white outline and a date
on the pavement of Plaza de Mayo
as final as the silhouette that's left
                after the bomb.

[GD]

Fingerprints

On the village square
where the Inca sundial
tries its best
to keep time
more accurately than the church clock,
the old men in their hats
wash their thumbs
in the fountain;
each one in turn
stooping over the water
before turning it blue
with the colour of his vote;

giving a new meaning
to "showing one's colours",
while the armed guards
supervise the queues
of colourful women
casting their votes
for Vecino or Salizar:
they have no choice,
democracy is compulsory,
it's a vote or a bullet
here on the banks of Titicaca
where the church towers

try their best
to cast their shadow
on the Inca temples;
on the market square,
thumbing the knick-knacks
every blue thumb
bears witness
to extending a helping hand to someone,
while the clean hands
wait their turn:
but despite the harshness
of the shadows
of guns and churches,
the marks
on the stubborn skin
are not everlasting,
they'll wash off,
and the fountain's water is blue
from the white man's ink,
and their thumbs are clean
as they race each other
to capture the sky and lake,
and catch the free sunbeams
like the Inca's sundial.

[GL]

Dust Truck Blues

We've all been
on the back of a truck sometime,
with miles of dust in our hair,
all been on the back of a truck sometime,
miles of dust in our hair:
money factory on the mountain,
and all the small change down there:

we've all knocked on a church door,
and found the church door locked to us,
all knocked on a church door,
found the church door locked to us:
for every one who kept his Bible
there are two who missed the bus:

we've all sung for the Americans,
the Americans pay us well,
all sung for the Americans,
the Americans have paid us well:
every dime is a harvest,
each golden dollar a summer bell:

> a season to drink and dance,
> and weep and embrace,
> a season to worry at dawn
> that the money's all gone…

we've all written about an honest woman,
learnt the lesson of her white robe,
all written about an honest woman,
and learnt the lesson of her white robe:
she don't come without bearing flowers,
her chariot comes down real slow.

[GL]

An Old Photograph

May was murder, a hooligan spring
that bruised the senses, hypocrisy thick
as the mist on Menai wood and the headlines all to hell;

rape and riot were inside-out
like a black-and-white negative; I inched through drizzle
to the evening service in case I hit on chemicals

that would colour the images:
words choked above empty pews,
prayers and yearnings dripped down the walls

and the hymns wrestled the rain that rapped on the window:
a siren startled the *seiat*, a Sunday-night ambulance
from the far side; still the picture would not come clear;

the tentative chemicals washed across it
and left it with white and black reversed,
a misty negative, and me
with the smile on my face dying in daylight.

[RP]

Emyr Lewis

Emyr Lewis (*b.* 1957) was born in London, brought up in Cardiff, and read English at Cambridge and Law at Aberystwyth. He now practises as a solicitor in Cardiff. He has won both the Crown and Chair at the National Eisteddfod, and writes in both the strict and free metres. Despite being a master of the *cynghanedd* metres, his work has an ironic twist which often lifts his work from the traditional mould. He now lives in Craig-cefn-parc in the rural hinterland of Swansea, and is married to the novelist and critic Angharad Dafis.

Drivel

In a warm bar one fine morn
I sat, and after midday
I kept on all afternoon
sitting there silently
enjoying, over my lemonade,
as I relaxed, hearing
the endless din of critics from the bar,
flashy-worded mercenaries,
in a pseudy synod
humourless and prim.

A fistful of post-modernists
and purist post-marxist bores
and a heap of post-structuralists
sprawling and drinking in droves,
arguing for hours on end
in learned brainspeak,
in words strident and strange,
about the most peculiar particulars
and twistings of the curious
theories of lit., like the entrails of lice.

Through the pub's night-turmoil
the academics got drunk.
Discourse became tongue-lashing,
civility became a yell,
sharp words after five pints
and fighting after six pints,
before one contentious jack-the-lad
united them by pointing
a finger at a strange young man
oddly clothed and pale faced,
and shouted, announcing
'I spy a bloody bard,
one of *Barddas*'s ratty rams,
squabbling's their great achievement,
unlearned *cynganeddwyr*
cywydd-ridden, fractious, sour.
The burble of their bunged-up rhyme's
subtlety-free, a warmed-up ditty,
it's death to our nation's ear,
the drone of tradition'.

He fell silent, and the pack roared
one hymnographoid 'Amen'.
The young man scratched
his head – they were loving it
mocking him, but he stood up.
Never was seen a runt so small
of size, since he was scarcely
more than bones in a weskit,
but he spoke up well,
like Siôn Cent from the first word,
and he swore, fervently,
'Unless it's strict it's not a poem.'

The bard was beating the tables
from ten till quarter to two
and he thundered his credo
in a *cywydd*, artfully strict:
'Our *hengerdd* is truly free,
our freedom sings throughout it;
we in our strict poems
lay claim to independence,
their constant music's our survival,
the free words of our culture.

'You dry baleful critics,
poemless save for spitting "Don't!",
there's no exaggeration
can image-forth your vast drivel,
weak lambs, following in a flock
the fruitless paths of the vers-librists
with their brave "experimental" bleatings,
pretend-poets, effete and foolish.
You are post-people, not knowing
the uncomplicated fact of what it is to live,
only post-existing,
sour, since you do not sing,
constricted by your theories
and drinking, you fragile flies.
You fleas, I am warning you,
away at once, before I
hurl the pack of you into the sea
as bacon for the lobsters.'

He paused, and the barman
tetchily asked me this:
'You, old man, you heard tonight
the two who've been squabbling,
so as to thaw their quarrel
adjudicate between two mules.'

I answered him, 'I wonder
if that would be wise, say?
Brother, since I'm not so bold,
no, I'll not adjudicate.
For me that would be folly:
I am the mystic Ancient

who has always plodded frailly
through old and eloquent *awdlau,*
I say my bit about the grave
and bumble about life's brevity.
Throughout my life my fate has been
to say my line and disappear
and I am going to prove
that now.'
                    And that was that.

[AUTHOR]

A Once-in-a-lifetime, Never-to-be-repeated Cywydd in English following a chance meeting with the late Allen Ginsberg

We talked poetic tactics,
of form, of the way we fix
in Welsh, the truculent words
in crazy little crosswords,
and wrap them in jagged rhyme,
our hectic bardic ragtime.

We talked, reserved, untactile;
one fleeting, cementing smile,
one brief arc, into darkness
now gone. Strange now, I guess,
that you wrote in your notebook
two words 'cow with', and then took
a breath, through lips that were bright
as only in the sunlight
lips can be that see and sing.
And once had sung like dancing
in love and, fearful, heavy,
told tales of mortality.

[AUTHOR]

Freedom

(two poems from the sequence)

This is the city of lost things, thrown away,
caught in the space between Sunday afternoon
and the rest of time; things that had the stamp
of souls upon them once; but not today.

In gutters, underneath the railway bridge,
and hiding in the borders in the park
safe from memory and significance
are passport photographs, a single shoe,

and whisky bottles now half-filled with dew,
and house keys, left-hand gloves, small change; the grime
drifts over them when dog-day breezes blow,
and rain beats down on them in wintertime.

They've not been buried, not been elegised:
there are no rites for the discarded things,
you may just curse them briefly now and then,
then let them go, don't think of them again.

*   *   *

In the imperfect time when we have the right
to dream a little, in the occasional pause
between obeying the merciless ticking
when we can feel the whole universe singing
its lyrics to us when the stars are bright,
in candle darkness, in the sound of cars,
there comes the night.

The imagination cannot plough up the street
into a fallow place where we can pray,
it cannot pick up the lost discarded things
whose elegy was not sung, imaginings
can't change the way of clocks, and so today
in the salem of our evening, it's sweet
to hide away.

Here is our well-fashioned time, our compromise
between the wild innocence of first loving

and the dust that we have been breathing for years,
London-wise, sophisticated as cities.
Between the trees where the Taff is flowing
we rest a last dance to the night-birds' cries,
one fine evening.

[GD]

Dawn
(three extracts)

Mad Magnet of a Wild Wind

Mad magnet of a wild wind
here and there whirlying,
spittering old newspapers
along the street, the stories
(yesterday so grand and weighty)
are playing touch in the mud
with the detritus, stray and wet,
of dirt city, until the
meaningless, textless roaring
of countless words becomes one.

See now this page-leaf
which was a shout of news,
which pounded the kingdom's boast;
great headlines are grey stodge.

Stale Spit is the Morning Train

Stale spit is the morning train
fag and dust and lack of space,
brimming over with elbows
and ten in a seat made for two,
cross men, grumpy in their seats
no wise word, no good morning,
frown-sharing on daybreak's train,
the lost crowd of the grey dawn.

This is My Book
(Old Man's Song)

'This is my book, in my hand
its handy leather has worn,
its spinecloth has ripped after
an age of laying down law,
its tissue decomposing
to a hole under dark covers,
turning to fog the golden
letters once so clear on the
old tool of conformity
I wielded to keep captive
so many saints of a Sunday
in the gospel's clutches.

This is the collar of shame,
uniform of my bit-faith,
this is the suit which I wore,
adornment in each prayer meeting,
its threads snaking apart,
its black fabric has become a hole.

I walk where there are no meetings,
silent through the universe's
remote, deserted chapel,
through the graceless, brotherless city,
in whose graveyard-grey pavements
my faith was snuffed out.
The Godhead's thread does not run
one stitch through our living weave.'

About him is the peculiar
synod of cats and dogs.

In his head is a small boy
in sunsmile of more cheerful times
holding his father's hands,
hands of a giant, hands of love,
two ghosts along the ghost of a beach
in the hot sun of a distant past.

[AUTHOR]

Gwyneth Lewis

Gwyneth Lewis (*b.* 1959) is a truly bilingual poet who was born in Cardiff and graduated in English at Cambridge. She then studied creative writing at Columbia and Harvard, before going to Oxford to write a doctoral thesis on the 18th-century Welsh literary forger, Iolo Morganwg. After periods as a journalist in New York and the Philippines, she returned to Cardiff as a TV producer. Recently she was awarded a NESTA fellowship to enable her to spend some years travelling around the world in a yacht, allowing her time and freedom to write. She has won acclaim for her poetry in both Welsh and English. Her first English collection, *Parables & Faxes* (Bloodaxe, 1995) won the Aldeburgh Poetry Festival Prize; her second, *Zero Gravity* (Bloodaxe, 1998), was shortlisted for the Forward Prize. Her third Welsh-language collection, *Y Llofrudd Iaith* ('The Language Murderer'), won the Welsh Arts Council Book of the Year Award. Its reinvention in English, *Keeping Mum* (Bloodaxe, 2003) is a Poetry Book Society Recommendation.

White Horse

As a child, I knew the privilege
of serving ponies: I was prince of the caravan
and led the horses through the damp wood
to the fields' slow fire, flowers like smoke
in the smouldering morning. The white horse
was my favourite. From pride – for he had no tail –
he insisted that a long red scarf be tied
tight to his stump so he could swat away flies
all day with silk. He'd find the trail
for the others as the sunlight's clock
gave hands to the thistles. Then he'd follow me back
to the stable's climate, where we two stood
so softly together that our sweet breath
formed a weather of purest happiness.

But what's precious is frail. One afternoon
the white horse was driven into a hedge
by a selfish woman who forced him to jump
and, in spite of a warning and a command
not to push him, she left him with a broken leg.
They shot him.

                Twenty years have passed since then
but still I look in the afternoon's hay
for the flame of his tail. Nothing's lost,

though it be broken. Today, I sense the white horse
in the morning mist with its chilly flanks,
I hear him in the salty spume as it leaps
onto the pikes of the rocks, immaculate beast.

[RP/AUTHOR]

The Mapmaker's Song

It's no labour of love, this document
that faithfully depicts, bay by bay,
the coast of Wales, showing each church tower,
noting every river's name, as if grace
might dwell in minutiae. I drew my lines
to save me from the harsh slopes' dazzlement,
disarming their souls with factual signs.
There's no longing in rocks – only power
to outlast weathers that cleanse and abrase,
grinding gravel and grit to a mindless mud.
I go on labouring – just like some god
who's impotent because he can't forgive,
re-drawing endlessly the same old place.
Since when has beauty been a way to live?

[RP/AUTHOR]

The Language Murderer
(three poems from a sequence of 37)

Interview with the Poet

I started to translate in seventy-three
in the school yard. For a bit of fun
to begin with – the occasional 'fuck' –
for the bite of another language's smoke
in the back of my throat, its bitter chemicals.
Soon I was hooked on whole sentences
behind the shed, and lessons in Welsh
seemed very boring. I started on print,
Jeeves & Wooster, Dick Francis, James Bond,

inside Welsh covers. That worked for a while
until Mam discovered Jean Plaidy inside
a Welsh concordance one Sunday night.
There were ructions: a language, she screamed,
should be for a lifetime. It was too late for me
already. Very soon, I moved to French, snorted Simenon
and Flaubert. Had to read much more
for any effect now. One night I OD'd
after reading far too much Proust.
I came to, but it scared me. For a while
I went back, Welsh only, but it was bland
and my taste was changing. Before too long
I was back on translating, found that three
languages weren't enough. The 'ch'
in German was easy, Rilke a buzz...
For a language festischist like me
sex is part of the problem. Umlauts make me sweat,
so I need a multilingual man
but they're rare in West Wales and tend to be
married already. If only I'd kept
myself much purer, with simpler tastes,
the Welsh might be living...
                                    Detective, you speak
Russian, I hear, and Japanese.
Could you whisper some softly?
I'm begging you. Please...

[AUTHOR]

The Forgetting Begins

Today the 'sigl-di-gwt'
became a *wagtail*.
I watched closely
as the stream's printing press
moved the day's newspapers
down from the mountains
to be torn up
in the village's shredder.

The *wagtail* didn't care –
he was self-assured
as before,

bowed deeply
to the light and the stones.
He didn't seem
to be a swifter bird
despite having fewer
consonants to carry.

The Cardiganshire *swallows*
squealed overhead,
their wings like a corkscrew
opening the sexy wine
of the evening.
Their cry
is an integral part
of my soul,
their energies
are deeper than language,
or silence, or pain.

[GL]

The Final Minutes

The end was dreadful. Inside, a dam burst
and blood was everywhere. Out of her mouth
came torrents of words *da yw dant*
i atal tafod, gogoniannau'r Tad
in scarlet flowers – *yn Abercuawg*
yd ganant gogau... – the blood was black,
full of filth, a well that amazed us
with its idioms – *bola'n holi, ble mae 'ngheg?* –
and always fertile, *yes no pwdin llo*,
and psalms were gathering in her viscera
and gushing out of her, proverbs, coined words,
the names of plants, seven kinds of woodpecker,
dragonfly, mountain ash, Michaelmas daisy,
then disgusting pus, and lost terms
like *gwelltor* and *rhychor*, her vomiting a road
leading away from her, a mighty army
abandoning its dwellings in the fortress
of her breath *gwŷr a aeth Gatráeth*.
And after the crisis, there was nothing to be done
but watch her die, as the saliva and sweat

366

of words poured out like ants – *padell pen-glin,*
Anghydffurfiaeth, clefyd y paill,
and in spite of our efforts, in the grey of dawn
the haemorrhage ended, her lips were white,
the odd drop splashing. Then she was gone.

[RP/AUTHOR]

Wholeness
(two poems from the sequence)

Llanbadarn Baptism 1843

The day they baptised
Margaret Ann
the Jordan
flowed through Llanbadarn.

As the river closed
above her head,
Margaret Ann heard the roar
of salmon breathing
and the water's weight,
its turbulent history,
a bond between her
and the minister.
He stood like a giant,
two pillars his legs
and the currents were black
as her sins, which spread
below and around her,
a deluge to drown her.

Her sister waved her parasol;
the saints stood like flowers
along the banks
of the crystal Rheidol
while along it, the lions
of Providence
roared out their blessings
to Aberystwyth
while she and the minister,

they both wore
the river like stockings
in hosanna style

while watching two worlds –
one rural, parochial,
the other divine –
both flowing together
while the Sunday hats
were ready for Judgement
and she, the bride,
our Margaret Ann,
was dazzling,
lovely, fully at one
with the brilliant sun
which blessed and protected
the sighing palms
that had sprung up
in fertile Llanbadarn.

Half

A person who's whole possesses four legs,
has forty fingers (that's counting all toes),
two heads and two brains to supervise
the marrow's factory inside the bones.
But a terrible longing fills those who know
that the soul is in half when it lives alone.

Love is a city of misplaced halves
who turn among fractions endlessly
in search of a mathematics where two
and two together always make three,
confounding all angles of being apart
and changing 'those others' into a 'we'.

All praise to those beings to dare to live whole,
who close on each other like heavy tomes
time after time, till their pages compose
private stories for each other's eyes,
classics which flower into public flames
which burn like exotic butterflies.

[AUTHOR]

Strip-Tease

After shutting the door on the rest of the party
and locking it – with the coats empty people
on the grave of the no-man's-land of the bed
and the howling of their owners still to be heard –
the cowboy turned to her: 'Now, sweet thing,
let's see how much you can really undress.'

She undid the buttons of her breasts
and tossed the sovereigns noisily to the night;
she slipped out of the stays of her ribs
and peeled off her skin like a shirt of smoke
that faded away in the sun of her heart –
in nakedness it becomes a visible planet.

He followed the burning course of her setting
to her legs' forest, where he became lost
forever in the flurry of her spirit.
But not before turning back from the abyss
to see the room where she'd been a girl
and the coats all praising her, raised into a choir!

[JPC]

Ifor ap Glyn

Ifor ap Glyn (*b.* 1961) was born and bred in London, graduated at the University of Wales, Cardiff, and now works in the media in the Caernarfon area. He is another performance poet who has toured widely with poetry shows at pubs the width and breadth of Wales and beyond. Consequently, his poetry has an immediacy which stirs the audience's imagination, and often creates laughter and tears. He won the National Eisteddfod Crown in 1999, with a series of poems based on his experiences as a teacher of Welsh as a second language. He jocularly claims to have been the only Welsh-language poet to have performed on the same platform as Tom Jones and to have been played on Radio 1.

The Cucumbers of Wolverhampton

I've made this alarming discovery –
it's been like a blow to the ear:
the cucumbers of Wolverhampton
are Welsher than people round here!

It's something I saw in the paper,
I could hardly believe my eyes,
But there it was in black and white –
and *The Sun* don't tell no lies.

I was thumbing around in all innocence
between the racing and the Page Three pets,
when I saw in this piece that our bodies
are nothing but chemistry sets!

Giblets and bones are what's inside me,
I'd believed until that day –
not calcium, potassium,
carbon and water –
even iron, so they say.

True love may well be likened to steel,
but there's iron in every man too;
there's iron in the bosom of every woman,
and silicon in the breasts of a few.

Although we're quite rich in iron,
we're seventy per cent water, or more!
(Though why the water doesn't rust the iron,
the scientists aren't quite sure.)
We're all H_2O, a full seventy per cent!
It's a fact you can't gainsay!
Gallons and gallons of Tryweryn am I
as I slosh along my way.

Now, the people of Bilston and Handsworth
may not sound as Welsh as they aughta,
but they drink what flows from Tryweryn
and they're seventy whole per cent water.

So they're Welsh by pipage, if not
parentage; the census is therefore wrong:
a barrel of Welsh red water
is each Leroy, Singh and Wong.

And so in the Midlands of England
there are ten million lost Welsh others;
isn't it time we pushed the border back east
to embrace our abandoned brothers?

It would solve all our problems with tourists:
they'd be living in Cymru too,
with Powys spreading to Norfolk,
and Gwynedd ending at Crewe.

A great *Sun*-reading brotherhood,
sharing alike both friend and foe.
I don't mind being on a par with the *Sais*
…but second to a vegetable? No!

Because now here comes the downside.
The paper then started to number
the contents of animals, plants and veg –
including the cu-bloody-cumber.

While there's no shortage of water in us,
cucumbers have ninety per cent!
The cucumbers of Wolverhampton
are Welsher than Gwynedd and Gwent.

So if some cheeky blockhead comes along
proclaiming to all in sight
that he's 'more of a Welshman than you',
don't reply 'You looking for a fight?'

Just put on a knowing smile and say,
'That's nothing, stop making a fuss –
the cucumbers of Wolverhampton
are Welsher than every last one of us.'

[NJ]

Englyns

Englyns are akin to scampi –
no one's sure exactly what they are,
and you're usually sorry you asked...
for anyone who fancies
that they can explain them
are about as engaging
as a talkative bore when you're busting for the bog,
a CSE in biology,
a member of the SDP,
or last week's *TV Times*.

It's in school that many first stumble upon them
...along with bullies,
the whiff, in the chem lab, of stew,
and everyone else's hand in the air
when you don't have the faintest clue.

They don't teach much that's useful
to you
in school
like:
how to unfasten a bra;
but they *do* teach you
such invaluable things as
how to deconstruct an *englyn*.
What's the use of learning how to strip down
the carburettor
when there's nothing more that you'd adore
than a driving lesson
in an *englyn* afire on cylinders four!

Englyns are not a kind of *bratwurst*...
a *bratwurst* has no trouble raising laughs...
especially if it's a "stand-up" *bratwurst*.

Englyns can't be compared to dogs.
An *englyn* will neither give rise to fleas,
nor fetch your new slippers as you take your ease,
it'll simply inform you that the old pair
were so much better than these.

Englyns are also unlike ashtrays;
they can hold things that shine
as well as what's ashen,
and no parlour should be without one
in case a poet should call.

Because *englyns* are ancient –
a kind of bardic bouncing cheque –
they're like last night's curry, inclined to 'repeat'
and after fifteen hundred years –
that's still pretty neat.

Writing the little devils
is as much as ever a fag,
but things will be somewhat different
when we've *englyns* that 'boil in the bag'.

[NJ]

I'm the Guy with the Gut

I jump, as I pass myself in a window;
I'm that guy with the gut.

Me – the young rake (literally);
thin as, in those teen photos,
who couldn't even get wet
in the rain without moving around.

It's disgusting taking this change on board
I'm barely halfway along
the allotted years of our lord;
I'll need a barrow for when
I hit the three score and ten.

I'm that guy with the gut...

I'm sporting the badge of decadent living,
the beery sessions, and then the Indians
but you can't hide the logo of middle age
under the lapel of your jacket:

it's a mantelpiece over my pants,
a bay window above my belt,
eaves, even.

I'm that guy with the gut…

In the bath I can tame it,
make it a sandbank in a circle of sea,
a round foothill rising meekly
beneath the Himalayas of my knees

but when I come from the water
like a hippo dripping,
the pulling power of Club Gravity
always draws the flubber towards the floor
it bulges like a Tesco bag
full of blancmange,
heavier than a sackful of Aberystwyth,
this, my conscience, and fellow traveller of the front…

I'm that guy with the gut.

And if I'm pregnant from my prodigality,
my wife, who's done the *llanddewibrefi*
four times with baby in the belly,
always gets back flat like a tray;
the crêpe skin of multiple parturition
is the only man-ifestation
that testifies to her-oism
and is also a witness
to my own laziness,
I who have bred forth
no more than a belly laugh or two
from my own abdomen…

but you have to laugh sometimes,
and learn to love your failings.
I'm the guy with the gut.

[AUTHOR]

Sonia Edwards

Sonia Edwards (*b.* 1961) comes from Anglesey, and she graduated in Welsh at Bangor. She now teaches Welsh at Llangefni Comprehensive School. Her published work includes novels, short stories and poetry. She has won the National Eisteddfod Prose Medal, as well as the Welsh Arts Council Book of the Year Award.

An Empty Place

She loves him from a distance
and her hands cup
the flame of her longing
as the night draws in.

He is the illusion
that sustains her hopes
fragile as tomorrow
among the soap suds;
clean plates gleam like jewels,
witnesses to the commitment made
so early in the day
when the church was cold.

And when afternoon grows into evening
pretending to be night
she lays the tables
for the lawful wedded husband with dirt on his hands,
placing her vows
neatly in front of him
between the knives and forks.

Tonight, with the day folded up in a drawer
she can lie beside the dream
that slips between them
into the empty space in the middle of the bed.

[SRJ]

Between Two Lovers

And her face said to him:
'I love you.'
There was no music
or flowers
or gaudy cards
haemorrhaging hearts –
only the grey rain
mottling the darkness
like the ravage of woodworm.

His nearness
warmed her
without their touching:
their eyes did that,
kissing the teardrop-coloured moments
that bound thoughts.

In his smile she saw
the years as if through soft lenses
as he remembered her
cocooned in a spent shyness
that was too drowsy to care.

Free now from the bonds of youth
she gave him her body
in the touch of her hand.

And words had no part to play.

[SRJ]

Aled Lewis Evans

Aled Lewis Evans (*b*. 1961) was born in Machynlleth, and graduated from the University of Wales Bangor. He taught for many years at Wrexham before training to become a Nonconformist minister. He has published a volume of short stories, a novel and a number of collections of poetry, including two volumes of translations, *Wavelengths* (1995) and *Mixing the Colours* (2000). His latest novel *Y Caffi* was published in 2002. He is now a freelance writer.

Alone

There's a vastness out there
with lights in it, shivering,
bright and coloured in the winter darkness,
in the ice which
bends the lights of Liverpool,
Chester and the whole of the border.
A fragile small hours place
murmuring to itself.

Through empty trees of Maelor,
the bitter wind lashes
and blows the edge of Whittington.
Here vanity
chokes
the neat suburbs,
empties their souls.
Oh yes, summer will come, it will,
but for now the Overton yew stays cold and poor
and the church's dust
covers our poetry, our places
and our history.

$*$ $*$ $*$

By the Clywedog river
the housing estates sit
slick and unwitting.
Their law is silence.
They don't track roots.
They are ignorant and brash.

Losing a language is an old-fashioned thing, a memory,
no new shame for the shameless new wealthy.
Along this border, this vague line, the watchers
sit comfortably. Seithenyn, suburban now,
and still idle. Seithenyn who let Cantre'r Gwaelod drown.

$*$ $*$ $*$

In these border lands
the people bottle their *hiraeth*
hide it, lose it,
hope it will vanish, be gone.

They want their belonging bottled,
that shame of yesteryear
cast like an X-ray
across our no-man's-land.

*　　*　　*

There's a reek of chips in Poyser Street
which sticks to the red brick houses.
An old man stares at the stones
in the churchyard,
studies their lettering   .
waits for the cold day to end
to leave his red prison
and the smell of chips and battered fish.

*　　*　　*

I'm an island in these borders
lapped by the warmth of others,
their valleys, their fair places,
always far away, over the hill.
I smile and talk about my
world as if it's real, believe in it,
without any first hand proof.

It's difficult, sometimes, to stick with
my Welshness, in this borderland of angst
and antagonism,
it's hard to keep the spirit alive.

When there's a *cymanfa*
my eyes go wet.
When we sing our anthem
I'm proud.
My island, other islands,
our voices move together.

It's a privilege and rare
to become a continent,
all of it Welsh.

Us,
me,
on the border.

*　　*　　*

The lights of motorways
English roadsigns
strange radio singing its sweet nothings,
us zooming, pushing, rushing across borders,
sloughing the darkness, going somewhere.

Town Centre
no mention of *Canol y Dref.*
Gwerndwnc, Rhydfudr and *Cae Deintyr*
are now The Dunks, Red Wither and Tenter's Square.
The way to avoid them
is to cross again that border,
Brynffynnon, Pen-y-bryn, Croes Eneurys are ignored.

The green of *Brymbo, Bwlchgwyn* and *Gwynfryn*
vanishes beyond the steelworks
which winks in the sunset,
darkening for a final time.
Life's fast lane
gets us to Chester, hedonism,
all that,
shallow pleasure at the end of
a dual carriageway,
conscienceless,
over the line.

Back inland there's the fox sun again, its warmth
hardly covering our naked forms
as Englishness picks and bends
at our roots.

We're welcomed here,
and we rejoice.
Along these borders we sun worship,
brown over Offa's Dyke
where the deep tan comes.

But I turn my face from
all this, from the heat,
and face instead the
steadfast silence of the hills,
the Welsh hills and solitude, mine.

[PF]

Elin ap Hywel

Elin ap Hywel (*b.* 1962) was born in Colwyn Bay, Denbighshire, but was edu-
cated at schools in London, Barry, Cardiff and Wrexham, because of her father's
peripatetic lifestyle as a minister. She studied Welsh and Irish at Aberystwyth,
and has worked as a translator for various institutions, and also as editor for
the Welsh women's press, *Honno*. She won the Literature Medal at the Urdd
National Eisteddfod in 1980, and published a volume in the *Beirdd Answyddogol*
(Unofficial Poets) series. Her latest book is *Ffiniau/Borders*, a bilingual volume
of poetry in collaboration with Grahame Davies. She is Fellow of the Royal
Literary Fund.

Thing

Neither of them –
not the technophobic vicar
nor his dim, agnostic daughter
– despite years of physics lessons –
understand the microwave oven.

They don't understand where the heat comes from.

'It's a bit like faith,' says the girl –
'it's invisible
colourless
it smells of nothing –
and yet, somehow, it changes things.'

And it's true.
Some unseen force
reconfigures mass and molecules,
transubstantiating fish and flour
to cod in crispy, steaming breadcrumbs.

The trouble is, there are so many rules.
Thick-skinned foodstuffs must be pierced with a fork,
thin-skinned ones protected
but NOT with foil, or everything
will either explode or fall in on itself.

They stand, these two, on the threshold of Christmas
and stare, blank-faced, at this miracle.

This is her dream; some night
she comes home late. In the kitchen
the only light is the oven-belly
where a jacket potato pirouettes through space
awaiting the firm and final ping.

On the plates, the table, the counter
on the bread bin, the floor, the fridge
her father has spread the feast –
a Christmas pudding studded with fruit,
a flood of custard,
a Titanic turkey
and eden of vegetables, fresh and green.

Bathed in unblinking, incandescent light
she draws up her chair, picks up her cup.

[AUTHOR]

Understanding Light
(in memory of Gwen John)

Sometimes
on Sunday afternoons
in a north light
she sees her face for what it really is –
a cold sun etches a cheekbone,
figuring the years' circles under her eyes.

At mass this morning
– *others at prayer in a world of light* –
she stares at the folds
in coif and wimple.
How can linen be the colour of ash?

Last night, by lamplight, she placed
a loaf of bread, a knife, on the table
and before eating picked up her pencil.

Tonight she will finish the sketch.
She will draw the cat, the rickety chair.
She knows the girl's head against the light

will be
the colour of a drop of blood,
drying.

[AUTHOR]

In My Mother's House

In my mother's house there are many mansions,
parlours all full of air and light
where the table is set for afternoon tea
and the shutters always open outwards
to a view of the sea without ships; dark-brown passages
which go on for miles, hot and airless,
ending in sculleries where the crockery totters
and something major's gone wrong with the plumbing.
Staircases which spiral down down down
past family photographs on flock-papered walls
– *Look, there's my grandmother. There's a weasel on her shoulder!* –
till they get to the bad place
that cellar that's full of charcoaled bones,
of children's skulls thin as blown eggs.

Tonight I'm trying to get to the bathroom,
a tiny Antarctic of marble and glass.
I've been here before once.
I played with the soap,
I loved the way it shot through my fingers,
leaving a snail's trail of tears behind
and I thought
If I could stick my head under the tap
the water might make me feel better.

I've been coming here each night since the funeral.
I've walked, danced, and wandered through the rooms of this house,
whose geography changes
quick as an hour-glass. I love the back kitchen,
the dresser carved from a hunk of bog-oak,
solid and black, more fruitcake than furniture,
with my uncle's initials gouged in its side.
The Staffordshire china dogs

stand guard over the willow-patterned plates,
their eyes as small and jealous as sloes.
Sometimes, if I'm lucky, they'll talk to me:
She went thataway. You only just missed her. She's in the corridor! –
and I'll catch a glimpse of the hem of her skirt.

Once, I'll never forget it, I went in
and there she was, in an armchair, by the fire.
She stretched out her hands to me, her fingers
harpists' fingers, slender and white.
I laced my fingers in hers. We said nothing,
each of us embarrassed that we'd been caught out,
fraternising, as it were, the wrong side of the veil.
I can't remember now how I got out of that room.
I look for it every time I go back.
Sometimes it's there, sometimes it isn't.
Sometimes her cup still sits in its saucer
Sometimes the fire is cold, cold ashes.

[AUTHOR]

Blue
(in memory of Derek Jarman)

There's a tortoise-man on TV. His skin
is so old, it's ancient, eternal, as if
seared to a husk by a sierra wind,
a peel without zest or sap.
A tortoise-man without a shell, whose head
jerks, unstoppably, towards the camera
– looking to see if the world's still there.

I want to touch him –
to reach, somehow, inside the TV,
my thumb longing
to smooth out the hollows under his eyes,
I want to place one finger on his papyrus cheek
and say thanks, silently

– for the gleam of silk, for glamour,
for powder and paint, for pain,
for gemstones, for candlelight,

for grapes, for strawberries, for wine,
for velvet, for a warm breath,
for excess. For elation. For gilding
the black and white screen with a rainbow eye –

colour by colour they fade and run
and there's only blue left, a blue
that's as true as the sky or the sea,
like the smoke rising from the morning's first cigarette
like petrol on a rained-on road,
a blue like the twist of salt in a packet of crisps –

blue too like a cardboard file, a nurse's skirt,
a surgical gown, an artery,
a knife's edge, a fading bruise,
like small grit sucked on by the tide
like the colour between the living and the dead
like the hard screen that's between you and me.

[AUTHOR]

Goddesses

Goddesses of Wales –
goddesses of broom, and meadowsweet and oakflower,
dry, rattling bones, claws buried deep in fur –

you weren't the ones who wobbled,
years ago, through my dreaming schoolgirl head.

I worshipped the little sprites, the come-day, go-day
quavering through the myths of Greece and Rome,
a rainbow one minute, the next a spring or tree,
wavering between two minds, two bodily forms,
trying to please some man, hide from some god,
changing their names, their selves, like choosing lipstick.
Echo, Eros, Psyche – sixth form nymphettes,
giggling behind their freshly shampooed hair.

I came to our goddesses slowly,
reluctant and painful, stubborn like drowning kittens.

With every bruise I've seen, each empty kiss,
each fallen ring, become apprentice Fury –
smelt the blood on your hands, the heat of the iron,
heard the skulls of children knocking on wind.

Goddesses of wild, mad, grief-stricken people,
of enormous silence, of terrible, unsaid things –
you're here tonight in the thin sound of the news,
stalking the room in your ragged silken gowns,
bone-weariness a bruise under shadowed eyes,
your skin crabbed like old apples –

yet lightning and thunder sing through your clouded hair,
your aprons gigantic knots around sagging bellies,
white clovers of anger still bloom in the print of your shoes.

In the sweep of your petticoats kingdoms crash and are gone.

[AUTHOR]

Meirion MacIntyre Huws

Meirion MacIntyre Huws (*b.* 1963) was born and brought up in Caernarfon,
and still lives and works in the area in a freelance capacity. He studied Civil and
Structural Engineering at Cardiff, but after a period working for Dŵr Cymru, he
became a graphic designer. In 1993 he won the Chair at the National Eisteddfod.
He is an accomplished master of *cynghanedd*, and representative of the 'second
flowering' of strict-metre poetry of the 1980s and 90s. He is frequently heard
on the popular poetry radio programmes, *Talwrn y Beirdd* (the Poets' Cockpit).

Window

Up to my hotel window
he came like some black cloud;
an old jack tar in tattered coat
and autumn trousers proud,
his whole world in a battered case
clasped tightly just below his face.

He peered into the thickened glass,
and fiddled with his shirt,
then cursed us all and cursed the world,
himself and heaven he cursed.
And then he stormed off in a huff,
so angry, and not big enough.

Was it a mirror, was it glass,
between the wretch and me?
I wonder did he see my feast?
The wine, the maître d'?
Or did he see a spectral curse –
his own reflection – which one's worse?

I'm older now, he's history,
but still, with coat and case
he haunts my hotel window,
reproach etched in his face.
He's croaked and buried now, maybe,
but oh, his eyes keep stalking me.

[GL]

Conscience

I haven't seen him, yeah,
I know – but he is there:
the man who's only words,
and the mouth that's always heard,
an incessant gainsayer:
my good brother – my betrayer.

He never goes away:
each time I try to stray
he stops me, I'm depressed
by this ever-present pest;
he is the meaning of strife,
he is the bane of my life.

And on St David's Day
can I escape? – no way,
he's in my leek and onion

soup: he's famine and starvation:
in the bread and fine wine he's
the thousands of Somalis.

He sits on the victim's knee
and points non-stop at me:
he's the lonely and the elderly,
his voice is every charity.
He's Sarajevo's caterwauls,
a boot in memory's balls.

In my petty world of whingeing
or my ocean of complaining,
he's the brown-paper-houses crowd,
the homeless ones crying out loud;
his endless roar reminds you
of the blind man's cry, the dole queue.

Oh! I'd give the sun to spend
just one hour without this friend:
and the whole world I would forfeit
for one summer without this prophet;
the man who's only words,
and the mouth that's always heard.

[GL]

The City

To my dream land I go
at night, to lighten my woe;
I row on a golden tide,
to a pleasant shore so wide;
steer my boat to a vast village:
the city that speaks my language.

Like all this city's hoi polloi,
the high life's mine to enjoy:
here, I've the right to choose,
and the right to vanquish my foes;
the right to speak Welsh freely,
without having to say 'sorry'.

The feast goes on all year
on snow-white tables here;
I drink from rivers of mead,
and wander the city, freed,
whilst in its gloomy kitchens
the strangers wash the dishes.

[GL]

Coat

I may wear a dawning smile for shirt,
my grooming you may note,
but still I long for the touch of the cloth
of my poorest greatest coat.

The coat that smelled of tavern-smoke,
that stayed my friend through much,
that felt the silk of a secret kiss
from smile to morning touch.

From mountain-side to marriage,
a servant, house and bed,
the coat that cried 'To battle',
experienced, well-read.

They wove it from a black sheep's wool,
and threadbare as may be,
when autumn winds turned colder,
it gave us sanctuary.
And he who took it took our past
and stealing it, stole me.

[GD]

Gerwyn Wiliams

Gerwyn Wiliams (*b.* 1963) was born in Pwllheli, and moved around with his family, spending periods in Chester, Llangefni, Welshpool, Newtown and Lampeter, before going to Aberystwyth to read Welsh. He wrote a doctoral thesis on the Welsh literature of the First World War, and published two highly acclaimed volumes based on his research. He is a critic of note, and whilst a student launched an iconoclastic journal called *Weiren Bigog* ('Barbed Wire'). He has been an editor of *Barn* (Opinion) and *Taliesin* (the literary quarterly of Yr Academi Gymreig). In 1994 he won the Crown at the National Eisteddfod. He is senior lecturer in the Welsh Department at the University of Wales, Bangor.

My Wales?

We live between the covers of books.
We lurk between them.
We've long since swapped
a white stick and a guide dog
for the visionary lenses of our books.
That's where Wales is at ease.
That's where she makes sense.
Spring makes its comeback
between the covers of each book
and bardic hope bursts from its leaves.
Confident, jam-packed,
our poems bulge with allusions
to Cilmeri and Glyndŵr
or phone Dewi Sant for help.
Who recognises them today –
imagery's methuselahs doggedly
scratching around for a grave?
Yet anarchy struts our streets.
Novelists impress on chaos
the structures of art.
Still…a beast banged up in a cage?
It's hardly the same.
Conjuring meaning from paper and ink?
That's cooking the books.
What the hell! I'll tell you this:
reading's safer than living.

[RP/AUTHOR]

Final Curtain

Is this how it will end?
Bussed like Chernobyl patients
in a snake thirty miles long
clean out of our country?

'Heard the news?
Traws and Wylfa
pissed radio-activity;
Sellafield, in a panic,
shat its load in its pants.'

And messed up our shores.

'All aboard! Your private colony
with self-contained identity
awaits beyond the border.'

Will we face the final curtain
as a knell sounds over our grave
and they screw down the coffin lid
on the corpse of the Welsh Problem?

And, amidst the desolation,
will a TV crew materialise,
raring to film the Finale?

'More tears! Less wailing! Cut!'

Once the whirligig of existence,
our dissenting, botched existence,
loses its fizz and slows to a crawl,
after saintfaganising every fart and fuck,
they'll be there to serenade our exit.

'They have lived.'

Or did we merely act our lives out
for the camera's benefit?

[RP/AUTHOR]

Forward March

There was a city
that veiled her face from the sight of the world.
And the world pitied the mystery
of the city's captivity
and campaigned to set her free.
But when the city turned
her credulous eyes to the eyes of the world
and surrendered her secret,
into her courts with praise
came McDonald's, Benetton, Coke.

There was a city.
Now it is free.
Free to be like the rest.

[RP/AUTHOR]

Washington

The Vietnam Memorial:
a destination for their grief,
directors of the western epic.

There was nothing
of the majesty of the Menin Gate,
the bugler's precision at eight
nor the bemedalled old men
who still remember.

There was no dignity:
not even Lincoln nearby
on the marble throne of his vision
could avert his gaze
from these people's amateurism:

caressing the granite
as if to awaken flesh;
tracing names onto paper;
stuffing wreaths
of tattered flowers
into the fissures between the stones;

their siege of cameras
colonising the scene.

Despite Hooson's daffodil
that wilted with shame,
we did not feel involved.

As day was disappearing,
I happened to look before leaving
into the smooth depths of the stone
and there I saw her approaching,
extinguishing our reflections.

She,
the small naked girl of the image,
rushing toward us still.
Her back a tapestry of napalm,
her dummy-mouth
shaping some primeval
'Mammy!' or 'Daddy!'

She,
arms reaching out
through stone.

She,
frail, insignificant,
piercing us
through the armour of our objectivity,
snaring us
in humanity's bonds,
denying us
the privatisation of grief.

[RP/AUTHOR]

Pledge

Because you're an infant in arms,
expelled from the nursery womb;

because you're eight pounds on the scales
and a ton of care in a cuddle;

because your eyes keep transmitting
cryptic telegrams between us;

because your plaited hands suggest
a wretch who's begging forgiveness;

because of all this, Marged Elen,
you're a siren flashing in my head,

I'm an ambulance always on call,
be it riot, fair weather or snow,

from sunrise to sultry midnight –
just waiting to succour you.

[RP/AUTHOR]

Grahame Davies

Grahame Davies (*b.* 1964) was born near Wrexham, and read English at Cambridge before going on to do his doctorate in the Welsh Department at the University of Wales Cardiff. He has published two collections of poems, and was Welsh Language Editor of *Poetry Wales*. His comparative study of T S Eliot, R S Thomas, Saunders Lewis and Simone Weil was published by the University of Wales Press in 1999, entitled *Sefyll yn y Bwlch* (Standing in the Breach). Another critical study is forthcoming from Seren. He lives in Cardiff and is a BBC Wales journalist.

DIY

The Workers' Hall could do with some work,
weeds are growing in the cracks of its grandeur;
and the slates of the roof have been stolen –
the slates of empty buildings
are one of the valley's last natural resources.

Hall, chapel, club:
a society's essentials once,
are now shells, museums without visitors:
like old people whose children have left them.
The community no longer needs them enough
to look after them.

That said, there's plenty of maintenance going on in the valley.
Hundreds are busy each day with hammer and saw;
but now it's every man for himself;
it's not common effort that builds an extension,
changes a kitchen, puts up a shed.

The DIY stores are the temples
of our individuality;
we spend hours of our leisure
in these out-of-town halls
prowling singly, in pairs,
along a maze of choices
with our world shattered in a thousand pieces
in boxes all around us.

We carry the components home
to the lonely privacy of our houses,
and, with nails and glue,
we try to make things whole.

As the old commonalities die,
everything is DIY.

[AUTHOR]

Waste

The old waste tip has gone;
the great snowdon of slag has been shoved aside
and in its place the private houses are growing like grass.

Imagine someone from Hollywood
creating his idea of an English village;
he'd do it something like this,
in mincing mock-Tudor.
They preen themselves on the tip's dusty stage
made up in black planks and plaster
like black-and-white minstrels,
a parade of parodies.

Private;
each one on its little separate plot,
too embarrassed to touch.
Toytown one-night houses;
a graveyard of little dwellings.
It's hard to believe a slagheap
could be defaced.

Devolution's come to the valley;
each house is independent;
the cells of a community's body
dividing, retreating;
the blood flowing from the veins of the terraces
to congeal in little coloured coffins like these,
with the junk of a fake past as company
through the long decay
– a little porcelain statuette of a miner with his pick,
soft cuddly dragons –
like the bric-à-brac of the ancient Egyptians' graves.

It's boxes within boxes, this life,
like a Russian doll –
the man in the car
and the car in the garage,
and the garage in the house
and the house in nothing.

No ties, no community,
no chain, no strength.

The chains of the valleys are loosening,
link by link;
the iron which challenged
the hammer of oppression
is rusting,
giving way.

[AUTHOR]

Liverpool

When I was a lad up in Flintshire,
a day to remember for me
was to take a trip over the border
to the city at the edge of the sea.

With her white towers on the horizon,
the world seemed to bow at her feet,
and we felt a pride in her accent
as we eavesdropped her talk in the street.

But now those same Merseyside accents
are no more the sign of a spree;
there's no need to travel to Liverpool
when Liverpool's travelled to me.

[AUTHOR]

Rough Guide

It happens inevitably,
like water finding its level:
every time I open a travel book,
I sail past the capital cities, the sights,
and dive straight into the backstreets of the index
to find that in France, I'm Breton;
in New Zealand, Maori;
in the USA – depending on which part –
I'm Navajo, Cajun, or black.

I'm the Wandering Welshman.
I'm Jewish everywhere.
Except, of course, in Israel.
There, I'm Palestinian.

It's some kind of a complex, I know,
that makes me pick this scab on my psyche.
I wonder sometimes what it would be like
to go to these places
and just enjoy.

No, as I wander the continents of the guidebooks,
whatever chapter may be my destination,
the question's always the same when I arrive:
'Nice city. Now where's the ghetto?'

[AUTHOR]

Red

You set the olives down beside the *feta*,
    and make sure the *ciabatta*'s looking nice.
You light the perfumed candle for the meeting,
    open the red wine, put the white on ice.

A little *antipasti* to begin with;
    a French *baguette* to soak up all that wine;
this is the way we meet to save our nation
    in CF One in nineteen ninety-nine.

I wonder what he'd make of this, your grand-dad,
    who risked a prison cell for Stalin's sake,
the one who raised the red flag in the valleys,
    the man the hungry thirties couldn't break?

The one who got invited out to Russia
    to get the Soviets' thank-you face to face,
and came back with a little bust of Lenin,
    that's now an ornament above your fireplace.

The one who earned the local rag's displeasure
    for calling meetings to arouse the mass,
I wonder what he'd make of his descendant:
    Welsh-speaking, nationalistic, middle-class?

I wonder. But you're still so like your grand-dad:
    cut from the same cloth, just by different means,
trying to cure the evils of injustice
    by painting all the world in red – or green.

[AUTHOR]

Llion Jones

Llion Jones (*b.* 1964) was brought up in Abergele on the north Wales coast, and he graduated in Welsh at Aberystwyth before gaining a PhD for his study of the work of T H Parry-Williams. He is now a Lecturer in the Department of Media and Communications at the University of Wales Bangor, specialising in language, literature and technology. He established a web poetry magazine for practitioners of the strict metres, which can be accessed at *www.cynghanedd.com*. With Myrddin ap Dafydd, he is one of only three who have won two of the major cultural awards in Welsh-speaking Wales – *Cân i Gymru* (A Song for Wales) and the National Eisteddfod Chair.

Illusions

As I Survey

Through the bustle and commotion
a siren's timely exclamation
is an urban exhortation;

on the railway tracks, the trains
reiterate high-speed refrains,
evensong as daylight wanes;

and to the sound of tyres
each weary soul retires
from the rush hour's ire;

hasty echoing feet
beat tonight's retreat
from the darkening street;

front doors shut in a while
on each terraced domicile,
curtains close in single file.

The mist falls like a sheet
over this everystreet,
empty cars are all you meet;

and unseen by the street lights
rows of cameras out of sight
take pictures throughout the night,

a recorded ritual
on some control booth wall
…I usually watch it all.

On the Threshold

The door shuts out the traffic's din,
he gives a grunt, stepping in,
casts off the burdens of the day
and lets his troubles fade away.

There's mail to be stepped over
under his feet like clover,
spreading like so many weeds,
epistles that nobody reads,
empty letters to be swept
to the skip of the unkept.

He skims the evening paper
in his cell, eyes a-caper,
from headline to headline he'll go,
so avid is he to know
what's what on the world stage,
the instant wisdom of the front page.

In his evening ritual he
half listens to the litany
recorded on his answerphone,
messages form people unknown
selling some miracle gain,
promising to call again.

In his familiar sanctuary
evening is and always will be
clear-cut steps, like Sunday church,
and from one to one he'll lurch
as regularly as the soap
that broadcasts in faith and hope
its small conventions, coming in.
Doors shut out the traffic's din.

Bricolage

Zap! zap! zap! the rhythm goes
pumping out the evening shows
as pictures come and pictures go
the pendulum swings to and fro
following the fleeting whim
desire is all: reality's dim.

This armchair life
is a world of illusion,
the channel-hopping routine
is his evenings' vain conclusion;
he scans the cosmos seeking naught
but iamges without a thought.

Zap! zap! zap! the rhythm goes
pumping out the evening shows
illusions come and go, role-play's
the passive rite that fills his days,
as awareness is drowned
in a mediocre sound.

By the fire he burns the bridges
between safe truth and lies,
in a fluid world where history's seen
through cruel cartoonists' eyes,
and past, present, future all are seen
as one upon the flickering screen.

Zap! zap! zap! the rhythm goes
pumping out the evening shows
from screen to screen, an effortless
wailing cry of emptiness,
of endless hours spent viewing
avidly, seeing nothing.

Party Political Bored-Cast

Ritually he slots his smile
between two programmes for a while,
a toothy smile that embraces
through the screen his people's faces,

400

the cheap smile, merciful, kind,
softening even the hardest mind.

How measured his words are,
his faith so plausible and pure,
politics of abstracts there
ready for the cameras' glare.

It's a game-show gimmick
expressed in a slogan, it's slick,
a respectable, pinstriped view,
and nicely ironed too,
with knotted tie and fine words, he
makes image his ideology.

But in these twilit seconds
memory's video beckons,
and as I press 'rewind'
see what's been left behind.

His stirring rallying-cry,
his hatred of every lie,
the revolution in his songs,
his urge to right all wrongs,
a sight in scruffy denim blue,
high on confidence anew.

Somehow the rebel's sway
is a treacly smile today,
and just a droplet of his passion
remains tonight, in his new fashion.

[GL]

Mererid Hopwood

Mererid Hopwood (*b.* 1964) was born in Cardiff and read Spanish and German
at Aberystwyth. After periods studying in Spain and Germany, she was a uni-
versity lecturer in London, before taking up a lecturing post in German at the
University of Wales Swansea. She has been involved in many translation projects
and has published a book of Welsh poems in German translation. She created
history by winning the Chair at the Denbigh National Eisteddfod in 2001, as
she is the first woman poet to win the Chair, which is awarded for a long poem

in the strict traditional metres. Now she is a freelance writer, and also teaches strict-metre poetry at Carmarthen, enthusing others – especially women – to learn the craft.

Rebirth

Reader, my story's an old one – and yet
it's an ever-true one,
it's always been – but each dawn,
in understanding, I'm re-born...

Unworldly as the crescent moon, we vowed,
fearless and innocent,
together we'd see, content,
the dawning each new day sent.

It wasn't so. Our world grew large, ballooned
bigger than our night's marriage:
youth, clichés and badinage –
we two were just air and rage.

We parted; lost each other in a dark wood
until the early fervour
of two warm hearts together
drew us closer, closer.

Pillowed on our forever
I float on the night's feather
tucked in your wing. Together

we ride the billowy bedding
of last night, nesting, nestling,
pretending that we're resting.

At daybreak we are parted
until we're reunited
in our lair, our white bed.

There we are joined together
in our long night. The feathers
that brush us rise and flutter.

*

Am I?! I can't quite credit
instinct's old, insistent writ:
I doubt the gift I'm given,
the miracle in my womb,
this nest of flesh; yet I feel
the fleeting spark is real –
a butterfly fluttering free,
a little moth inside me,
turning, tossing, here and there,
it wakes me, a bright shiver.
Feeling its *frisson* in me
I know this being to be.

I doubt the gift to begin
but somehow I know its meaning:
I can't deny, you see,
your little smile inside me.

Under my hand, melody
rising from flesh moving free:
an erratic fist begins
pounding its tabla of skin,
this is your heart, its beating
the metre of all the singing.

Your hand's touch leaves a trace.
I see, here, the future's face,
your angle-elbow outpacing
my waist, elastic-seeming.
Playing your merry mayhem
till the small hours, little man
you and I have fun and games,
complicit in our pastimes.

A tiny baby's being:
my lineage on the screen
and maybe I myself am
in that blurred half-square of scan.
Black and white: between them lies
the seed of all our stories.
That drop in the sac of tears
another me, the future years:
this, the one that will remain,
is different and yet the same.

My story, your history, one circle
closing, rings infinity.
You see – this is our story,
this is what binds you and me.

*

Tonight our star is rising – in my chains,
tonight, I am singing:
I feel your bonds unravelling:
your freedom-day is dawning.

It moves me to tears, your crying – pure heaven,
sum of my years' longing
in my pain, I am flying –
your shout is a nine months' hymn.

Tonight, with nine months' harvesting in my lap
my heart is overflowing:
the love of nine moons waxing
completes me, all-embracing.

In this love, now plain to see
I know I am more than me.

Your birth tonight is my new coming
to love and to the true understanding
of 'mother', 'father', beyond my past knowing
a brand-new life in a world that's shining
in this rainbow present, at once I fly
to your tomorrow, your future being.

Eager, I knock – the doors of my loving
are opening still in your blue eye's dawning.
I'm born again just through your being,
so full of mirth and joy and laughing!
Happy babbling mimic, one smile from you
is like words exploding, a new beginning.

*

But in your bed, tonight, in darkness
lying in a silence that cannot fool us
like a sheet of ice, my tenderness,
an agony that's beyond all sadness.
Cold hands on my fragile baby's skin,
I notice the fever of real illness.

Today is the day I know despairing
as I watch my white-wax love slowly melting
to the candle's end, guttering, dying.
I am silent. I can't speak of his leaving.
He is so young, his joy at an ebb.
His smile is forced where once he was laughing.

*

Come little one, the sunset
spills its gold. Time to fetch
and lay to rest your playthings:
the long, cold night is coming.
Come, and hear my story
about the dawn, and let me
hold you close for the last time
in the warm nest of bedtime.
Twine your white hands round me tight
before you yield to the sunlight.
Come, your new day will see
a King and His mystery.
Sleep, my sweetest princeling,
your endless day is fading.

*

In a tiny wreath I find
your secret plan entwined:

to today I plant a root
plucked from yesterday's shoot.
Tomorrow it may turn
this black earth to a garden.

Above the grave, my simple prayer
is silent: may You be there.

And if tonight old questions come and go
I won't ask any more. Let them to and fro.
I'm a mother. I don't dare doubt for long
that beyond the words there's a truth we know.

*

My message and its history are old,
older than this story:
the choice is ours, you see:
rebirth lies in you. And me.

[EaH]

Tudur Dylan Jones

Tudur Dylan Jones (*b.* 1965) is a member of the prominent Parc Nest family (son of John Gwilym Jones, nephew of T James Jones and Aled Gwyn Jones, all three recipients of major Eisteddfod awards). He was brought up in Bangor, and graduated at the University there. He teaches Welsh at Ysgol y Strade in Llanelli, and lives in Carmarthen. In 1995 he won the Chair at the National Eisteddfod, when his own father was the Archdruid who officiated at the ceremony, and in the same year as his uncle Aled Gwyn Jones won the Crown.

The Great Glasshouse at the National Botanic Garden of Wales

On the banks of Tywi river there's a rainbow of one shade
spreading its amazement in sunshine and in rain.

It's not the silver rainbow that reflects our coloured planet
yet the hues of all the world are blooming underneath it,

drinking the gift of sunshine which shines through all the panes,
igniting power that drives through all the roots again.

And on the banks of Tywi there's the circle of creation,
the singing of a blackbird, a longing that is ancient.

There is a dome of clear glass
that rolls the sunbeams into grass.

By Tywi there's sowing,
there's harvesting.

And on the banks of Tywi this rainbow arc will stay
reflecting light from dawning until the end of day.

[EaH]

Gardening

The man who spreads the cow-muck
and tills the fields is in luck?
Bollocks! That man with the spade's
a sad git, a renegade.

An idea occurred to me –
move to town asap,
and so I came to garden
a back yard in Carmarthen.

I saw that nextdoor's lot
was full of peas and what-not,
while I sat home, on the skids,
with creeds like giant triffids.
My garden is nothing but
a long rectangle or rain-smut
soaked, under feet of snow,
watered by drizzle, not elbow.

The sun shone on him next door,
that Medwyn of a neighbour,
his bulbs are his *raison d'être*,
his bower, his greatest pleasure.
Drunk on wires and nets
– laureate of the privets!
The Thrower of onion-sets,
Bowering of hanging baskets.

His plot is an oasis
sculpted from shit. It is
a garden in a story
blooming with plants flow'ring free.
Weeds? Not *his* enemy –
they live next door – with me.
His weeds are microscopic,
his thistles such little pricks!
Good God, the briars in my field
have roots of Llanwern steel.

The weeds began to argue.
Off I went to B and Q.
Into the shop I went
to buy my arsenal. I spent.
Seeds, and books in tandem
showing me where to shove them;
to give this garden a go,
I needed to talk plant lingo.

Manage your veg with free verse,
Begonia for beginners.

Once I planted one small pea.
This was exhausting for me
in itself. One little sphere,
round and green I put down there.
Despite the tears, pain and sweat
I never saw that pealet.
That orb, all by itself,
is down there still, on the shelf,
doing sod-all, I presume;
an existentialist legume.

My spade is growing rusty;
my greenhouse is produce-free,
devoid of all tomatoes
while I, oh sad forker, doze.
If the lawn sees an eggshell
of rain – Atlantean swell,
the flowers are all very sick;
the weeds are quite fantastic.

Birds from Hawaii migrate
to his plot to seek a mate –
they'd not come from Caeathro
to perch on my patio.
RSPB? Forget it!
I never saw a single tit.

This plot, my quarter acre!
this Somme-like, muddy failure –
a garden not evergreen
as much as never-been-green...
Right! Damage limitation!
In two hours 'twas bare again.
I levelled the lot, and pronto,
flames rose from the Flymo.

And so sorriest of men,
I scorched-earth my own Eden.
The man who spreads the cow-muck
and plants a mess – oh, wish him luck!

[EaH]

Elin Llwyd Morgan

Elin Llwyd Morgan (*b.* 1966) is the daughter of the poet and academic Derec Llwyd Morgan and the novelist Jane Edwards, and was born in Cefnbryn-brain in Carmarthenshire. She graduated in French and Spanish at Aberystwyth, and then worked as a journalist and editor. Now she lives in Dyffryn Ceiriog, and is a freelance writer and translator.

The Contemporary Jezebel

She sucked the happiness
from his life and left him flaccid;
savaged the spirit,
ravaged the soul
and ripped the heart
to bloody gobbets.

And everything about her
provokes longing,
making him writhe
in agony
when she breaks
into his dreams.
There's a switchblade in her beauty,
belladonna in her kisses
and a merciless charm
polluting her bloodstream.

She has childbearing thighs
and lungs full of dust,
but physical perfection
has always been tedious.
And it's the memories
that sting:
her catnapping on the bed
and him at the desk writing;
her photographs on the walls;
the murderer in her eyes sometimes;
her voice on the phone from a far country;
her body voluptuous and supple
and unfaithful.

And that's what wrecks everything,
turns love into hatred,
turns life into bile.

There's a twisted thrill in killing,
like the power of the hunter
and the speed of the skier,
leaping through the sky
high above all feeling
save for the rush and the laughter,
the sun's heat and the healthy
bite of the fresh air.

But somewhere in Wales
in a rainy grey town
someone's heart lies
broken and bleeding
while her intact heart
bleeds in pity –
not that that
alleviates the anguish
nor revives the bliss,
for there's no comfort
in knowing,
in his blackest hour,
that the contemporary Jezebel
owns a conscience.

[RP/AUTHOR]

Schizo de Picasso

Sitting by the inlet
looking at the sunset
cursing fate
and the crazy
mixed-up world
that makes my heart retch.

Picasso said that every woman
is either a goddess or a slut.
I am a goddesslut,

welcoming good and bad folk
into my life
filling buses with those that are nice
and falling in love with the misfits.

The sunset is so romantic
as it penetrates
the island's arsehole,
but I feel lost in spite of the
sex and drugs and rock 'n' roll
that keep the killjoy gods at bay.

Something is missing
in my prodigal life,
some sin I haven't proven,
some god I haven't woven
into the complex pattern
of my make-up.

Before the sunset sucks me into
the beached bowels of loneliness,
reach your hand out for me again;
I'll be a goddess
and a slut for you,
a schizo for Picasso.

[AUTHOR]

Your Ostrich Nature

Hesitantly,
I say that you
remind me
of an ostrich
with its head
buried
in a desert
of glass grains,
like millions
of dirty panes
piled on top

411

of each other
in the microscopic world
of your brain.

Staring
through the density
of the windows,
the world
outside you
is distorted,
as if you were
squinting
at a skeleton
savaged
by a lingering illness
and the squalor of senility
after twenty centuries
of suffering.

But
your shoulders
aren't strong enough
to bear the world's burden
like Mr Atlas,
Father Christmas and Christ.
The stalk of your neck
has been broken,
your liver pickled
in a lethal cocktail
of daily poison.

I offered you my hand
to pull you out
of your lifestyle
of sand.
I waded into
the bloodbath
and drank with you
to spare you from having
to enter the cavern
of awful oblivion
on your own
– but in vain.

The solitude
which stifles you
has gone beyond
the succour of company,
and arms around you
are less necessary
than the content of the bottles
fuelling you on.

You gazed into the eye
of the sun for a second
and decided
that being
buried alive
was less dreadful
than being blinded.

[RP/AUTHOR]

Ceri Wyn Jones

Ceri Wyn Jones (*b.* 1967) was born in Hertfordshire, and brought up mainly in
Cardigan, and he graduated in English at Aberystwyth. Formerly head of Eng-
lish at Ysgol Dyffryn Teifi in Llandysul, he is now editor for Gwasg Gomer,
Llandysul, and lives in Cardigan. He learnt to write in *cynghanedd* from novelist
and poet T Llew Jones, and is well-known as a member of one of the *Talwrn y
Beirdd* teams. He won the National Eisteddfod Chair in 1997.

Honour
To the first child born after the IRA ceasefire

This mild child's not turned her face
to the spyhole of our race;
so cannot see she will inherit
the certain shaming of the spirit.
She's not been bothered about blood
or the nagging tooth of nationhood.
She's not scrawled slogans of the schism
or learned her Semtex catechism

413

or glimpsed us as we grind the bones
of children on sectarian stones.
    Still, pretty soon she must discover
    that life is one side or the other.

[RM]

Influence

*(My father's family hail from Blaenau Ffestiniog,
which is overlooked by the Moelwyn mountains.)*

In these screes, I cannot see
a sign of my ancestry,
or find, in this slump of slates
their chisel strokes, undated,
nor find their names, their faces,
their gravestones, – a single trace.
And yet, my father's fathers
are in my bones, and they are
the tumbled rocks. They swear and sing,
a catch in my own breathing.
The metres of this country
are stone on stone inside me.

[EaH]

Legacy

(extracts)

Blow after blow is the farm's blight –
and its branches are bruises bright
to her who sees dawn as night.

Selling-up and its clamour,
the fall of the auction hammer,
are driven coffin-nails for her.

A legacy's made public
in raised thumb, and gestured trick:

414

a shrewd count behind each curse,
low and bleat now are commerce.
With the gleanings of husbandry,
the gear of field and dairy,
her country – her kin's tomorrow
are ground under a hammer's blow.

There's mourning in each minute
and Mam, who's no mam, is mute.
She yields: turns from the fields of fuss
to stare at the silent storehouse.

Her son's face are its features:
she sees, she remembers all…

      *   *   *

Echo. Shriek. Scattering crows.
Screaming-scrambling hedgerows,
and a rickyard re-echoes.

The echo that soils the pitcher
is heard in the clay's ear,
cleaving to the clover.

In a wood the knell of wings
rings awhile; and then silence –
as fine as a leaf's fall.

Above the still farms nearby,
on a breeze, gunshot abroad
in unquiet quiet calls.

All morning fixing his fence,
dead to all but Parc-y-Fedwen,
Boyce doesn't even unbend.

As he sets his rusty snare,
Hughes sees all in his wallet –
not a glimpse past Nant-y-Glog.

If at all, John Cilbronne
heard without regarding
the morning-shattering shot.

His mother heard – without suspecting,
and to the needles' clicking
just carried on her knitting.

It's one o'clock – she's on her feet.
It's one o'clock. It's time to eat.
First to the yard – then to the gate –
Where is the boy? Why is he late?

She calls his name, then calls him names: calling
with no one to answer. Till each building,
with twelve dozen echoes ringing,
mocks her call, gutter-to-roofing.
She, in her failure, opens wide the door,
from wordless yard onto the storehouse floor.

She sees the silence of her dying days,
amid grey straw and rusting coulter blades.
She sees the furrow torn through dower land:
where corn had ripened, now a nightmare's sown.
There, garnered in his blood, swim gathered seeds;
and on the whitewashed walls her heart-wound bleeds.

        *   *   *

The funeral empties each farmstead, each yard,
outbuilding and cowshed.
We come from homes widespread
to play-act over the dead.

The cwm wears its ready mourning: we crowd
in crow-black adorning,
and with clichéd tears weeping,
for a stranger our hands wring.

        *   *   *

Then from grief's formality
to the loose-tongued bar we flee.
But spit-and-sawdust rhetoric,
and sagas half-comic
of lost cows, and broken fence
end in tomes of sober silence.

At the bar, the glasses bring
a night's pontificating.
In flowing pints the least fluent,
liquor-high, grows eloquent.
They recreate, thought and deed,
in the bar, him they buried.

'He was odd, just a half-wit;
not normal, an old hermit',
spat Cilbronne to all present,
as Hughes nodded his assent.
Said Nant-y-Glog, for all to hear
of his reclusive neighbour,
'His field was his world, as it were;
not like us – who see further'.

In the bottom, but beyond our sight,
the empty glass holds truth a-right.

      *   *   *

And, after dwelling on his lonely life,
we all turn back to far-off croft and farm:
all to be broken by the rusted plough;
each one to bleed, to waste away unseen.
We turn to till our fields of debt and stone,
a fellowship where each man walks alone.

Echo. Shriek. Scattering crows.
Screaming-scrambling hedgerows.

[DWJ]

Elinor Wyn Reynolds

Elinor Wyn Reynolds (*b.* 1970) was born in Treorchy, raised in Carmarthen, and read Welsh at Aberystwyth and Oxford. A versatile poet, fond of public performance, she recently toured Wales with a multimedia poetry show, *Lliwiau Rhyddid* (Colours of Freedom) with Ifor ap Glyn and the Bara Caws theatre company. She has worked in the four corners of Wales, and is now a freelance writer and broadcaster. She has been resident poet on the radio, a word-juggler, teacher, a TV presenter and hopes to be a lot more besides, soon.

I Had a Really Good Idea for a Poem in Cynwil Elfed

Like a child playing peek-a-boo with me,
the idea astonished me by leaping out into the middle of the road
in Cynwil Elfed, boldly, to shock me.
Screech of car tyres and the smell of rubber like brimstone
in my nostrils
ready to cause a literary accident in rural Wales.
A Really Good Idea for a Poem
hitting me with the wet, smelly mackerel of the muse, happily,
slap across my chops.
'Hey! You! I'm a Really Good Idea for a Poem!'
And then it climbs up to the roof of the chapel
just out of reach of my starved, uninspired, grasping fingers...
Blast you! Really Good Idea for a Poem!
for escaping to a rooftop
to skulk among the slates again.
Don't linger to tempt me!
Vanish into the night. Go on. Get lost!
Leave me here untouched.
What are you, anyway?
What kind of poem will you be when you are born?

I am the scent of a feather falling from the sky,
an unexpected car journey to nowhere,
a nightmare where nuns are crying,
wailing, crazy laughter in an empty quarry,
caressing the silk of a luxurious nightdress, the memory of
        something which never existed
the fragile spirit of mourning trees – that kind of thing I suppose.

Poet, never sleep – in case you lose a gem –
that one shining white poem that will make you famous,
invest you as a poet beyond your words and ragged verses.
Learn to jump high, to the middle of the soft, quiet current of
        the breeze
to snatch that Really Good Idea for a Poem from there
to hold it firmly in your hands and cherish it.

[GD]

The Night I Won the Crown in the National Eisteddfod of My Dreams

It didn't take much to write, must've come from the heart.
Yes, I surprised myself to tell you the truth,
and my mother too,
especially when you remember the tragic standard of my written work
in school.
The kids aren't talking to me at the moment,
I left supper half done to be extra early in order to dodge the
Gorsedd.
I wasn't sure that I'd won at all,
being a girl, you know,
but I got somebody to compare my chromosomes
with the winning *nom de plume*
before going to the Pavilion,
and it was me – a chance in a million

I wasn't going to stand when the trumpet fanfared
thought I'd avoid any fuss, indeed,
but when I saw the searchlights whirling
through space, looking for a poet in the pitch black
the urge came over me like a cold sweat
to jump
and throw myself on a bright beam,
catching its tail and squeezing it so tight that I fly through the firmament
way, way above the chattering crowds,
a cultural trapeze act, beautiful, but deadly
showing my second best knickers to the Archdruid
and doing a loop-the-loop around the Mistress of the Robes
before dive-bombing the little dancing girls with their pretty flowers,
baring my teeth
to see if their petals shake and fall,
a shower of posy-poems on stage…
how embarrassing…

I don't remember a thing after that.
The poem?
Oh yes, there's a message there
for anyone who wishes to hear it.

But it's very quiet, a whisper,
it can tickle an ear,
excite the heart and the blood in the veins.
Yes, I wrote it with somebody special in mind
but I doubt if he was listening.
I cried words onto a page,
full of pain, hurt and salty wetness,
full of laughter too and beautiful singing
but he did not notice,
not even
when the eyes of a whole nation
were upon me.
When the righteous rays of Wales' sun were beating down on me alone,
warming my body,
leaving the cold, empty wind to whip through the rest of the country
for a while.
He must have been looking at something else,
listening to a different song,
watching the horizon, looking for the promise of something different.
Me, it seems I'm a poet with no voice.

[AUTHOR]

Mererid Puw Davies

Mererid Puw Davies (*b.* 1970) was raised on a Welsh-speaking hearth in Lancashire, before the family moved to north-east Wales. She read German at Oxford, and spent periods studying and researching on the Continent. Her doctoral thesis involved a feminist study of aspects of German literature. She now lectures in German at University College, London.

Over a Drink

Come on then my sweet
let's be cruel tonight

and let's catch up
with that girl they call love
that foolish elf

who never sees sense
who always forgets
to leave her glassgreen wings at home
when she sashays by like summer

let's be cruel tonight
and give her a call

that trusting child
with the heartstopping smile
all eden's glory in her hair
holding out gifts, brilliant leaves in her hands

let's call her now
that girl they call love

and as payback for something
(that slips my mind now)
let's cut off her hair
pierce her palms
put out her eyes

and between us, smiling
transfix and tear

over a drink

those stupid, greenglitter wings

[AUTHOR]

Computers Are Poets Too

We close the door, shut out all sound, this is a ritual. We open the
current.

We talk.

This is a conversation through glass. An exchange in little live neon
words,
fireflies in the screen's knot garden, with none of the halting, raw
touching of some hand on a page that'll perish.

We talk.

And this computer isn't so different from the ones which
      pace hearts and score life's rhythms.
This computer with its lights and pulses isn't so different
      from my own light heart.

We talk.

We are abroad. I teach it my language.

And shining answers come back to me, as though from the far side
    of Europe,
    electric shocking. Only the computer and I understand.

We talk.

And my own language, my old writing: I see their shapes shift.
In a silver surface, fire flowers, lucid lucent procession, brilliant heralds,
     brighter than anything you've ever seen.

We talk. The computer is a poet.

[AUTHOR]

A Poet on 'Poets on Poets': And Other Poems
(thinking partly of Francis Ponge)

D's giving a talk called 'Poets on Poets'. I nearly didn't go.

It's a very learned talk. D is very learned. Today, I'm very learned
    too – but learned
        different things from those in D's talk,
        and so, it's hard to listen.

D too is a poet. Does this qualify or disqualify him to talk on this topic?
        Perhaps it doesn't matter.
Perhaps there's some mystic pleasure in this, these endless reflections,
    this hall of mirrors,
   between the topic and the one who speaks to it. Perhaps the topic
    speaks to him.
        Perhaps it's the speaker who's spoken here.
       Or perhaps, of course, it doesn't matter.

But D's voice calls up the consonances of the Anglo-Welsh canon
and the words

lift off the page

glittering. Unexpected. Like resurrection.

And to me, not listening too hard: it's a soundtrack to what I learned,
all dislocated,
today. About some artist, seeing the work of some other artist,
in all the splendour of a chapel in Italy. And saying:

I too will be a painter!

And isn't every painting, isn't every poem, a statement on what's
before it,
what went before, what lies before it?
The creator's response is a critic's response.

All of us, then, we glorious poets, we noble painters, D's seriously
famous poets,
even the learned D himself –

we all wear two hats

(as poets as critics)

that is, I mean:

we've all got two heads.

And so, here I am then, not listening too hard – notwithstanding two
heads and two sets of ears –
the words are like pebbles, rolling, sonorous on the floor on the ceiling,
never mind that I'm not listening:

the voice ripples on, making poems of poems which are quite different
poems,
which make no sense at all, are brilliant irrelevance,
and this is far greater and oh how much sweeter

than any obedient attention.

[AUTHOR]

NOTES

T Gwynn Jones

Argoed (31): T Gwynn Jones himself devised the story of Argoed, but it is based on the Roman conquest of pre-Christian Gaul, and could easily be read as a parable for modern Wales under English siege.

Pro Patria (36): This is an earlier and uncharacteristic poem by T Gwynn Jones, which relates the true story of a Welsh soldier in the Boer War. In this excerpt from the long poem, the soldier tells of his experience to a Welsh nurse who tends him in hospital. The title is of course ironic, coming from a man who described himself as 'a pacifist with the emphasis on the fist'. This poet turned away from realism in his mature work, and yet returned to it in his later years.

T E Nicholas

Caernarfon Circus, 1969 (46): This refers to the investiture of Charles as Prince of Wales at Caernarfon Castle. It was widely felt in Wales that this was a ruse by the politicians to use the Prince as a puppet to create an impression of unity between Wales and England. The ceremony was ironically held in a castle built by Edward I who conquered Wales in the 13th century. There were many protests against the investiture, and two activists were killed by their own bomb. See also poems by T Glynne Davies (206, 435*n*) and Gerallt Lloyd Owen (285, 438*n*).

Dewi Emrys

Pwllderi (48): The title is the name of a rocky cove on the north coast of Pembrokeshire not far from Strumble Head. The poem itself has been written in the strong, colourful dialect of the area, which is almost as different from formal Welsh as Lallans is from English.

W J Gruffydd

This Poor Man (51): Gruffydd had an academic interest in medieval Welsh myth, and alludes in this poem to the Mabinogion. Arawn was the king of Annw(f)n or the Celtic Otherworld. Caer Siddi was the high court of that otherworld. Rhiannon is a prominent figure in the Four Branches of the Mabinogi, and her birds had the power to entrance the living into sleep and to awake the dead.

R Williams Parry

Hedd Wyn (60): These two short series of *englynion* are an elegy on the death of Ellis Humphrey Evans (*see* 66-67), whose bardic name was Hedd Wyn (White Peace). He was killed in action in France in the summer of 1917, six weeks before he was declared the winner of the Chair at the National Eisteddfod. His empty chair was draped in black. Trawsfynydd was the village in Meirionnydd (Merioneth) where he was born on a small-holding called Yr Ysgwrn, and where he was a shepherd.

The Geese (61): The Great Market (y Farchnad Fawr) where geese were sold before Christmas seems to be a premonition of the Last Judgement (y Farn Fawr).

A E Housman (62): This poem was written in 1936 as an elegy on the death of the poet well-known for *A Shropshire Lad*. Housman was an agnostic who seemed to regard this world as the worst of all possible worlds, and R Williams Parry seems to have seen him as a kindred spirit.

J S L (63): R Williams Parry was outraged at the imprisonment of John Saunders Lewis following the 'fire in Llŷn' incident of 1936. This sonnet shows Saunders Lewis to be something of an outsider in the Wales of the 20s and 30s, due to his Merseyside background, his Catholicism and his challenging political views. R Williams Parry is acerbic towards his academic colleagues in their ivory tower.

Wales 1937 (64): Another ferocious sonnet arising from the aftermath of the 'fire in Llŷn'. The penultimate line refers to the burial place of Wales's greatest hymn writer, Williams Pantycelyn in the 18th century (Llanfair ar y Bryn in Carmarthenshire), and to the birthplace of his contemporary, Goronwy Owen, a very different person who was a fluent writer of poems in the traditional metres, but also an excessive drinker (born at Llanfair Mathafarn Eithaf on Anglesey).

Mortality (65): This sonnet was written in response to the call from a younger generation of poets for committed poetry which engaged with contemporary issues. Branwen is the character in the Four Branches of the Mabinogi who married the King of Ireland, but suffered insult and humiliation at the Irish court. She tamed a starling and sent it to Wales with a message telling her countrymen of her sorry plight. The Welsh decided to sail to Ireland and fight a war of revenge. They were victorious, but only seven of them survived. On returning to Wales, Branwen died of grief and was buried in Anglesey. The fig tree referred to is the one condemned by Jesus for not bearing fruit. Arianwen is a young dead girl described by John Morris-Jones in a modern poem. These three examples of mortality span the period from prehistory, through Christian times, to the beginning of the 20th century.

T H Parry-Williams

Tŷ'r Ysgol (68): The School-house where T H Parry-Williams was brought up in the village of Rhyd-ddu at the foot of Snowdon.

Llyn y Gadair (69): A lake near the poet's home in Rhyd-ddu.

Saunders Lewis

A Vineyard Placed in My Care (77): This is an extract from the verse-play for radio, *Buchedd Garmon*, written while Saunders Lewis was awaiting trial at the Old Bailey in London for his part in the controversial 'Tân yn Llŷn' arson attack on the bombing school at Penyberth. The play was broadcast on 2 March 1937 when the author was already in prison. This seemingly benign play based on early 5th century history in Gaul and Wales was pregnant with meaning to its first audience. The speech by Emrys is a rousing plea to the Welsh people to stand up for their Christian heritage and national traditions in the face of the threat from English secularism. He is addressing Garmon or St Germanus, the Bishop of Auxerre in Gaul, who led the Britons to victory at the battle of Maes Garmon in 430.

Scene in a Café (78): The scene is set in the university seaside town of Aberystwyth in mid-Wales, and the poem alludes to evacuees from London and other cities who lived there during the Second World War. The 'white gloves' is an ironic reference to the Victorian concept of Wales as 'the land of the white gloves' – a country without crime.

The Deluge, 1939 (79): Central to the imagery of this poem about the ravages of the Depression in the industrial valleys of south Wales in the 30s is the Deluge in the book of Genesis, chapters 6-9. 'Lethe milk' alludes to Lethe, a river in Hades in the Greek underworld, whose waters brought oblivion.

'Mond pension': It was Sir Alfred Mond who organised a campaign to improve the lot of industrial workers by increasing their pension.

'They turned cow's milk into sticks of umbrellas': Refers to the absurd economics of the period, whereby milk was sold cheaply for the manufacture of umbrella handles, whilst the price of milk for mothers was quadrupled.

The third stanza of the second section bristles with Classical allusions, including a reference to Virgil who depicts the Golden Age of the Sabines in central Italy. It was Virgil who also prophesied the birth of a Babe, subsequently thought to be a reference to Christ's birth.

The third section of the poem charts the political situation in the decade leading up to the Second World War, from the slump of 1929 on the Wall Street stock market, to the rise of Hitler as successor to Bruening, with references to the Anschluss in Vienna, the 'Peace in our time' Munich agreement, the invasion of Bohemia and subsequently the whole of Czechoslovakia, and the massacre of the river Ebro, one of the bloodiest battles of the Spanish Civil War.

'Dragon's teeth' is an allusion to the Greek legend of Cadmus killing a dragon. When he sowed the dead dragon's teeth on the land, armed men sprang therefrom, and fought against each other.

Mary Magdalen (82): Mary was one of the women who stood by the Cross and who went to the grave of Jesus with the intention of anointing his body. The poem refers to the account given in John 20, when Mary finds the grave empty, and later sees the resurrected Christ, although not recognising him at first. It is he who tells her: 'Do not touch me.' The 'night of the senses' recalls St John of the Cross's concept of abstinence from sensuous pleasure. Niobe was a character in Greek mythology whose children were all murdered, and who was herself transformed into stone by Zeus at her own request. Thomas was of course the doubter who needed to put his finger in the mark of the nails on Christ's body before he could believe that he was resurrected from the dead – a luxury denied Mary.

Et Homo Factus Est. Crucifixus... (84): The title, meaning 'And was made man. He was crucified...' comes from the Nicene Creed which is recited in the Catholic Mass. Caiaphas was the Jewish high priest who said it would be good for one man to die for the people. Tiresias was the blind prophet in the Greek legend of Oedipus.

Chance Child (85): A vociferous anti-Marxist, and anti-Modernist in the theological sense, Saunders Lewis rejected the evolutionary view of human development, and therefore did not accept the Marxist dream of an Utopian classless society, or Teilhard de Chardin's Christian interpretation of evolution as directed towards perfection.

Prayer at the End (86): The poet rebutted the claims of some critics that this poem was one of despair in the face of death, and referred his readers to the theology of some medieval mystics in Germany and the Netherlands who emphasised the impossibility of comprehending the meaning of God. He said that 'death itself is therefore a prayer, a prayer at the end'.

Cynan

Monastîr (87): Here the mature poet and committee man recalls the heady days of freedom he spent as a soldier in Macedonia, and he satirises the small-mindedness of institutionalised religion.

The Prodigal Son (88): This is an excerpt from Cynan's Crown-winning poem of 1921, 'Mab y Bwthyn' (literally, 'Son of the Cottage'), which tells the story of a country lad torn from his supposedly innocent rural background to face the lurid temptations of a soldier in a totally alien environment. *Felin Fach* literally means 'Little Mill' and *Nain* 'Grandmother'.

Alun Cilie

The Old Chapel (91): Although the word *gwerin* literally means 'folk', its connotations are wider in Welsh. It conveys a concept of an idealised common people who were both cultured and religious. The fact that the Welsh gentry became anglicised in the wake of the Act of Union of England and Wales in 1536 meant that Welsh speakers belonged to an unprivileged class, and yet, through the 18th-century 'circulating schools' of Griffith Jones, and the Methodist Revival, these people became the upholders of poetry, music, religion and even radical politics during the 19th and 20th centuries. It was often claimed that the University Colleges of Aberystwyth and Bangor were built with the pennies of *y werin*, and the prevalence of institutions of higher education in Wales was a symptom of the desire of ordinary folk to rise in the world. Even today, Welsh people in high offices often proudly claim that they have sprung from this ordinary but noble class.

Gwenallt

Dartmoor (93): Gwenallt spent time as a prisoner in Dartmoor as a result of his stand as a conscientious objector in the First World War.

Rhydcymerau (95): The poet's family on his father's side came from this rural village in Carmarthenshire, and in his youth he spent a great deal of time there during school holidays. The farms of the area were sold to the Forestry Commission, thus bleeding the area of its people and its culture. The 'manuscript of Peniarth' refers to the main collection of medieval Welsh manuscripts housed at the National Library of Wales in Aberystwyth.

The Hedgehog (97): Nanteos is a mansion on the outskirts of Aberystwyth where the remains of a wooden cup were housed, and this cup was believed to be the Holy Grail. In this poem the hedgehog seems to bar the poet's Christian pilgrimage to see this cup, and looms in his mind as a symbol of the introversion of secular and pagan modernism.

The Dead (98): In the third stanza there is a play on the meaning of Merthyr in the name of the industrial town of Merthyr Tydfil in Glamorganshire. The Welsh word means 'martyr', and the neighbours who came from there were nicknamed 'y merthyron' or 'martyrs'.

Iorwerth Peate

Nant yr Eira (101): This is a nostalgic poem about a district in Montgomeryshire where some farmsteads were in ruins. The name translates as 'Snow Brook'.

Roncesvalles (102): A pass in the Pyrenees where Roland was killed whilst fighting in Charlemagne's army in Spain. This Roland is the hero of the famous French poem, *Chanson de Roland*.

Airstrip St Athan (103): This poem refers to the military airport in the picturesque Vale of Glamorgan. The places mentioned conjure up the villages and churches of the Vale whose harmony seems threatened by modern development. Bethesda was the chapel associated with the hymnist, Thomas Williams, and Eglwys Brywys is the church in a nearby village. As this book goes to the press, we hear of proposals to extend the military zone of St Athan, which makes Peate's poem even more telling. Some people predict that virtually the whole of the Vale of Glamorgan could become a military zone.

J Kitchener Davies

The Sound of the Wind that is Blowing (104): J Kitchener Davies was suffering from cancer when he wrote this death-bed poem. In it he confronts himself, questioning his motives at various stages in his life, from his upbringing in Cardiganshire to his adult life in the Rhondda Valley during the Depression of the 30s and afterwards, when he was an active campaigner for the Welsh Nationalist Party, and a committed Christian. But it is only as he faces his final destiny that he realises the full implications of salvation.

R Bryn Williams

Patagonia (111): A Welsh colony was established in Patagonia in

Argentina in 1865, when a group of settlers travelled on a small ship, the *Mimosa*, to Porth Madryn or Puerto Madryn, in an attempt to create a new Wales free of oppression and poverty. They settled in the arid land of the Camwy Valley, and suffered great hardship. Yet Welsh-language culture flourished, especially its religious aspect, and chapels were built, and books and newspapers published. Almost miraculously, the Welsh language still survives in small pockets of the colony, and there have been recent attempts to re-invigorate the Welsh heritage.

T Rowland Hughes

Crib Goch (116): This is a ridge at the top of a craggy rock in Snowdonia, and a challenge for climbers.

Salem (116): This poem is based on a picture painted by Curnow Vosper and displayed in the Royal Academy in London in 1909. The picture is a portrait of Siân Owen, an old woman in traditional dress, inside Salem, a tiny chapel in Merioneth. The portrait became famous when reproduced as an advertisement for a brand of soap.

Caradog Prichard

Earthly Turmoil (120): This long poem failed to win the Crown at the 1939 National Eisteddfod for the absurd reason that it did not conform with the title set for the competition. Its subject is suicide, and the poet in his autobiography relates an incident when he himself seems to have subconsciously attempted suicide.

Waldo Williams

Preseli (125): Waldo Williams learnt Welsh in the area at the foot of this ridge of mountains in north Pembrokeshire. In 1946 the British Government announced that 16,000 acres of land from this area would be taken over for the purpose of military training. As a pacifist, Waldo was distraught at hearing the news, and wrote this poem as a kind of protest. The places named in the poem can easily be found on a map of the area. Yr Efail refers to Efail-wen, which is associated with the Rebecca Riots of the 19th century, and was therefore a literal and metaphorical smithy.

A Summer Cloud (126): The poet was living in Lyneham, Wiltshire when he composed this poem, and the houses named at the beginning were probably in that area. He noticed how people seem to have a strong need for roots. This surrealistic poem is open to many interpretations. The second stanza is generally taken to convey the nature of the Welsh poetic tradition, and the third may refer to the prose tradition. In Wales, history has more to do with chronicling the development of literature than with kings and queens. Yet the summer cloud of the title annihilates the concreteness of the house of tradition, and the poet is mesmerised in an anguished existential solitude of self-questioning. Only towards the end of the poem does objective reality flow back through his veins.

After the Mute Centuries (128): This poem pays homage to three Welsh Catholic martyrs who lived in the latter part of the 16th century and the beginning of the 17th.

In Two Fields (130): This poem is based on a mystical experience which Waldo Williams had between Weun Parc y Blawd and Parc y Blawd (Flower Meadow Field and Flower Field) – two fields in Pembrokeshire. It relates to his religious experience (vivid, yet unspecific in theological terms), which leads him to meditate on the relationship between people, as both individuals and nations, and at the end of stanza 5 there is an allusion to The Book of Revelations, 22.2: 'And the leaves of the tree were for the healing of the nations.' The image of a fountain of love which sheds healing leaves is the ultimate expression of Waldo's belief in the brotherhood of man. The people of all nations congregate on these two fields in the poem. At the end there is an apocalyptic vision of the Exiled King reclaiming his kingdom, and he is the quintessential peacemaker.

A Young Girl (131): Her remains are preserved in Avebury Museum, and she belonged to nearby Windmill Hill, about 2500 BC. Archaeologists tell us that her people were farmers who lived together in peace.

Three English Poets and England (132): The first English poet is Thomas Hardy (see the beginning of *The Dynasts*). The second is John Keats who stayed in Winchester (a centre for the Belgae in pre-Roman times) in 1819, and found much inspiration for his poetry there. 'This world is a vale of soul making' comes from one of Keats's letters. Keats called his poetry 'the leaves of his tree'. The third English poet mentioned is William Cowper, who wrote the line: 'I was a stricken deer and left the herd', and when his country was celebrating the victories of the Seven Years War, he wrote 'O for a lodge in some vast wilderness'. This poem has echoes of Waldo's visit to the Quantocks with his future wife, Linda, in 1940 (the area where Wordsworth and Coleridge wrote *The Lyrical Ballads*), and also of the years he spent in England (Huntingdon and Wiltshire) after his wife's untimely death.

W R P George

Armstrong and Aldrin on the Moon (150): 'Cauldron of man's rebirth' is a reference to the *Pair Dadeni* [Cauldron of Rebirth] that appears in the second of the Four Branches of the Mabinogi. Caer Arianrhod is the Milky Way.

Moses Glyn Jones

The Old Light (159): 'Goleuni Parc y Blawd' refers to the 'sea of light' which Waldo Williams described in his poem 'In Two Fields' (130), in which he describes a mystical experience he had between two fields in Pembrokeshire. See the note on that poem (432).

The Living Spring (160): Cian, Iestyn, Pedrog and Tudwal are four Welsh saints associated with Llŷn.

Alun Llywelyn-Williams

When I Was a Boy (162): *Gwennan Gorn* was the name of the ship on which Madog sailed in his quest for a sceptred island, according to Welsh legend.

On a Visit (163): This is based on the poet's experience in Belgium during the Second World War.

In Berlin – August 1945 (165): The poet described Lehrter Bahnhof as a railway station 'where at the end of World War II some of the many thousands of wretches were unloaded who were driven out of those lands in the east that Russia had given to Poland'. He also explained that Zehlendorf was a suburb through which the Russians, after surrounding the city, made their final attack. He remarked that Theater Des Westens was a relatively undamaged playhouse in the British sector of Berlin. Llywarch Hen and Heledd were characters in 9th-century sagas depicting the suffering of war and its aftermath. Roath Park is in Cardiff.

Eluned Phillips

Ties (169): See the note on 'Patagonia' by R Bryn Williams (430-31). This poem by Eluned Phillips is a kind of short story. It begins with the emigration of a farming family to Patagonia because of oppression. They rebuild a new Pant Glas (the farm's name at home in Wales, literally meaning 'Green Valley') in the new Welsh colony in Argentina. 'Llynlleifiad' is a Welsh name for Liverpool, from where they sailed, and *Y Faner* (The Flag) was a Welsh newspaper which whipped up support for the establishment of a Welsh colony in South America. *Mimosa* was the name of the ship on which the colonists sailed. *Hiraeth* is of course that most untranslatable of words, loosely meaning longing or nostalgia. Then the story leaps forward to 1982, and to the contemporary Pant Glas back in Wales, whose son joins the army, and during the war against Argentina he finds himself on the warship Sir Galahad. Wounded, he reminisces about his home back in Wales, and who comes to his bedside but an Argentinian soldier, but a Welsh Argentinian, from Cwm Hyfryd (Pleasant Valley) in Patagonia. They communicate haltingly in Welsh, and despite belonging to opposing warring factions, their Celtic roots tie them together.

J Eirian Davies

Bafflement (189): Apart from its castles, Wales's most prominent architectural characteristic is its Nonconformist chapels, many now closed or put to commercial use. They have usually been named after places in the Holy Land, such as Bethel, Moriah, Nazareth, Ebenezer, etc.

Emyr Humphreys

On the Guincho (192): The Guincho is a beach in Portugal famous for its lobster restaurants.

Poughkeepsie (193): The poem takes its title from the name of a town in upstate New York that Americans tend to make rather a joke of. According to that most American of publications, the *Encyclopedia Britannica*, its meaning is 'the reed-thatched-shelter-by-the-little-spring', a faraway but unmistakable Anglo-Saxon echo of the kind of tourist translation with which we are so familiar in Wales in the form of Llanfairpwllgwyngyllgogerychwyrndrobwllllantysiliogogogoch. (As a matter of interest, although unrelated to the poem, this long-drawn-out name of a village in Anglesey was made up by a tailor in the middle of the 19th century, and is a kind of joke on tourists who think of it as authentic and try to twist their tongues around it.) The Peter Williams mentioned in this poem was an 18th-century Biblical commentator who published an annotated edition of the Welsh Bible in 1770, subsequently reprinted many times. It became popular as a family Bible, where family names were written. Clogwyn Du'r Arddu is the name of a crag in Snowdonia.

John Roderick Rees

Brenin Gwalia (194): The stallion's name literally means 'The King of Wales'.

Gareth Alban Davies

The Wild Geese (195): Coalmining was one of the main industries of south Wales, and the Miners' Strike of the mid-1980s generated a great deal of passion. By now the industry faces its demise.

T Glynne Davies

Ruins (203): The story of this poem revolves around Jo, who mourns the loss of his lover. The poem is about the ruins of his personal life as well as about the decay of rural Wales.

Caernarfon, July 2, 1969 (206): See the notes on 'Caernarfon Circus, 1969' (425). Llywelyn was the last legitimate Prince of Wales, and he was killed in 1282. Owain Glyndŵr (Owen Glendower) was of course the 14th-century hero who tried to regain Wales's independence. See also poems by T E Nicholas (46, 425*n*) and Gerallt Lloyd Owen (285, 438*n*).

Dafydd Rowlands

The Village (225): The 'Utopia on the summit of Gellionnen' is a quotation from Gwenallt's poem, 'The Dead' (98). It refers to his disillusionment with his early Marxist dreams which he imagined on the top of Gellionnen mountain in the Swansea Valley. Adelina refers to the world-famous opera singer, Adelina Patti, who built her own opera house at Craig-y-nos in Breconshire. Ellis yr Ysgwrn was the poet Hedd Wyn (Ellis Humphrey Evans) who was killed in the First World War (66). Thomas Davies was a local boxer.

Dic Jones

Lamentation (236): The hospital where the poet's daughter Esyllt was born and died was at Glangwili, Carmarthen.

T James Jones

Dyfed Devastated (246): 'Category A': primary schools in Dyfed were categorised according to the main language of tuition. A Category A school was one at which Welsh was the medium of education. Some English incomers protested at this, and formed a pressure group called 'Education First'.

Thursday (247): This poem comes from a sequence of poems called *Cerddi Ianws/Janus Poems*, jointly written by T James Jones and the American poet, Jon Dressel. The Welsh version was submitted for the Crown competition at the 1979 National Eisteddfod, but although they were judged worthy of the prize, they were disqualified because they had been entered under a joint authorship. Two poets could not wear the same crown! More importantly, they took as their subject the unsuccessful referendum on devolution which was held in 1979. They express the deep anguish of the poets at what was for them a shattering result.

Face to Face (248): A kind of sequel to *Cerddi Ianws/Janus Poems* was published in 1997, entitled *Wyneb yn Wyneb/Face to Face*. This is a sequence of poems to celebrate the victorious referendum for a Welsh Assembly held in 1997. The same process of co-authorship was at work here as with the earlier sequence.

T Arfon Williams

Quarry (249), *Foam* (249), *May* (250), *One-day Snow* (250): Strict-metre Welsh poetry is agonisingly difficult to translate, and with these *englynion* the translator Emyr Lewis decided to offer two alternative versions, the first in each case being a fairly literal rendition, and the second attempting to convey the spirit of the stanzas.

Eirwyn George

Family (251): The Wicklow Hills of the Irish Republic are visible from Pembrokeshire, and there have been close ties between Pembrokeshire and Ireland, not just because of the ferry connection between Fishguard and Rosslare, but also because of common Celtic roots. The 'Cymry' are the Welsh. Erin is of course Ireland. The poem mentions the Easter Rising in Dublin in 1916 and the Maze Prison where many Irish nationalists were held.

Meic Stevens

Sylvia (272): On reading *The Bell Jar* by Sylvia Plath, the singer remembered another Sylvia he met in the 60s. A classical pianist and a true (rebellious) child of the period, she too shared the same sad fate as that of the poet. This song also tries to capture the struggle for women's liberation.

Derec Llwyd Morgan

Bow and Arrow (275): This is a poem in the *cywydd* metre written in the tradition of medieval messenger poems. The poet came from Carmarthenshire, and his girlfriend (his future wife, the novelist Jane Edwards) lived in Niwbwrch on Anglesey. 'Cwm Aman' is the Aman Valley, and 'Môn' is Anglesey.

Registering the Little One (276): The poet's daughter, Elin Llwyd Morgan (also featured in this anthology, 409-13), was born in 1966, the year when Gwynfor Evans was elected the first MP for Plaid Cymru (Welsh Nationalist Party) to represent the Carmarthen constituency. At that time, it was impossible to register a birth in Welsh. Dafydd Iwan is the popular singer (also represented in this anthology, 273-74).

Meirion Pennar

Branches of a Mabinogi (281): The Mabinogion is a collection of 12 medieval Welsh tales which include three Arthurian romances and *Pedair Cainc y Mabinogi* ('The Four Branches of the Mabinogi'). The word *Mabinogi* here roughly means 'a tale about youth'. The youth whose tale is told in these tales is Pryderi, the son of *Rhiannon*. *Teyrnon* was the king who brought the lost child back to his mother. *Annwn* is the otherworld. *Ceridwen* was the alleged mother of Taliesin in the myth which evolved around the 6th-century poet. It was she who brewed a magic potion in her cauldron, drops from which would imbue a person with the gift of poetry. *Gwydion* is a magician who is one of the main characters of the *Pedair Cainc*, and through magical ruses he helps his brother *Gilfaethwy* to rape the virgin Goewin, for which both brothers are punished by Math by turning them into animals who have children from one another. Gwydion is also involved in the creation of the woman made of flowers, Blodeuwedd. *Manawydan* is the main character in the third of the *Pedair Cainc*. He takes Rhiannon as his wife, and they – together with Pryderi and his wife Cigfa – are the only ones who remain in Dyfed after an enchantment befalls it, and the area is enveloped in mist. It is *Llwyd fab Cil Coed*, or the *Grey* one mentioned in the poem, who was the magician responsible. Other allusions reverberate through this poem, including an echo of the line in Aneirin's 6th-century poem which says that swords sound forth in the heads of their dead warrior sons.

Gerallt Lloyd Owen

The Shame of Llanfaes (283): It was Siwan, the wife of Llywelyn Fawr (Llywelyn the Great), who was buried at Llan-faes in Anglesey. Her husband established a house of Franciscan friars therein to pray for his wife's soul. *Mona* is Anglesey. *Edward* is King Edward I of England, who conquered Wales in 1282 and whose grand castles at such places as Caernarfon are a visual and living image of that conquest.

Cilmeri (283): It was near this village in Breconshire that Llywelyn Ein Llyw Olaf (Llywelyn the Last) was killed by the English, and this marked the end of Welsh independence. Llywelyn's head was taken to London as an exhibit of the conquest, and his trunk buried at the abbey of Cwm-hir, not far from Builth Wells.

The Man on the Horizon (284): This is a poem to Saunders Lewis (77), one of the founders of Plaid Genedlaethol Cymru (The Nationalist Party of Wales) as it was then called. The poem refers to his imprisonment for his part in the arson at the bombing school in Llŷn in 1936 (see also 19, 427*n*).

To the Death (285): This bitter poem was penned in reaction to the investiture of Charles as Prince of Wales in Caernarfon Castle in 1969. (See also poems by T E Nicholas [46, 425*n*] and T Glynne Davies [206, 435*n*]).

Nesta Wyn Jones

Beaches (290): The poet recalls the death of her loved ones, including her grandmother, *Nain*.

Robat Powell

Heysel (296): The poem refers to the tragedy at the Heysel football stadium in Belgium.

Alan Llwyd

The Hawk Above Felindre (297): Felindre is on the outskirts of Swansea, where the poet used to live.

The Bull of Bryncelyn (298): Alan Llwyd was brought up in the Llŷn Peninsula, and this poem depicts a scene on the farm of Bryncelyn.

The Moons of Llŷn (302): R S Thomas, Wales's foremost English-language poet, served as a priest in the parish of Aberdaron in the Llŷn Peninsula. The place-names mentioned are located in that area. *Tir na n-Og* is the Land of the Young Ones in Irish mythology. It was there that *Osian* fell in love with Nia Ben Aur (Nia of the Golden Tresses) who was the king's daughter.

Gwynn ap Gwilym

Penyberth (306): Penyberth was the mansion near Pwllheli where an RAF bombing school was established in the mid-30s, against the will of the local Welsh-speaking population. There were outcries throughout Wales at the decision to locate it there, and Saunders Lewis (77, 427*n*), D J Williams and Lewis Valentine set fire to the buildings in 1936 for which they were imprisoned. This became known as the 'Tân yn Llŷn' (Fire in Llŷn) incident.

Einir Jones

Ffynnon Grandis (311): This is the name of a fountain.

Grey (315): Nant Ffrancon is a pass in Snowdonia.

Menna Elfyn

Cell Angel (315): This is a poem about a youth Menna Elfyn met during a visit to a residential school while compiling the book *Hands Off* (Save the Children's Fund/Welsh Women's Aid). The violent-natured youth tried to prove (unsuccessfully!) that he could play the piano.

Nothing but Curves (319): 'In the US they take their lingerie seriously, calling them "engineering projects". In Welsh, the word *bronglwm* years ago would send people into fits of laughter as the vocabulary of sexual politics had not yet become part of the acceptable poetic vocabulary. This tries to redress that...' (Menna Elfyn)

Rice Papers (321): 'I spent many weeks in Vietnam in 1994 and 1995 researching a documentary for S4C. During my first visit I was looked after by the cultural department of the government and a woman called Trinh.' (Menna Elfyn)

Geraint Løvgreen

Life's Dovey Junctions (332): Dovey Junction is a tiny railway station 'in the middle of nowhere' between Aberystwyth and Machynlleth. It is a desolate spot in the middle of a marsh, where time seems to have stopped.

Myrddin ap Dafydd

'A Language is only Words' (338): The translator Tony Conran supplies the following notes:

As the whole point of this poem is the loss that is suffered in translation, it seems even more paradoxical than usual to translate it. One's only excuse is that such a poem is quite crucial to any discussion of what translation and language-loss imply. In several cases I have had to make the meaning more overt than it is in the Welsh. Even so, it is virtually impossible to do without notes. I am indebted to the poet for his help with these – which by no means cover everything – and with some of the phrasing in all three poems; though of course he is not responsible if I've made any mistakes.

Line 1: 'Mountain' echoes for instance Ceiriog's 'Aros mae'r mynyddau mawr' ('Still the mighty mountains stay') which has come to refer to the Welsh heritage in general. *Line 3:* Tryfan the mountain in Snowdonia is known locally as Y Benglog, the Skull. *Line 7:* 'lleuad uwch y cwm' ('moon above the valley') refers to a lyric by Hedd Wyn to Cwm Prysor. *Line 12:* 'yn y gors' ('in the marsh') means the same as the English "down in the dumps". *Line 13:* The owl of Cwm Cowlyd or Cawlwyd was one of the three ancients of the world in the Mabinogion tale *Culhwch ac Olwen*. *Line 14:* refers to the legend of March's ears from Pen Llŷn. *Line 17:* 'giants' – Tre'r Ceiri (town of the giants) is a famous hillfort in Llŷn. *Line 19:* 'bogs don't sprout feathers' – but in Welsh they do: cotton-grass is called 'plu'r gweunydd', feathers of the bogs or moorlands.

The Poet's Insurance Risk (339): *Sain* is a type of *cynghanedd*. 'Traws stretch' refers to the long straight stretch of road south of Trawsfynydd in Gwynedd.

Gwenllian (340): 'the ivy crown': The head of Llywelyn the Last was paraded through London crowned with ivy.

Siôn Aled

Sunset Over Llŷn (344): Llandanwg is in Ardudwy, not far from Harlech. *Catraeth* is Catterick in the north of England, where a bloody battle was fought around 600 AD. This battle, where almost all the soldiers of the Brythonic war-band were killed, is commemorated in Aneirin's poem *Y Gododdin*. *Gwrtheyrn* or Vortigern was an early 5th-century Brythonic king. His language would probably have been a very early form of Welsh. Place-names mentioned in the poem are in the Llŷn Peninsula.

Dylan Iorwerth

Sand (345): Druidstone is in south Pembrokeshire, where the poet and his family spent holidays with Dafydd Vernon Jones's family at a seaside hotel.

Iwan Llwyd

The Disappeared (351): These are poems to the disappeared people commemorated 'on the pavement of the Plaza de Mayor' in Buenos Aires.

Old Photograph (355): This poem comes from Iwan Llwyd's Crown-winning sequence *Gwreichion* ('Sparks'), which was a tribute to Bruce Chatwin, and there are echoes in the poems of Chatwin's book about the Australian Aborigines, *The Song Lines*. They also obliquely refer to the years following the débâcle of the first devolution referendum held in Wales in 1979, the bleak years of Thatcherism.

Emyr Lewis

Drivel (356): *Barddas* is the monthly journal of the *Cerdd Dafod* Society, a platform mainly for strict-metre poets or *cynganeddwyr* (poets who write in *cynghanedd*). The *cywydd* is one of the most popular strict metres, first popularised by Dafydd ap Gwilym in the 14th century, but still going strong. *Siôn Cent* was a medieval poet who used the *cywydd* metre. *Hengerdd* is a term sometimes used for the oldest Welsh poetry. *Awdlau* are long odes in the strict metres, popular with the medieval *Gogynfeirdd* and also the type of poems traditionally associated with the Chair competition at the National Eisteddfod.

A Once-in-a-lifetime, Never-to-be-repeated Cywydd in English following a chance meeting with the late Allen Ginsberg (359): The American Beat Poet Allen Ginsberg visited Wales in the mid-90s and was overawed by the large congregation of Welsh-language poets who attended a *Cerdd Dafod* conference at Aberystwyth. He is reported to have exclaimed: 'Are all these people *poets*?' This poem by Emyr Lewis is not strictly a translation, but he writes almost exclusively in Welsh, and this *cywydd* could be regarded metaphorically as a translation.

Gwyneth Lewis

The Language Murderer (364): These poems come from a volume of the same title which is made up of a sequence of 37 poems. They purport to be from a secret police file. The volume is a kind of poetic detective story. To quote (in translation) from the blurb: 'If a language can die, someone can kill it. Who is responsible for the body on the stairs and the death of our mother tongue? The poet? The archivist? The farmer or the butcher?...At whom will Carma, the Detective, point a finger? Are you sure that you are not to blame?' The 'torrent of words' in Welsh in the poem 'The Final Minutes' are a mixture of quotations, proverbs and resonant words. The meanings are as follows: *Da yw dant i atal tafod* – A tooth is a good barrier for the tongue; *gogoniannau'r Tad* – the Father's glories; *yn abercuawg yd ganant gogau* – cuckoos sing in Abercuawg (from a 9th-century poem); *bola'n holi, ble mae'ngheg* – my stomach asking where my mouth is; *yes no pwdin llo* – yes, no, calf's pudding (a nonsensical phrase); *gwelltor* and *rhychor* – the left- and right-hand oxen in a plough-ing pair; *gwŷr a aeth Gatráeth* – men went to Catraeth (from Aneirin's 6th-century poem, *Y Gododdin*); padell pen-glin – kneecap; *Anghydffurfiaeth* – Nonconformity; *clefyd y paill* – hay fever.

Wholeness, Llanbadarn Baptism (367): The medieval church of Llanbadarn is in Aberystwyth, and the river Rheidol flows to the sea there as well.

Ifor ap Glyn

The Cucumbers of Wolverhampton (370): This poem plays on the fact that Welsh water is exported to England. This has often created protests amongst Welsh people concerned about the fact that Welsh-speaking villages have been drowned to create reservoirs. The most notorious example was the drowning of the village of Capel Celyn near Bala in Merioneth to create the Llyn Celyn reservoir in the early 1960s. Despite the unanimity of Welsh MPs and the Welsh public in general, a Liverpool City Council bill was pushed through Parliament by a Conservative Government. This led to a campaign of direct action by Welsh Nationalists. *Tryweryn* was the valley in which Capel Celyn was situated.

Englyns (372): An *englyn* is today a four-line stanza in *cynghanedd*, one of the most basic of the strict metres. Its roots can be traced back to our earliest poetry, when it was a three-line stanza. The plural in Welsh is *englynion*, but in this rendering, the English plural ending has been used, to give the form *englyns*.

Aled Lewis Evans

Alone (377): This is the product of the poet's period in 'the border country', very much aware of the cultural tensions involved. The poem refers to areas in north-east Wales as well as places over the border in England. *Cantre'r Gwaelod* was the land which was drowned beneath Cardigan Bay, according to legend. The best-known version of the legend lays the blame for the drowning on *Seithenyn*, the keeper of the dyke, who let the water in when he was drunk. According to folk memory, the bells of the church of Cantre'r Gwaelod can be heard on a calm day. *Cymanfa* is a hymn-singing festival. Offa's Dyke is the dyke built in the 8th century as a boundary between the lands of King Offa of Mercia and the territory of Wales itself.

Meirion MacIntyre Huws

Conscience (385): The patron saint of Wales is *St David* whose feast day is celebrated on March 1st. The leek is one of the national emblems of Wales, and it is customary to serve leek soup on St David's Day.

Gerwyn Wiliams

My Wales? (389): Llywelyn Ein Llyw Olaf (Llywelyn the Last) was killed at *Cilmeri* near Builth Wells in 1282, and this marked the end of the independence of Wales. *Glyndŵr* was Owain Glyndŵr (Owen Glendower) (*c.*1354-*c.*1416), the national hero who saw himself as the Prince of Wales and successor to Llywelyn Ein Llyw Olaf. Despite his failure to secure Welsh independence, he has been an inspiration to Welsh patriots up to the present time. *Dewi Sant* (St David) is the patron saint of Wales.

Final Curtain (390): There are two nuclear power stations in Wales, one at *Trawsfynydd* (or *Traws*) in Merioneth, and the other at *Yr Wylfa* on Anglesey.

Washington (391): I D Hooson wrote a popular romantic lyric on the daffodil (*Hooson's daffodil*) which somehow seems irrelevant in the context of the Vietnam war.

Pledge (392): This poem is about the poet's newly-born daughter, Marged Elen.

Elinor Wyn Reynolds

The Night I Won the Crown in the National Eisteddfod of My Dreams (419): The main poetry competitions at the National Eisteddfod are those of the Crown and the Chair, and the awards are made in colourful ceremonies held in the main Pavilion on the Eisteddfod Field. There is a procession of the *Gorsedd of Bards* (in green, blue and white robes), and the ceremony is led by the chief officer of the Gorsedd, known as *Archdderwydd* or *Archdruid*. *The Mistress of the Robes* is the officer responsible for the bards' costumes. A troupe of young children perform a 'flower dance' in front of the winning poet. The identity of the winner is kept a secret, and he or she is asked to stand in the audience when his/her *nom de plume* has been called to a fanfare of trumpets.

ACKNOWLEDGEMENTS

We are grateful to the copyright holders cited below, as well as to the publishers of the original poems for their kind permission to include the translations in this volume. Some of the translations in this anthology have already appeared elsewhere, and we also thank the original publishers for their permission. Every effort has been made to trace copyright holders and publishers, and we apologise for any inadvertent omissions from the list below.

T Gwynn Jones: Non Davies, Llandaf; **Dyfnallt:** Geraint Dyfnallt Owen, Shrewsbury; **I D Hooson:** Emlyn Hooson, Llanidloes; **Dewi Emrys:** Nina Watkins, Isle of Wight; **Isfoel:** Jon Meirion Jones, Llangrannog; **Wil Ifan:** Brian Evans, Cardiff; **R Williams Parry:** Pat Robinson, Conwy; **T H Parry-Williams:** Lynn Davies, Denbigh; **Saunders Lewis:** Mair Saunders, Bwlch-y-groes; **Alun Cilie:** Jon Meirion Jones, Llangrannog; **Prosser Rhys**: Eiddwen Jones, Cheadle; **J Kitchener Davies:** Manon Rhys, Cardiff; **R Bryn Williams:** Nan Griffiths, Minffordd; **J M Edwards:** Emyr Edwards, Y Barry; **T Rowland Hughes:** Alun Williams, Hereford; **Gwilym R Jones:** Silyn Jones, Denbigh; **Caradog Prichard:** Mari Prichard, Oxford; **Waldo Williams:** Eluned Richards, Aberystwyth; **Euros Bowen:** Huw Euros Bowen, Llanaelhaearn; **Aneirin Talfan Davies:** Geraint Talfan Davies, Cardiff; **Pennar Davies:** Hywel Pennar, Cardiff; **Gwilym R Tilsley:** Gareth M Tilsley, Rossett; **Harri Gwynn:** Eirwen Gwynn, Tal-y-bont; **Moses Glyn Jones:** Nia Coupe, Llangefni; **Alun Llywelyn-Williams:** Alis Llywelyn-Williams, Bangor; **Rhydwen Williams:** Huw Rhydwen, Penderyn; **Dyfnallt Morgan:** Eleri Morgan, Bangor; **J Eirian Davies:** Siôn Eirian, Cardiff; **T Glynne Davies:** Aled Glynne Davies, Cardiff; **Dafydd Rowlands:** Marged Rowlands, Pontardawe; **R Gerallt Jones:** Sŵ Gerallt Jones, Dôl-y-bont; **T Arfon Williams:** Einir Wynn Williams, Caeathro; **Gilbert Ruddock:** Meinwen Ruddock, Cardiff.

The poems in the original Welsh were published by the following: **Gwasg Gomer**, Llandysul: poems by T Gwynn Jones, Dewi Emrys, Isfoel, T H Parry-Williams, Saunders Lewis, Cynan, Gwenallt, J Kitchener Davies, R Bryn Williams, Waldo Williams, Euros Bowen, Moses Glyn Jones, J Eirian Davies, Einion Evans, Dafydd Rowlands, Bryan Martin Davies, Dic Jones, R Gerallt Jones, T James Jones, Eirwyn George, Donald Evans, Nesta Wyn Jones, Robat Powell, Menna Elfyn and Siôn Eirian; **Gwasg Dinefwr,** Llandybie: poems by T E Nicholas, J M Edwards, Caradog Prichard, Aneirin Talfan Davies, Pennar Davies, J Gwyn Griffiths, W R P George, Harri Gwynn, Rhydwen Williams, T Glynne Davies, James Nicholas, Bobi Jones, Gwynne Williams, Derec Llwyd Morgan, Meirion Pennar, Gwynn ap Gwilym and Geraint Jarman; **Gwasg Gee**, Denbigh: poems by T E Nicholas, I D Hooson, R Williams Parry, Prosser Rhys, Iorwerth C Peate, T Rowland Hughes, Gwilym R Jones, Alun Llywelyn-Williams, Dyfnallt Morgan, R Gerallt Jones and Gwyn Thomas; **Cyhoeddiadau Barddas**, Llandybie: poems by Dyfnallt, Pennar Davies, Moses Glyn Jones, Gareth Alban Davies, John FitzGerald, Bobi Jones, Bryan Martin Davies, R Gerallt Jones, T Arfon Williams, Gwynne Williams, Gilbert Ruddock, Donald Evans, Dewi Stephen Jones, Alan Llwyd, Mihangel Morgan, Siôn Aled, Emyr Lewis, Gwyneth Lewis, Aled Lewis Evans, Grahame Davies and Tudur Dylan Jones; **Llys yr Eisteddfod Genedlaethol/The National Eisteddfod Council**: poems by Wil Ifan, Gwilym R Tilsley, Geraint Bowen, Eluned Phillips, D Cyril Jones, Einir Jones, Siôn Eirian, Dylan Iorwerth, Llion Jones, Mererid Hopwood and

Ceri Wyn Jones; **Y Lolfa**, Tal-y-bont: poems by J Gwyn Griffiths, Meic Stevens, Carmel Gahan, Siôn Aled, Ifor ap Glyn, Gerwyn Wiliams, Elin Llwyd Morgan and Mererid Puw Davies; **Gwasg Gwynedd**, Caernarfon: poems by Gerallt Lloyd Owen, Gwynn ap Gwilym, Einir Jones and Sonia Edwards; **Gwasg Carreg Gwalch**, Llanrwst: poems by Huw Jones, Geraint Løvgreen, Myrddin ap Dafydd, Ifor ap Glyn and Meirion MacIntyre Huws; **Gwasg Prifysgol Cymru/University of Wales Press**, Cardiff: poems by Emyr Humphreys; **Cyhoeddiadau Modern Cymreig**, Liverpool: poems by John FitzGerald; **Seren**, Bridgend: poems by Elin ap Hywel and Ceri Wyn Jones; **Poetry Wales**, Bridgend: poems by Elinor Wyn Reynolds; **Cymdeithas Lyfrau Ceredigion**, Aberystwyth: poem by John Roderick Rees; **Dafydd Iwan and Recordiau Sain**, Llandwrog: poem by Meic Stevens; **Gwasg John Penry**, Swansea: poem by Alun Cilie; **Gwasg Taf**, Cardiff: poems by Iwan Llwyd; **Annwn**, Caernarfon: poems by Iwan Llwyd and Gerwyn Wiliams; **S4C/Hughes a'i Fab:** poems by Dylan Iorwerth, Llion Jones, Mererid Hopwood and others.

Most of the poems in this anthology were newly-commissioned by the editors, but some translations have already appeared elsewhere. We have made every effort to trace the original publishers, but if there are any omissions in our list, we apologise. Thanks are due to the following: **Seren**, Bridgend for translations which appeared in *Welsh Verse* (Tony Conran) and *Oxygen* (ed. Amy Wack & Grahame Davies); **Gwasg Gomer**, Llandysul for a poem in *Poetry of Wales 1930-1970* (R Gerallt Jones), for Joseph P Clancy's translations in *Twentieth Century Welsh Poems*, for Jon Dressel and T James Jones's poems in *Cerddi Ianws/Janus Poems* and *Wyneb yn Wyneb/Face to Face*, for Tony Conran's translations of poems by Waldo in *The Peacemakers* and for Elin ap Hywel's and Grahame Davies's poems in *Ffiniau/Borders*; **University of Wales Press**, Cardiff for poems from Emyr Humphreys's *Collected Poems* and for poems from Saunders Lewis's *Selected Poems* (Joseph P Clancy); **Gwasg Gee**, Denbigh for poems from Alun Llywelyn-Williams's *The Light in the Gloom* (Joseph P Clancy); **King's College, London** for poems from *Modern Poetry in Translation* (ed. Dafydd Johnston); **New Native Press**, North Carolina for poems from *Writing the Wind* (ed. Thomas Rain Crowe); **Collins**, London for a translation by D Myrddin Lloyd in *A Book of Wales*; **Gwasg Dinefwr**, Llandybie for poems from Bobi Jones: *Collected Poems* (Joseph P Clancy); **Bridges Books**, Amsterdam for Gwyn Thomas's poems from *Living a Life* (Joseph P Clancy and the author); **Bloodaxe Books** for poems by Menna Elfyn in *Cell Angel* and *Cusan Dyn Dall/Blind Man's Kiss*; **Perpetua Press**, Oxford for translations of Waldo from *After Silent Centuries* and *Remembering Jerusalem* (Rowan Williams); **The Asheville Review**, North Carolina for Joseph P Clancy's translation of a poem by Bobi Jones; **Poetry Wales**, Bridgend for poems by Ifor ap Glyn and Elinor Wyn Reynolds. Thanks are due to **Lowri Gwilym** for permission to include translations by her father, Gwyn Williams, **Rhiannon John** for a translation by her father, D Myrddin Lloyd, and to **Gwydion Thomas** for translations by his father, R S Thomas.

Some poems have appeared under different imprints, but we have endeavoured to refer to the earliest publication wherever possible.

INDEX OF POETS & TRANSLATORS

329